MW01629948

DR. MEIR WIKLER

BEHIND CLOSED DOORS

OVER 45 YEARS OF HELPING PEOPLE
OVERCOME THEIR CHALLENGES

MENUCHA PUBLISHERS

Menucha Publishers, Inc.
© 2018 by Dr. Meir Wikler
First Impression - August 2018
Second Impression - October 2018
Typeset and designed by Beena Sklare

ISBN 978-1-61465-713-2

Published and distributed by:
Menucha Publishers, Inc.
1235 38th Street
Brooklyn, NY 11218
Tel/Fax: 718-232-0856
www.menuchapublishers.com
sales@menuchapublishers.com

Printed in Israel

בס"ד

שמואל קמנצקי
Rabbi S. Kamenetsky

2018 Upland Way
Philadelphia, PA 19131

Home: 215-473-2798
Study: 215-473-1212

בעזהשי"ת יום ג' אדר תשע"ח

כבוד הרב הגאון החשוב מו"ה שליט"א

שמחתי מאד לשמוע שמגדלים תורה וגדולה במקום

דואגים בבני — כן יעלה כמ... ...

...

...

...

...

(718) 436-1133

RABBI YAAKOV PERLOW
1644 - 48TH STREET
BROOKLYN, NY 11204

יעקב פרלוב
קהל עדת יעקב נאוואמינסק
ישיבת נאוואמינסק - קול יהודא
ברוקלין, נ.י.

בס"ד

Wednesday 2-28-'18.

I have known Dr. Meir Wikler for many years, and am familiar with his approach and accomplishments. Dr. Wikler combines Torah knowledge and therapeutic experience in his practice of helping people. Certainly this new book will re-inforce this record and serve as a medium of Chesed to those who need sound professional advice with a mature Torah understanding.

Rabbi Yaakov Perlow

בע"ה

דוד צבי שוסטאל
בית מדרש גבוה
לייקוואוד, נ. דז.

לפ״ק

כבוד ידידי יקירי הרב ר' מאיר ווקלער שליט״א

הנני כבר מאות מדוקדן ונעימת מנגד כונת [רן]
הלוואת לאור ספר דגאות רסאא הנפש, וגונו רבוף
ונאצא כעולוגות הרינטג משן אאטג ולורלעיף ש/ג ענב
ודיני אצר ונאאיסאן להרדה הרדה כלי ענונ [הגן] סנוף
ולגבדיצא רבינג הרבוננג קרצבלייג.

ובן כאיא האנבגות שקירל מאמין לגלי הצבג הב
הילא תאנצקה שליא אלישא ונהוני פרלור אליא האנגיף
ועדן הבצהאא קעבסגא דקוט״ קרין ואתיף להונ הלפעע
ספו כ'ג. ורגן שלבפ דבג ניהדג ועוג [קתו
לריכבא אאת יגנב מעני שליא רעובסיג לרון ו
ואוגר הבגסוסר נספפ ונהאשיף ע/ג דיתבאא לאל מאון
כביא לואג ו/גוגו אעגגו אד ב, ילגא שלא נגו

דידכאג ר,

דוד צבי שוסטאל
טוב אשר נעם יבן
לייקוואוד יצ״ו.

*This book is dedicated
with heartfelt appreciation to all those
individuals, couples, and families
with whom I have been privileged to work,
who honored me with their trust
and who have allowed me to participate in
their growth and actualization.
As David HaMelech declared,
"Mikol melamdai hiskalti —
From all those I have taught
I have become wise" (Tehillim 119:99).
The vast majority of my clinical knowledge
I have learned from you.
And for that I will be forever grateful.*

Contents

Introduction
— *The Purpose of This Book*

When people hear how long I have been in the mental health field, there is one question they ask most often: what changes have you seen in your practice from when you started out until now?

Typically, I answer lightheartedly, "The greatest change I've noted is that when the phone rings, interrupting a therapy session, it is now most often the patient's phone. And when I started out, it was the other way around."

However, for those such as yourselves, who are reading this book and who are interested in a more thoughtful reply, I answer that there is much greater acceptance and utilization of professional mental health services in our community today than there was half a century ago. Moreover, there are many more *frum*, licensed therapists available today than ever before. When I entered the mental health field, you could count the number of *frum* therapists on your fingers. Today, they number in the thousands. Finally, in the past, it was a common communal attitude that if you became a therapist or consulted one, your Yiddishkeit was called into question. Today, *baruch Hashem,* that is no longer the case.

As a result of these trends, there is also a parallel increase in the community's interest in the benefits and outcomes of psychotherapy. Newspapers and magazines, for example, now carry articles on mental health topics that would have been literally taboo years ago. One purpose of this book, therefore, is to take the reader **behind closed doors** to provide an intimate view of the therapeutic process as it unfolded in some of my more memorable case histories from close to half a century of clinical practice.

In addition, during my years of practicing psychotherapy and family counseling, I have developed Torah-true, time-tested therapeutic techniques, some of which are short and simple, to help people overcome many widespread emotional, psychological, and family challenges. Along the way, I have tweaked these approaches to make them even more effective and easier to employ. The second purpose of this book, then, is to share these strategies after having whittled them down to their barest essentials.

In the *Haggadah Shel Pesach,* after we recite the list of the *Eser Makkos*, we proclaim, "*Rabi Yehudah hayah nosein bahem simanim: d'tzach, adash, b'achav.*" At first glance, it appears that Rabbi Yehudah simply created a pneumonic device by taking the first letters of each *makkah.* What did Rabbi Yehudah accomplish with that? And why was it included in the Haggadah?

The Vilna Gaon, in his commentary on the Haggadah, explains that all of the *makkos* were written on Moshe *Rabbeinu*'s staff, which clarifies the earlier passage, "*U'v'osos, zeh hamateh.*" Rabbi Yehudah's opinion, then, is that only the *roshei teivos* of the *makkos* were written on the staff.

Rav Shamshon Raphael Hirsch, in his commentary on the Chumash (*Shemos* 7:15), elucidates a deeper significance to Rabbi Yehudah's grouping of the *makkos.* The first two *makkos* in each group took place only after a warning was given. The third in each group occurred without warning. Furthermore, the first group was meant to reveal Hashem's power on water and land. The second group was inflicted to demonstrate Hashem's control over living creatures and human beings. And the third group was intended to declare Hashem's dominion over the air.

Rabbi Yehudah's *simanim*, therefore, contain much more meaning and significance than their simply being abbreviations. In a similar vein, the clinical techniques and therapeutic strategies included here represent much more than simple prescriptions and homework assignments. They represent the distillation of much of my education, training, and clinical experience working with thousands of individuals, couples, and families.

Each technique is presented together with at least one case that illustrates how it was applied to a real-life situation. Needless to say, all of the names and identifying information have been thoroughly disguised in each case history to protect the privacy of the individuals involved. Any similarities to people the reader might know or has heard of, therefore, are purely coincidental and serve only to prove how prevalent these situations and conditions really are.

Hopefully this book will enable the reader to become more knowledgeable about the inner workings of the therapeutic process. And, in some cases, the reader may even be able to use the techniques described here to overcome his or her own personal struggles or those of someone close who may be confronted with one or more of the issues covered.

In addition, novice and experienced therapists may find useful tools here which they can add to their own repertoires, making them even more effective and successful than they already are in their practice of the noble profession of helping others. And finally, volunteers who work for *chesed* organizations serving disadvantaged or challenged clients may be able to use these techniques to assist them in their *avodas kodesh*.

In short, this is my attempt to share with others what I have learned about coping with and overcoming many of life's hurdles. And, hopefully, readers will be able to benefit from the strategies contained here to achieve greater life satisfaction, peace of mind, and success in their *avodas Hashem* — for themselves, their families, and their fellow Yidden.

Meir Wikler, DSW
Brooklyn, New York

Acknowledgments

I welcome this opportunity to publicly proclaim my heartfelt gratitude to Hashem Yisbarach for the *siyata di'Shemaya* that enabled me to complete this memoir of my almost half a century of clinical practice in psychotherapy and family counseling. "*Mah ashiv la'Hashem kol tagmulohi alai* — How can I repay Hashem for all He has bestowed upon me?" (*Tehillim* 116:12).

Moreover, I would also like to acknowledge the following people who contributed to this book and without whom its publication would not have been possible.

Rav Shmuel Kamenetsky, *shlita, rosh yeshivah* of the Talmudical Yeshiva of Philadelphia, for his personal guidance, *hadrachah*, and his generous *haskamah*;

Rav Yaakov Perlow, *shlita,* Novominsker Rebbe and Rosh Agudas Yisrael of America, for his *shiurim*, private counsel, and his unstinting *haskamah*;

Rav Dovid Schustal, *shlita*, *rosh yeshivah* of Beth Medrash Govoha in Lakewood, for his warm encouragement and his gracious *haskamah*;

Rabbi Dr. Abraham J. Twerski, MD, for his decades of inspiration and friendship and his treasured endorsement;

Rabbi Paysach Krohn, for his enduring friendship, valued advice, and his enthusiastic support;

Rabbi Yaakov Salomon, LCSW, a *yedid ne'eman*, for his creative contributions to this book and all aspects of my professional life, and for his uncompromising personal commitment to me in times of both joy and challenge;

Dr. Gail Bessler, Dr. Larry Bryskin, Dr. Rashi Shapiro, Dr. Bentzion Sorotzkin, and Dr. Elin Weinstein, the current members of the ongoing professional peer-supervision group to which I have belonged for the past thirty-four years, for providing me with a fertile forum in which to cultivate many of the concepts, insights, and formulations included here, and for their encouragement to compile and complete this book;

Mr. Hirsch Traube, publisher and CEO of MENUCHA PUBLISHERS, and **Mrs. Esther Heller,** editorial director, for their vote of confidence by agreeing to include me in the MENUCHA "family"; and to the following highly skilled and dedicated MENUCHA staff: **Mrs. Bracha Steinberg,** for her expert editing of the manuscript, **Mrs. Chaya Baila Lieber,** for her faithful shepherding of the manuscript through all stages of publication, and **Mrs. Beena Sklare,** for her creative layout and design of the book;

Sarah, Yeshaya, Miriam Baila, Shloimy, Dovi, Rivky, Tziporah, Menachem, and Shoshana, for always giving me so much *nachas*, and a*chronah*, *achronah*, *chavivah*, my wife, **Malka,** for her faithful support and patient indulgence throughout my career, for which she deserves all of the credit for whatever I have accomplished with Hashem's help. Of her it may be said, "That which is mine and that which is yours — all belongs to her" (*Kesuvos* 63a).

CLINICAL DEPRESSION

CHAPTER 1

Dream Analysis
— *Rebbetzin Tzirel Cohen*

The World Health Organization (WHO) estimates that approximately 5 percent of the world's population, or 350 million people, suffer from some form of major depression each year. The National Institute of Health (NIMH) estimates that about 7 percent of all Americans are clinically depressed.

Everyone feels sad at times. That is not depression. When someone experiences intense sadness that lasts at least two weeks, which is accompanied by feelings of hopelessness, loss of energy, appetite, and/or interest in activities that had been previously pleasurable, then the person is considered clinically depressed. Such people may even feel suicidal, making treatment literally a matter of life and death.

All of the voluminous research studies on the outcomes of different treatments for depression arrive at the same conclusion. While medication, or psychopharmacology, and individual psychotherapy are both effective, the treatment of choice is to combine both. At times, however, people are averse to one or the other, which limits the options available to the clinician. And Rebbetzin Tzirel Cohen was one such patient.

When Rebbetzin Cohen initially called, I erroneously assumed she was calling to make a referral. She was the middle-aged wife of Rav Naftali Cohen, *shlita,* the well-known *rosh yeshivah* of a prominent local post-high school yeshivah and the daughter of another well-respected *rosh yeshivah* of an out-of-state *yeshivah gedolah.* I was, therefore, somewhat surprised when she said over the phone that she was calling to schedule an appointment for herself.

Rebbetzin Cohen was a petite, put-together woman who had earned a reputation for helping others — both collectively, through communal *chesed* and tzedakah projects, as well as individually, through her *hachnasas orchim* and constant open-door policy. It was awkward and uncomfortable, therefore, for her to be on the receiving end of a listening ear.

"There is a Yiddish expression," she told me with a nervous smile at the start of the initial consultation, "which goes *ich veis nisht mit veliche leffel m'est dos.'* It means, 'I don't know with which spoon to eat this.'"

She went on to explain that while she had referred many others for therapy during her approximately two decades as a rebbetzin, this was the first time she was consulting one for herself. When asked why she had come, she presented all of the classic symptoms of clinical depression.

"What was the *makkeh b'patish*, the final straw, that prompted your call?" I asked.

"Well, I was just walking down the sidewalk the other day," Rebbetzin Cohen explained, "and I felt so weak that I thought I was going to fall. So I reached out for a small tree that was nearby and grabbed hold of it for support. Then I burst into tears. I can't even tell you what made me cry. A neighbor came by and asked if I needed help. I just shook my head and tried to pull myself together. She asked why I was crying and I told her that I honestly didn't know. She said, 'Maybe you'd better speak with someone,' and I realized she was right. That was when I called you for this appointment."

When I later told Rebbetzin Cohen that she was suffering from depression, she was not surprised. She informed me that her mother had suffered from bouts of depression, although she did not know whether her mother had ever received treatment for it.

I then reviewed with her the treatment options, recommending a combination of medication and therapy. Rebbetzin Cohen was adamantly opposed to taking any kind of medication. She proudly informed me that all of her six children were born naturally. She strongly believed in alternative and natural remedies, and she was willing to do whatever was necessary to avoid taking any psychotropic drugs.

I reluctantly agreed to work with her without her taking medication. I did, however, reserve the right to revisit the issue later if I felt it was absolutely necessary. In the meantime, however, considering the severity of her depressive symptoms, I suggested that we meet more than once a week to intensify the effectiveness of the therapy, and she readily agreed to this treatment plan.

During the initial stage of our work, I explored Rebbetzin Cohen's early childhood experiences, looking for the psychological roots of her depression. She proved to be a very nonresistant patient, who freely shared both her childhood memories as well as her feelings associated with those experiences.

Both of Rebbetzin Cohen's parents were Holocaust survivors. Although neither spoke extensively about their wartime experiences, the traumas each suffered were readily apparent. Her mother was a strict disciplinarian. And while Rebbetzin Cohen was never physically abused, she did tell about how terrified she was when she saw her mother humiliating and beating her younger brother in full view of the other family members one day. Her father was much more lenient, but he reserved his physical and verbal affection for his sons. This left the young Rebbetzin Cohen starved for emotional nurturance, which she craved all of her life.

The yearning for closeness with her father and the rejection she felt from him, combined with the vicarious trauma of witnessing her brother's abuse, caused Rebbetzin Cohen to develop disturbing, recurrent masochistic fantasies. These were not obsessions, because she was able to control these thoughts. But they generated within her feelings both of pleasure as well as self-loathing, which only added to her guilt, anxiety, and depression, leaving her feeling inadequate, worthless, and unappreciated.

One example of the impact Rebbetzin Cohen's childhood had on her adult functioning will suffice. Rabbi and Rebbetzin Cohen had been married for a few years when they saw that their apartment was infested with roaches. Eager to save the expense of hiring an exterminator, Rabbi Cohen purchased insecticide at a hardware store and decided to fumigate their apartment himself. Not being familiar with the use of such products, however, he neglected to properly dilute the poison, and when he completed the job, the stench from the insecticide was undeniably intense.

Rebbetzin Cohen meekly suggested to her husband that perhaps he had erred in his application of the product and maybe they should consult a professional after all. Rabbi Cohen confidently declined, saying he was sure that by morning the smell would dissipate.

That night, Rebbetzin Cohen still had misgivings about the extermination project. She feared not only for her own safety and that of her husband, but also for the safety of their infant daughter. Not having the self-esteem or confidence to trust her own judgment, she did not assert herself in any way with her husband. Instead, she simply opened the window of her and her husband's bedroom a crack (even though it was the dead of winter) and slept together with her child next to the window, breathing in the cold, fresh air.

In the morning, Rebbetzin Cohen noticed that her baby looked listless. She went immediately to the pediatrician's office and recounted the tale of the previous night. After examining the infant, the doctor informed her that had she not slept with the baby next to the window, the child might not have lived through the night.

Rebbetzin Cohen cited this episode as an example of how low she felt about herself. Such insights took months and months of intensive work on both our parts to uncover. This was no short-term case by any means. The process of exploration and discovery can be compared to peeling an onion, removing one thin layer at a time.

One of the many tools used in the course of my work with Rebbetzin Cohen was dream analysis. As Chazal have taught, "A dream that is not interpreted is like a letter that has not been read" (*Berachos* 55b). Interpreting dreams in therapy, however, is not like looking up words in a dictionary. It is more of a collaborative process between therapist and patient, in which the patient is guided to explore his or her associations with the dream. The process can be compared to digging a mine in which the discovery of one lode can lead to another and another as the miner digs deeper and deeper into the mountain.

Shortly after we began working together, I informed Rebbetzin Cohen that analyzing her dreams would be helpful in uncovering the contributing factors causing her depression. If she could remember any, I instructed her, she should be sure to write them down and bring them in so we could discuss them together. In spite of her initial insistence that she never remembered her dreams, she managed to provide an abundant supply of rich dreams for analysis, which led to the insights described above. A few representative examples should suffice.

Early on in our work, Rebbetzin Cohen started a session by proudly informing me that she had remembered a dream from two nights before. This was the first dream she shared with me.

"Please tell me what you remember," I instructed.

"I was talking with Dr. Klein, my obstetrician, in his office," Rebbetzin Cohen began. "I had asked him something about a normal pregnancy. I recall feeling very comfortable with him and very confident in him. And I also had the feeling that he really cared about his patients."

"Now tell me what you think the dream means," I said.

"It just means that he was on my mind because I have been planning to call him," Rebbetzin Cohen replied matter-of-factly. "I have a medical question I want to ask him."

"Presumably," I explained, "there are many things on your agenda that you are planning to do. If you dreamed about this and remembered it, it may have some relevance to our work. Can you see any connection between the dream and/or the feelings associated with it and our work?"

"Well, if you put it that way," Rebbetzin Cohen said, tilting her head, "then perhaps the connection is that I'm having similar positive, hopeful feelings about your being able to help me."

A few months later, Rebbetzin Cohen presented the following dream. "I was sitting in class as a girl. The teacher was someone who was very critical. I was sitting all the way up front in the first row. My classmates were all complaining about how critical the teacher was. Then later, at recess, we were all talking about how the teacher had been picking on us during class."

"What comes to mind in connection with this dream?" I asked.

"Well, perhaps the teacher represents you, Dr. Wikler," she replied sheepishly.

"How so?"

Rebbetzin Cohen blushed slightly and averted her gaze. "Maybe I've been feeling that you are too critical of me," she said.

"Have I said or done anything recently that you felt was critical?" I asked.

"Well, at the end of our last session," Rebbetzin Cohen said, looking at me, "you told me I should be more assertive with my mother-in-law, who is always on my back. I guess I felt criticized by you for that. Of course, I realize that maybe I am too passive with her, and maybe I should speak up for myself more. But that was always something that has been difficult for me to do."

"And why do you suppose that is?" I asked.

"Well, I suppose I wasn't raised to be very assertive," Rebbetzin Cohen continued. "After all, my mother was somewhat on the tough side. And we children were taught to obey our elders and never to question them.

"The truth is that I do feel very intimidated by my mother-in-law. Last week, she came to the yeshivah for Selichos. When she walked in, I felt tense just seeing her. Then she took a seat all the way up front.

"Hmmm," Rebbetzin Cohen mused, "now that we're talking about my being more assertive, perhaps I'm feeling more confident lately in my relationship with my husband. And maybe I'm a bit uncomfortable speaking up for myself. I guess we should talk more about that next time; I see my time is up for today."

A few weeks later, Rebbetzin Cohen shared with me the following dream. "I was getting my family ready to go to the concentration camp. I was putting many layers of clothing on my children, and I was stuffing food into their pockets. During the whole time, I was feeling very much in control. And as odd as it sounds now, I was not feeling at all frightened or upset."

"An interesting dream," I noted. "Now tell me, what do you think the layers of clothing represented?"

"Um, let's see," Rebbetzin Cohen said, furrowing her brow. "Maybe they were like a protection of some kind."

"And who were you trying to protect?" I asked.

"Well, in the dream," Rebbetzin Cohen said, "I was protecting my children. But I've already learned that dreams are always about the dreamer. So maybe it means I am trying to protect myself."

"So what might you want to protect yourself from?" I asked.

"From you?" Rebbetzin Cohen asked tentatively.

"Why would you feel the need to protect yourself from me?" I asked.

"I think it's very important to me to please you," Rebbetzin Cohen confessed. "I really want you to approve of what I say. The thought of you disapproving of me in any way is very scary for me."

"I wonder when you've felt that way before," I thought out loud. "Who in your life did you want to please and feared would reject you?"

Rebbetzin Cohen's eyes teared up as she reached for a tissue. We sat in silence for what seemed like a long time. Glancing at the clock, however, I realized only two minutes had passed. Then she practically whispered, "I felt that way about my father. He was such a revered leader in the community where I grew up. Everyone respected him so much. And I was so proud that he was my father. I desperately wanted to be special to him. And, and…I can remember now how jealous I was of my brothers, who had so much private time with him when they learned together. As a girl, I never had that opportunity."

Eventually, Rebbetzin Cohen learned to appreciate herself even if she had never received the kind of emotional nurturance she needed from her parents. Along the way, she increased her self-confidence and discovered that she aspired to go back to school, which she did. She completed her bachelor's degree in two years, using credits she had earned in seminary, and she eventually went on to complete a master's degree in social work. Now she works part time at a family service agency in the community.

In her capacity as staff therapist, Rebbetzin Cohen has spoken with me about some of her clients, whether she was referring them to me for therapy or getting treatment histories from people I had worked with who were now seeking help from her agency. Occasionally during these phone calls, she would mention the work we did together in helping her climb out of her depression, and she would marvel at how far she has come since those dark days many years ago.

CHAPTER 2

Delayed Grieving
— Shayna and Yidel

Depression is often caused by buried conflicts and unresolved issues in a person's past. At times, it also comes from childhood traumas that were not adequately addressed. The dormant emotions can suddenly surface in response to a specific trigger. And even though the trigger is not the cause of the depression, it must be dealt with effectively in order to help the person regain her emotional wellbeing, as was the case with Shayna.

Many years ago, a Modern Orthodox couple in their mid-thirties, Shayna and Yidel, initially consulted with me for help in managing some garden variety sibling rivalry between their two children, a seven-year-old boy and a nine-year-old girl. During the initial session with Shayna and Yidel, I gathered some critical family background information.

"I can hear from your accent," I said to Shayna, "that you were not born in this country. Where are you from?"

"I was born in Romania," Shayna replied.

"So where were you during the war?" I asked.

"We were in hiding until the last year, when my family and I were taken to concentration camp," Shayna responded quite matter-of-factly, showing absolutely no emotion.

"You must have been very young," I said, quickly doing the math in my head.

"I was six and my sister was four," Shayna said.

"Do you remember any of what happened there? Or have you repressed all memory of that nightmarish ordeal?"

"All I remember is that when we were separated from our parents, my mother said to me, 'Be sure to take care of your sister.' Of course, that was totally impossible. And later the same day, my sister was taken away from me and I never saw her or my parents again."

I was numbed by what I had heard and I cringed as I imagined that gut-wrenching scene. What struck me with almost as much force, however, was the total lack of emotion in Shayna's voice as she told me her story.

We returned to the reason the couple came to meet with me, as Shayna and Yidel related numerous examples of typical, age-appropriate sibling rivalry. I asked if they could return the following week with both children and they readily agreed.

The following week, I suggested that the family play one of the board games I have in my office, while I observed their interaction. All four family members were stiff and uncomfortable playing in my presence. As I silently watched, however, everyone relaxed and began focusing more on the game than on me. Sure enough, halfway into the session, the two children got into a little squabble, giving me the opportunity to observe how the parents intervened. This provided me with ample evidence to confirm what I already suspected — that Yidel and Shayna were somewhat micromanaging their children.

The following week I met with Yidel and Shayna alone, without their children. At that session, I offered them guidance on how to avoid the micromanaging pitfall. Both parents were eager for the instruction and promised to implement my suggestions. A week later, they reported that they already saw an improvement in their children's behavior and we agreed to end our short-term relationship.

I assumed our work was done and I never expected to hear from this couple again. Six months later, I was somewhat surprised to receive a desperate call from Yidel. "Shayna has become so depressed that she literally cannot get out of bed," he explained. "She has not been able to cook, shop, or even take care of the kids. I have to get the kids ready for school every morning by myself and I'm coming late to work. Can you please help us? If this goes on any longer, I'm afraid I'll lose my job."

"When I saw you six months ago," I said, "Shayna wasn't depressed. When did this start?"

"It's been almost two weeks now," Yidel answered. "It all started when our dog, Sandy, died. We are all sad about it. But Shayna has literally gone off the deep end. Can you help us?"

"I can try," I said. "But you'll have to bring her to my office so I can speak with her."

"She stays in bed all day," Yidel repeated in a frantic tone of voice. "I'll try and see what I can do. If I can get her to come, when can you see us?"

I gave Yidel an appointment for the next day, as this was clearly an emergency, and they arrived on time for their appointment. One look at Shayna and I could see that she was suffering from a major depression. She made no eye contact and answered my questions with either a shrug of her shoulders or a monosyllabic grunt.

Yidel, however, filled me in on more details. "We do not have a yard because we live in an apartment," he began, "but Shayna insisted that I bury Sandy. I had to go out to the shoulder of the highway behind our building to bury her. Then the next day, Shayna told me she thought Sandy was still alive. She made me dig up the grave to prove to her that Sandy was indeed dead. Ever since then, Shayna just lies in bed and cries. Our house is falling apart and I don't know how much longer we can go on like this."

To say I had never encountered anything like this before would be an understatement. I was as baffled as Yidel. While he was talking, I began reviewing in my mind what I knew about this family. About halfway into the session it hit me. Shayna was having a delayed reaction to her sister's death many years earlier. As a six-year-old concentration camp inmate, Shayna could not allow herself to grieve for her sister. In order to survive, she had to suppress her emotions and focus on getting through each day. Now, almost thirty years later, she felt safe and secure enough to allow her normal feelings of grief to surface, having been triggered by the death of the family pet. In order to help her overcome this depressive episode, I reasoned to myself, I would have to treat the dog as a surrogate for Shayna's sister.

"Tell me, Shayna, do you have any pictures of Sandy?" I asked.

Shayna perked up slightly at my question and gave me the first full sentence of the session. "Of course," she said. "We have loads of pictures. You know we first got her when she was only a puppy."

"Where do you keep the photos?" I asked gently.

"We have them in a shoe box," Shayna answered, a bit intrigued by my questions.

"She must have been a very special dog," I said, convinced that my initial hunch had been correct. "I'm sorry that I never had the opportunity to know her."

Shayna nodded in agreement. "Yes, she was a very special dog. She was more like a member of our family and we all miss her very much," she said, dabbing the tears from her eyes.

"Okay, now here's what I want you to do," I instructed. "I want you buy a large scrapbook and fill it with pictures of Sandy. This should be a family project. After all, you really need to work on this to honor her memory. Let the kids help you decide which photos to include. And maybe the kids can draw pictures of Sandy and write a poem about her. Take your time with this in order to do it right. And then all four of you should come back to see me with the scrapbook in about two weeks so you can show it to me.

Yidel and Shayna left my office with a sense of purpose and with a plan. I was not sure what things would be like, if and when they returned. I was hopeful, however, since I had not heard from Yidel during the intervening two weeks. If the plan was not working, I reasoned, I would have received another SOS call from him.

Two weeks later, Yidel, a much less-depressed Shayna, and their two children returned...with their scrapbook. The children were carrying it and proudly presented it to me as soon as they walked in.

"Wow," I said. "This is beautiful. You all really did a great job with this."

I then cradled the scrapbook in my hands and gently, slowly, and reverently turned the pages, commenting on each page. "What a good-looking dog," I said. And, "It looks like she had a lot of personality." And, "What a cute bow she's wearing here."

As I reviewed the scrapbook, all four family members beamed with pride. "I can see you all worked very hard on this," I said. Then I read out loud the poem the children had written. "Did you do this all by yourselves?" I asked them.

The two children nodded bashfully.

Just before the end of the session, I asked the most important question, one I was almost too afraid to ask. "How are things going at home now?"

Yidel responded enthusiastically, "Things have really gotten back to normal. In fact, shortly after we left your office last time, Shayna began resuming her daily routine."

I never shared with Yidel and Shayna what my assessment was of the cause of her depression. I did not feel it was necessary. The goal was to get Shayna back to normal, and since that was clearly achieved, I saw no reason to offer any interpretations. When we ended that session, I told Yidel and Shayna to feel free to call again at any time. Since I have never heard from them again, I assume that they never again needed help.

CHAPTER 3

Bipolar Disorder
— Mendy, Usher, Toby, & Nesanel

What is bipolar disorder? It used to be called manic depression, which was a more descriptive term. At the risk of oversimplification, bipolar disorder is a condition that includes periodic episodes of moderate to severe depression as well as episodes of mania. The depressive episodes are characterized by the same symptoms as clinical depression. The manic episodes are marked by feelings of grandiosity, unlimited energy, and increased impulsivity. During a manic phase, for example, the person may feel little need for sleep, may spend money indiscriminately, and/or work intensely for extended periods. In extreme cases, one may even become temporarily psychotic, suffering delusions, which are beliefs disconnected from reality.

While psychotherapists have emergencies sometimes, they are rarely the kind of Shabbos ones that Hatzolah members deal with on a regular basis. It is with great clarity, therefore, that I recall my first Shabbos emergency.

I was seated at my Shabbos table, lingering over my tea and cake together with my family and guests, when I heard a knock at the door. I asked my daughter to answer it, and she returned to the table, saying someone needed to speak with me. I got up and went to the door myself.

A *yeshivah bachur* I recognized from the neighborhood was standing outside and asked to speak with me privately. Outside in the driveway, he explained that he had been sent by one of the rabbanim in the neighborhood, who I knew, to bring me to his home. It seemed that another *bachur*, who was spending Shabbos with the *rav*, was acting strangely and the *rav* wanted me to see him.

"Go back to the *rav* and tell him to call me on Sunday," I said, "and I will be glad to give him an appointment for his *talmid*."

"No, you don't understand," the *bachur* said. "He wants me to bring you now. He feels it's urgent and can't wait until after Shabbos."

I was not sure whether this was a genuine emergency or not. Nevertheless, I decided that it would be best to be safe, rather than sorry. I agreed, therefore, to accompany the *bachur* to the *rav*'s home, which was not very far away.

"Just let me *bentsh* first," I said, "and then I'll come with you."

When I arrived at the *rav*'s home, he was effusively apologetic for disturbing me on Shabbos. Then he explained that one of his *talmidim,* Mendy, and his *chavrusa*, who had come to my door, were spending Shabbos at the *rav*'s home. During the seudah, Mendy began to act strangely. The *rav* attributed the bizarre behavior to exhaustion and quickly finished the seudah. Then he sent the two *bachurim* to bed. When Mendy's *chavrusa* came out of their room and reported to the *rav* that Mendy was still behaving bizarrely and not going to sleep, the *rav* thought I should see him.

As I entered the room where Mendy was sitting up in bed, his *chavrusa* walked out, giving us privacy. What I saw before me was a classic case of a manic episode. Mendy was talking nonstop about a long string of unrelated topics. His speech was rapid and intense. He barely made eye contact, and he appeared almost to be talking to himself. He was talking about recent incidents in his yeshivah. The subject matter of his monologue, however, bore only a thin thread of coherence. There was also a brief display of delusional thinking when he mentioned that the brightness of the street lights confirmed the veracity of what he was saying.

After about fifteen minutes of my sitting with Mendy without saying a word, I wished him a *gut Shabbos* and left his room. Then I shared my assessment with the *rav*.

"Is he at risk of hurting himself?" the *rav* wanted to know.

"He is not actively suicidal," I said, "if that's what you're asking. It probably would be best, however, for him not to be left alone."

"What can be done to calm him down?" the *rav* asked.

"He's going to need medication," I explained. "And the sooner he gets it, the better. I don't think anything can be done to calm him down until he's properly medicated."

The *rav* thanked me profusely and apologized again for calling me over on a Shabbos. Then he walked me to the door. On Sunday evening, the *rav* called to tell me that he had someone take Mendy to the local mental health center on *motza'ei Shabbos*, where he was diagnosed with bipolar disorder, given a prescription which was immediately filled, and now was acting much more normally.

While Mendy's delusional thinking was minimal, another patient, Usher, had more severe delusional ideation.

Usher was in his mid-forties, a married wholesaler of industrial cleaning products. He worked together with other relatives at the successful family business. When he called for an appointment, it was clear that he was not in crisis, because he asked for an appointment for the following week.

When Usher came in for his first appointment, he informed me that he had been diagnosed with bipolar disorder many years earlier. He had been hospitalized twice as a result of manic episodes, and he was currently stabilized on a low dose of medication prescribed by his psychiatrist.

"What's the reason you wanted to meet with me?" I asked after Usher finished summarizing his treatment history.

"I'm coming to you because you are a religious man, in addition to being a psychotherapist," Usher explained in his soft-spoken manner. "My psychiatrist is not even Jewish. I wanted to discuss something with you that I felt my psychiatrist would not fully understand."

"Okay, sure," I encouraged. "Please go ahead. What would you like to discuss?"

"I want to know if you feel I have a responsibility — I mean as a *frum* man, that is — to let people know that I am the Mashiach," he said very matter-of-factly.

Is he pulling my leg? I wondered, stifling a smile from spreading across my lips. "How do you know this?" I asked, reflecting his matter-of-fact tone.

"Oh, Hashem told me," Usher said. "Not recently. Actually, it was about four years ago, around the time of my first hospitalization, that Hashem communicated with me. At that time, however, He wanted me to keep it a secret because He felt it wasn't the right time for me to reveal myself. And I haven't. But recently, with everything that is going on in the world, I was thinking that maybe I have a responsibility to let people know. In other words, I think people would want to know already who is the Mashiach."

"So you want to know from me," I said, trying to absorb what Usher was telling me, "whether I think you have a responsibility to the world to let people know that you are the Mashiach. Do I have it straight?"

"No, not exactly," Usher clarified. "I want to know if I have a responsibility *to the Jewish people* to let them know I am the Mashiach. I don't feel I have any special responsibility to the non-Jews."

"Have you ever mentioned this to your psychiatrist?" I asked.

"Oh, she knows that I am the Mashiach because I told her right away," Usher said with a brush of his hand. "But I can't ask her this question because she isn't even Jewish."

"I see," I said, stalling for time. "Well, uh, regarding your question, what would you do if I told you that I did not feel you had any responsibility to reveal yourself now?"

"Oh, I would accept that," Usher said. Then he added, "But I would want to know what your rationale was."

"Uh, suppose I said that I felt you have not yet fully recovered from your last hospitalization?" I asked. "After all, you are still taking medication, which you need, and you told me earlier that you still feel a bit weak sometimes during the day."

"That's true," Usher said in a reflective tone of voice. "I did say that. Okay, then, I guess I'll still keep it to myself. Come to think of it, if Hashem really wanted me to reveal myself now, He probably would have told me. And He hasn't communicated with me directly in over four years. Well, I'm really glad I came to see you and we were able to discuss this."

I told Usher to feel free to come back at any time, which he did, approximately once a year for the next five or six years. And each time he came, the content of the session was almost exactly the same, except for a few minutes at the end, when he would fill me in on the major developments with each of his children.

Maintaining the proper regimen of medication is vital to the successful treatment of bipolar disorder. And this is clearly illustrated by the next two case examples.

Toby was a middle-aged housewife with seven children. When her mother suffered a debilitating stroke and had to spend months in a rehabilitation facility, Toby found herself spending hours at her mother's bedside. As an only child, the burden fell on her shoulders. As a result, she was unable to fulfill her wifely and motherly responsibilities to the level she would have preferred.

Meals for Toby's family were graciously provided by a local Bikur Cholim society. And shopping and laundry were taken care of by friends and neighbors. The one major area that wasn't being attended to, however, was homework help for her children.

Toby's husband worked long hours at his bakery and hardly ever returned home before their children went to bed. As a result of his and Toby's not being at home most evenings to help them, their children's grades suffered significantly.

When Toby's mother finally returned home after her lengthy rehabilitation, Toby was determined to help other families in the same predicament as she had found herself. This gave rise to a new *chesed* organization called Homework Helpers. It started modestly. Eventually, however, it mushroomed into a major, well-respected community service.

When Toby called me for an appointment, I assumed she wanted to discuss her pet project. I quickly learned, however, that she had a much more personal agenda. She was having some minor marital issues about which she wanted my advice.

Toby was a no-nonsense, goal-oriented person. She filled me in on the facts and nothing but the facts. And she presented only information which had a direct bearing on the reason for her requesting to meet with me. Then she added the following somewhat shocking disclosure.

"In order for you to understand me fully," Toby said without hesitation, "there are a few other things I think you ought to know. You are not the first therapist I have seen. I had a breakdown six years ago and was hospitalized briefly. I was diagnosed with manic depression and I am currently taking medication for it. I know that I will need to take it for the rest of my life. And I also know that as long as I take my medication, I can function normally, which I have been doing for the past six years."

This revelation really startled me. I had heard of Toby before meeting her, and I had been impressed by her and her selfless work for the community. But now I had even more respect for her for three reasons. Firstly, she had accomplished so much in spite of her mental health challenge. Secondly, she had the courage to seek help and risk the shame of disclosing the facts of her condition. And, finally, she had unabashedly accepted the reality of her needing to take medication in order to control the symptoms of her illness, which, unfortunately, not everyone suffering from bipolar disorder does.

One who falls into this latter category is Nesanel, an expat Israeli in his early forties who moved into my neighborhood and began frequenting a shul where I used to daven. Nesanel was never a patient of mine; our relationship was strictly social. In addition to seeing him in shul, he eventually became one of our regular Shabbos guests.

From the outset, Nesanel was very open about his life, his personal views, and his mental health condition. He was suffering from bipolar disorder, was on medication, and was receiving disability benefits as a result. He was personable, gentle, and had an easy time making friends in the community. In fact, ours was only one of many homes into which he was regularly invited for Shabbos meals.

One week, Nesanel was scheduled to eat the Shabbos day seudah with our family, but never showed up. This was very uncharacteristic of him. For the rest of the day, I and my family were concerned about him. I even walked over to his apartment and knocked on his door, but no one answered. Later that night, I learned from another neighbor that Nesanel had assaulted a policeman and was being hospitalized in the psychiatric ward of a local hospital. The next day I wanted to visit him, but learned that he had been discharged. A few days later, I met him in shul and asked what had happened.

"I think the cop and I had a little misunderstanding," Nesanel explained with an embarrassed look on his face. "I was acting a bit manic and he approached, asking if I was all right. I mistakenly thought he was coming to arrest me. I certainly hope I did not cause a *chillul Hashem*, because the cop could easily see that I am a Yid."

"I'm sure they include dealing with psychiatric emergencies as part of their training," I replied, trying to reassure him. "But tell me, aren't you taking medication to prevent such episodes?"

"Well, I was," Nesanel told me. "But last week I was feeling so good that I thought perhaps I really didn't need the medication anymore. So I stopped taking it, thinking that I could always go back on it if necessary. It seemed to me at the time that I really had nothing to lose. Of course, seeing that I landed in the hospital, I realize now how flawed that line of reasoning was."

Nesanel went on to assure me that he would not make the same mistake again. Over the next two years, however, he did make the same mistake again. And each time, after suffering a manic episode, he ended up in the hospital.

After the last episode, he decided to move to another state, where he felt the climate would be more suitable to his needs.

Nesanel's attitude toward taking his medication is not at all uncommon. Many people who suffer from bipolar disorder experiment with going off their medication against their doctor's advice. And in each case, they learn the hard way that this can have serious consequences, as illustrated by Nesanel's experience. So for this reason, I was especially impressed by Toby's attitude.

Facing the Underlying Issues
— *Mordy and Chaim*

While the chief complaint of anyone suffering from depression is always the depression itself, that is often only a symptom of some underlying conflict which the person has suppressed for many years. The basic approach to help lift the person out of his depression, therefore, is to help him face the issue(s) he was trying to avoid. A good illustration of this process was my work with Mordy, a high-powered, highly successful political consultant in his early fifties.

As a result of Mordy's line of work, he had cultivated personal relationships with many well-known political figures. Mordy had a habit of name-dropping the many former and current elected officials with whom he lunched, attended meetings, or spoke to over the phone. To be quite honest, I initially felt somewhat intimidated by the impressive cast of characters Mordy was interacting with on a regular basis.

In addition, Mordy always wore finely tailored, three-piece suits and occasionally used terms or expressions I did not know, requiring me to ask for definitions and explanations. Finally, Mordy was also well connected with prominent rabbanim and community leaders, giving him an aura of power, influence, and prestige.

"I just can't seem to concentrate anymore," Mordy complained to me at the initial consultation. "I also cannot seem to stay asleep at night. I go to bed and have no trouble falling asleep. But then I wake up around 3:00 or 4:00 and cannot fall back to sleep. I've also been losing weight, although considering my size, that may not be such a bad thing."

"Tell me more," I coaxed.

"Well, I don't know what else to say," Mordy said, shrugging his shoulders.

"How long have you been feeling this way?" I asked.

"I'd say about six to eight weeks," Mordy replied, nodding his head.

"Has anything happened within the last couple of months which you think may have triggered this change?" I probed.

"Well, I did suffer a major loss almost three months ago," Mordy reluctantly revealed. "I had invested a considerable sum of money in a business venture that looked very promising. Believe me, I'm not an impulsive investor; this was the first major investment I ever made."

"Tell me what happened," I coaxed.

"In short, I lost everything," Mordy said, shaking his head. "I suppose I have a right to feel depressed. I lost over $100,000, and there seems to be no chance of my getting any of it back at this point."

"Wow, that is a lot of money," I confirmed. "How has that impacted on your daily life?"

"Oh, I'm still working and earning a living — and a very comfortable one, at that," Mordy replied. "How is it impacting on my life? I'll tell you. That money was not all mine. I had to borrow most of it. And now I'm over $80,000 in debt. I've never been in debt before, and I can't stand the feeling of owing others that much money, which I see no way of paying back right now. It's just making me feel completely down and out."

"I hope you won't take this the wrong way," I said, "but I have to ask you if you've thought of hurting yourself recently."

"You want to know if I'm feeling suicidal," Mordy stated. "No, I'm not feeling suicidal now. But to tell you the truth, I did feel that way when I first learned that I had lost all of that money."

"And when you felt that way," I asked, "did you have any particular plan in mind?

"Yes, I did," Mordy confirmed. "I was alone on the parkway one night, coming home from a meeting, and I thought I could kill myself by having a car accident. So I started driving at ninety-five miles per hour. A few minutes later, though, I got hold of myself and slowed down."

Considering the severity of Mordy's depression and the suicidal risk he posed, I referred him right away to a psychiatrist for medication. I also gave him another appointment so we could begin the task of exploring the underlying causes of his current crisis.

Certainly, losing so much money would sadden anyone, I explained to him. Not everyone, however, would consider suicide as an option.

"Depression often serves as a lid on unwanted, unpleasant feelings," I clarified. "Let me give you one of my favorite *mashalim*. Suppose you have a leaky hot water faucet and call a plumber to fix it. The plumber gets to work under the sink, and while he's in the middle of the job, you come into the kitchen and turn on the cold water faucet to get a drink.

"Nothing comes out of the faucet and you become irate. 'I called you to fix my hot water faucet,' you holler at the plumber. 'There wasn't any problem with the cold water. But you've been working here for almost an hour and now I don't have any hot *or* cold water. What good are you, anyway?!'

"The plumber pulls his head out from under your sink and says, 'Hey, mister, calm down will you? Let me explain to you what's going on here. I know you don't have a problem with your cold water faucet. I'm not working on that one. But you see this valve down here? That's your main water valve. I had to shut that off so I could work on your hot water faucet. Otherwise the water would shoot up and hit me in the face while I was working. This valve controls all the water in your home, hot and cold. When I'm finished, which will be soon, I will turn this back on and you will have both hot *and* cold water.'

"You see, Mordy," I continued, "the hot water faucet represents your unwanted, uncomfortable feelings. The cold water faucet represents your other, wanted feelings. In order to insure that your unwanted feelings do not surface, your mind must shut down *all* your feelings. And the valve that shuts down your feelings is called depression."

Mordy understood and accepted my crash course on depression. What unwanted feelings was he suppressing, he wanted to know.

I told him that we would need to discuss his childhood experiences in order to answer that question.

"My childhood was fine," Mordy protested. "Why is that therapists are always looking into the past? Why can't depression be caused by current circumstances? You said yourself that owing so much money would make anyone feel depressed."

"I did say that," I acknowledged. "But I believe there is more to it than that. Why are you so resistant to reviewing your childhood with me?"

"I'm not resistant," Mordy protested. "I'm just not sure I believe in all this psychobabble about underlying causes for depression. Like Ed Koch said at a recent reception for Jewish community leaders, 'I don't care about the underlying causes of crime. I just care about getting criminals off the streets and into jail.'"

Mordy was a tough sparring partner. We went back and forth on this issue for another couple of sessions, interspersed with his complaints about how frustrated he was that he could not get back to himself following his investment debacle.

By about the fourth or fifth session, Mordy softened his opposition and began speaking about his younger years. "We were quite poor when I was growing up," he said. "As a result, my mother had to work part time as a seamstress to supplement my father's meager wages as a soda salesman. They both worked hard to support us. So I suppose they didn't have much patience for us when we were growing up. I certainly don't blame them for that. And I understand that the financial pressures they were under put stress on their relationship. So they really didn't have much *shalom bayis.*"

"Did they quarrel a lot?" I asked.

"You could say that," Mordy conceded reluctantly.

"I don't want to put words in your mouth," I said. "Why don't you describe their relationship for me and how you felt about it."

"Okay," Mordy said. "They fought a lot. And it wasn't done in private. It was out in the open, in front of us kids. I was the youngest and it scared the heck out of me. Then, if I went to my mother for reassurance or comforting..."

Mordy buried his face in his hands and shook his head. When he finally looked up, I could see his eyes were moist. He reached for a tissue and blew his nose, making a loud, honking sound. Then taking a deep breath, he blurted out, "Wow, I never realized how strongly I felt about this. To be honest now, I think I did feel some resentment that my mother was never really there for us. But I don't hold it against her in any way."

"Mordy, do you feel guilty about resenting the conditions at home when you were growing up?" I asked.

"No, of course not," Mordy shot back. "I don't feel guilty about... well, maybe I feel kind of ashamed of myself for being critical of my parents. After all, they worked so hard to support us."

"Mordy, you can be *makir tov* and *mechabeid* your parents for all they did for you," I said, "and still feel bad that you did not receive the nurturance and emotional support some children take for granted."

In the weeks that followed, Mordy came to terms with his difficult childhood and his conflicted feelings toward his parents. He learned that he could feel sorry that he missed a lot as a child, while at the same time feel grateful for what he did receive. And it was not long after that that he found his energy and enthusiasm levels return to their normal levels.

At the end of only a few months of, albeit intense, therapy, Mordy announced his desire to terminate our weekly meetings. "Don't get me wrong," he said with a wry smile. "I really appreciate how you've helped me. You're a really nice young fellow. And I know I would probably enjoy continuing to schmooze with you once a week. But George Pataki has his eyes on the governor's mansion and asked me to join his team. So I think I'm going to be too busy for the next year or so. I'm sure you understand."

Facing underlying issues is difficult for everyone. In the end, Mordy was finally able to do so. Others, however, are simply not ready, for one reason or another. Consider, for example, Chaim's case.

Chaim was a retired *sofer* in his mid-sixties when he was first brought to see me. I say "brought" because he was so depressed, he never would have been able to come on his own. His married daughter had to drive him to my office each week.

"After my cataract surgery," Chaim explained, "I haven't been able to see well enough to work. You know, in order to do *safrus*, you really need to see very clearly. So I don't think I'll ever be able to do that again."

"How about your learning *sedarim*?" I asked. "Have you been able to keep up with your *shiurim* and *chavrusos*?"

"No, not at all," Chaim said, looking at the floor. "I'm so depressed; I cannot even leave my house. In fact, one of my *chavrusos* comes by every day to ask me to learn with him and every day I tell him I just can't. I'm surprised he keeps coming. It's been over two months, but he doesn't give up. I guess he's pretty stubborn."

"Why stubborn?" I asked. "Maybe he really cares about you and misses learning with you."

"No, I don't think so," Chaim said with a wave of his hand.

"Have you considered taking medication," I asked.

"What are you talking about?" Chaim challenged. "I've been seeing a psychiatrist for three months and I've been taking all the medications he prescribes. But they don't help at all. When I started with him, he said it would take six to eight weeks before I would see any results from the meds. It's been twice that long already and I haven't seen any change. In fact, the reason I'm here today is because my psychiatrist suggested I try therapy. I wasn't really interested, but my children insisted I come."

"Do you go out of the house at all?" I asked. "Do you go to shul?"

"I used to daven *vasikin* every morning," Chaim replied. "Now I barely make it to shul on Shabbos morning. In fact, I don't even take out the garbage because I'm afraid I'll meet a neighbor, and then he might say, 'I haven't seen you in a while. Are you okay?' I just wouldn't know how to answer him."

"How long have you been unable to work?" I asked.

"Oh, I know what you're thinking," Chaim said. "You're thinking that I'm depressed because I can't work anymore, right? Well, if that were the case, I would have been depressed for two years already, because that's when I had to stop. So there goes your theory about that."

"How do you get along with your children?" I asked, looking for the sore spot that triggered this depressive episode.

"All of my children are happily married and I get along with them fine. In fact, it was my married daughter who brought me to your office today. I used to drive myself, but now I feel I cannot do it anymore."

"Because of your vision problem?" I asked.

"No. I can see well enough to drive," Chaim said. "It's because I don't have the energy."

"And what about your marriage?" I asked. "Do you get along with your wife?"

"We get along," Chaim said after a slight pause.

I then launched into a brief discourse on the possible causes of depression. Chaim listened halfheartedly. When I finished, I proposed that we discuss Chaim's early childhood memories, looking for clues to account for his current crisis.

"I don't have any memories from childhood," Chaim countered. "So what would we talk about?"

"We don't need everything," I explained. "We'll make do with whatever you can recall."

As he had warned me, Chaim remembered very little from his childhood, which sounded unremarkable. Nevertheless, we spent the next few weeks going over whatever he managed to recall, but uncovered no pay dirt.

At that point, I suggested we take a different tack. Chaim was making small, but significant progress. For example, he resumed his *seder* with the one *chavrusa* who kept coming to his house. In reporting this to me, Chaim greatly downplayed the significance of this development. I proposed, therefore, that we focus for the next few weeks on helping him learn how to give himself more credit for his accomplishments.

Chaim consented to this plan less than halfheartedly. His small flame of hope of recovering was almost completely extinguished. After almost six months of medication and therapy, he had seen very little progress. He was feeling completely discouraged, and frankly, so was I.

At that point I reached out to colleagues for advice. I was baffled by Chaim's case and truly wanted to be more helpful to him. The colleagues I consulted pointed to the curious fact that I had not had any contact with his wife. She had never accompanied him to any of his appointments and she had never tried to reach me by phone. Perhaps I should initiate contact with her, they recommended.

But before I had the chance to act on my colleagues' suggestion, I received a call from Naomi, Chaim's married daughter who had been driving him to my office each week.

"I'm not asking you to reveal any confidential information," she said very respectfully. "But I'm really concerned about my father. He's talking about stopping the therapy, but my brothers and I want him to continue because we know therapy takes time and we still believe it can help him. So the reason I'm calling is to ask if you have any advice as to how we can be helpful to our father."

"I'm glad you called," I responded. "I would like to speak with you about this. Before we do, however, I must ask if your father knows that you are calling."

"No," she said. "He doesn't. Is that a problem?"

"Well, I cannot speak to you without your father's permission," I explained. "The right way to go about this is to tell your father that you would like to talk to me. If he agrees, tell him you would like to do so in his presence by joining him at his next session. That way, he won't feel we are talking behind his back."

Naomi said she would ask her father as soon as she got off the phone with me. She then showed up with Chaim for his next appointment.

"Is it all right if your daughter sits in with us today?" I asked Chaim when I greeted him in my waiting room.

"Okay," Chaim said. "I have nothing to hide."

Before I had a chance to ask Naomi any questions once we were all seated, she began speaking. "My brothers and I are all very concerned about our father. He's not really improving. Now I'm not a professional, but I feel that with depression there usually is some core issue causing the problem in the first place."

"You may not be a therapist," I cut in, "but you certainly sound like one. I'm very impressed with your perspective on this."

Naomi brushed off my compliment and continued. "So I've been thinking about what might be contributing to my father's depression, and I suspect that he may not have been fully forthcoming about things you really need to know in order to understand the whole picture."

Naomi paused and then turned to her father. "I don't want to hurt you, but I think it is very important that we are fully open with Dr. Wikler. Do I have your permission to speak about you and Mommy?"

Chaim nodded his approval. Then Naomi turned back to me and continued. "I think it started with my grandfather, my mother's father, but I'm not really sure, because I wasn't around when my parents got married. But it was never a secret that my grandfather did not like my father. I'm not sure why. That was just the way it was. And as far back as I can remember, my parents never really got along. They used to quarrel often when we were growing up. It's quieted down somewhat during the last couple of years since my father has been out of work. But I wouldn't say it represents an improvement. I think they are still at war, only now it is more cold than hot. Has my father shared any of this with you?"

I shook my head. Then I turned to Chaim and said, "I guess you misled me. Didn't you say that everything was fine between you and your wife?"

"That's not what I said," Chaim corrected. "You asked me if I get along with my wife and I answered that we get along. You didn't ask me *how* we get along. You only asked *if* we get along. So I didn't mislead you."

"Now that your daughter has put this on the table," I said, "would you be willing to discuss this with me privately next week?"

After a long pause, Chaim replied, "I'll think about it."

"What is your hesitation?" I asked. "Why would you not want to discuss this with me? Perhaps I can help you with what obviously must be a great source of stress in your life."

"Look," Chaim snapped, "I've already spent six months with you without accomplishing anything. I'm not sure that I want to invest any more in this. But I'll think about it."

Later that week, Chaim called to tell me not to hold his slot open since he had decided not to continue. I suggested that we have at least one final session to conclude our work properly. Chaim was not interested. And when I offered to refer him to another therapist if he was dissatisfied with me, he declined. I understood then that sometimes people are simply not ready, willing, or able to face the underlying issues that trigger their clinical depression.

SECTION II

INDECISION

CHAPTER 5

Building Confidence

— *Chaya*

As Chazal have taught, "There is no greater joy than resolving an uncertainty" (*Tzeil HaMaalos* 38). Conversely, there are few conditions in life which are more stressful than being gripped by indecision. For most people, periods of indecision are mercifully brief and infrequent. For others, however, these episodes can stretch on interminably, causing excruciating heartache and emotional turmoil.

It was in just such a state that Chaya, a perky, otherwise upbeat housewife in her early forties, first consulted with me.

"In order to understand my current dilemma," she began with a coquettish smile, "I'm going to have to give you a lot of background information."

I encouraged her to fill me in as she saw fit. Chaya then started from before she and her husband, Shloimy, married.

"I was a bit of a rebellious teenager," Chaya said with a mischievous grin, "and so my parents wanted to marry me off as quickly as possible.

Since Shloimy came from a good, *heimische* family, my parents agreed to the *shidduch.* I wasn't even twenty years old when we married.

"Shloimy had been a smoker before we met," Chaya continued. "That wasn't something I wanted. But Shloimy promised he would quit before the *chasunah*, and I believed him. During *sheva berachos*, I caught him smoking. He told me he had quit, but simply took a cigarette to take the edge off the pressure of all the simchahs."

"What you are telling me," I cut in, "took place over twenty years ago. Maybe you could bring me more up to date?"

"Well, *you* said I should start wherever I wanted," Chaya countered.

"You're right. I did," I confessed. "Okay. Please go ahead."

"I caught Shloimy with cigarettes again about a week later," Chaya continued. "That was when he told me that he really hadn't quit smoking. He explained that he had *tried* to quit. But he was addicted. And quitting was just something he was unable to do. He begged me to understand that he did not *want* to smoke. It was just that he *had* to smoke."

"At the time, all I wanted was to have a happy home, and I wasn't about to let this stand in the way," Chaya said, tearing up as she prepared to tell me the rest of her story. "So I accepted the smoking and naively thought that was the end of it.

"About six months later, I discovered that Shloimy also smoked marijuana. I didn't even know what that was. But when I showed it to a friend of mine who is more 'with it,' she told me what it was. Of course, I confronted Shloimy about this right away. At first, he tried to deny it. But when I presented my evidence, he confessed. Then he revealed to me that he had started smoking marijuana in yeshivah. He was quick to assure me that he was not addicted to it, and he promised not to smoke it ever again.

"I probably shouldn't have, but I believed him. No, I should say I *wanted* to believe him. I was already expecting our first child. I didn't want to be a single parent. And I knew I could not go back to live with my parents. So I just hoped that he would keep his word.

"Things weren't great. We had our ups and downs, like any other couple. We had three kids. Shloimy got a better job. We bought a house. And I felt as if we were living the American dream. Then, about six years ago, I came home and found Shloimy sitting on the floor with his eyes glazed over. There was a syringe on the floor next to him. And that's when I first discovered that he was doing cocaine.

"To say I was livid would be putting it mildly. I was more than furious. I was hurt, angry, and felt totally betrayed. I took the kids and ran to my sister's house. After I put them to sleep, I cried in bed for the rest of the night. Shloimy came over the next day and begged me to come home. I couldn't stay with my sister, and I had nowhere else to go. So, like a fool, I came home.

"For a month, we slept in separate bedrooms. Shloimy bought me chocolate and flowers every day. He swore he would never take drugs again. And he even promised to begin attending Narcotics Anonymous meetings. He cried when he begged me not to leave him. He sounded so sincere. So I believed him. No, I should say I *wanted* to believe him. I felt I had no other choice. Where was I going to go with three kids? I felt there was no other option but to stay and make the best of it.

"From that point on, however, I've never really felt secure with Shloimy. I keep wondering, is this what I want for my kids? Do I want to expose them to drugs in their own home? Do I want them to know their father is a drug addict? On the other hand, divorce is simply out of the question. Shloimy makes a good living, in spite of his addiction. I'm not working. And I have no other source of income. My father is no longer living and my mother cannot support me.

"So why am I here now, you probably want to know," Chaya said, making eye contact with me for the first time since she began her story.

"Well, yes, that would be helpful," I agreed.

"This week I was straightening up around the house and I found more drugs," Chaya said, her eyes moistening again. "There is absolutely no way I can stay with Shloimy any longer, and there is also no way I can leave him. So I realized I needed to speak with someone and that's when I called you."

Chaya took a deep breath after completing her story. She reached for a tissue and dabbed at the corners of her eyes. I assured her that we could certainly work together toward the goal of helping her resolve her dilemma.

Over the next few sessions, I explored with Chaya all of her options. Marriage counseling was out of the question. She felt she was past that. After all, she felt she could not trust Shloimy any longer. No, she felt this was her issue to resolve.

Getting a job was something she agreed would help. But she had no marketable skills. She was never any good as a student. And it would be even more difficult going back to school at her age.

Chaya desperately wanted to avoid breaking up her family. Her oldest daughter was only a couple of years away from *shidduchim*, and she dreaded to think what a divorce would do to her prospects "on the market" if that were to happen.

On the other hand, the thought of staying in the marriage at that point was truly abhorrent to Chaya. She resented Shloimy's betrayal in continuing to use drugs in spite of his promises to quit. And she felt the unspoken tension between them would be toxic for her now five children. Finally, she feared how having a drug-addicted father living at home might damage her children. In short, Chaya was very deeply mired in her indecision.

Chaya attempted to resolve her dilemma by asking me to make the decision for her. "What do you think I should do?" she bluntly asked me one day.

"You have friends, relatives, and rabbanim you can ask for advice," I responded. "That is not how I can best help you. Furthermore, I don't have to live with the consequences of your decision. You do. The best way I can help you is to enable you to make the decision yourself so that you will be able to live with whatever decision you make."

Chaya reluctantly accepted my offer. And the first stop on our journey together was taking a closer look at the dependent nature of her personality and her lack of confidence which seemed to make it more difficult for her to resolve her dilemma. In order to do so, we needed to explore the roots of her nature in her childhood experiences.

"You described yourself, initially, as having been a rebellious teenager," I began. "Tell me more about that. In what way were you rebellious? And what do you suppose prompted you to be that way?"

Chaya then shared with me that her father had been a Holocaust survivor. He had a strict, authoritarian parenting style which clashed with Chaya's "free spirit." He had a "my way or the highway" approach to parenting. Nothing short of total obedience was acceptable to him. Any word or facial expression that sounded or appeared to him to be disrespectful was met with his uncontrolled fury. While Chaya had initially described both parents as "loving," she apparently felt sufficiently comfortable with me three months into our work to share with me that her father had also been physically abusive.

"I recall one day," Chaya reported in a voice much softer than she typically spoke in, "my father had rebuked me for something. I don't really remember what it was. I didn't say anything, but I must have smirked at him. I was about fifteen at the time. He smacked me so fast that I didn't even see it coming. He hit me so hard across the face that my nose started bleeding. And I remember the blood was gushing so profusely from my nose that I had to cup both hands in front of my face to keep the blood from pouring onto the floor."

"I guess it's hard to build self-confidence if you are treated like that," I observed.

Chaya, surprisingly, had not made the connection between her lack of self-confidence and the manner in which her father had treated her. Over the next few weeks, however, she was able to see the cause-and-effect relationship.

Once we had uncovered the roots of her lack of self-confidence, Chaya and I next focused on steps she could take to repair the damage to her self-esteem. Chaya had never had a real job. She wanted to work for many reasons. She liked the idea of earning her own money. She felt that having a job would make her feel more empowered. And it would definitely raise her self-esteem. The problem for Chaya, not surprisingly, was that she simply could not decide what type of work she wanted to do.

I had Chaya peruse the want ads in the newspaper just to familiarize her with the types of jobs that were available. Consistent with her nature, she was very compliant. This exercise, however, failed to spark an interest in any line of work.

Next, I had her order a college catalogue. My purpose was to expose her to even more career options. This too failed to help Chaya find an occupation to pursue. She was as stuck in being unable to decide what type of job she wanted as she was unable to decide what to do about her marriage.

Parallel to this, Chaya was focusing on the day-to-day issues she was dealing with while raising her children and continuing to live with Shloimy. Each week she came in with yet another dilemma or challenge with which she needed my help, relegating the unresolved questions about her marriage and her yet-to-be-determined career to the back burners.

After about a year and a half of my working with Chaya, she felt more confident, less helpless, but still undecided about her marriage and her career. At that point, I realized that Chaya needed more encouragement than she was able to get from our weekly sessions. So I referred her to my colleague, Dr. Rashi Shapiro, for group therapy in addition to the individual therapy she was receiving from me.

Chaya took to the group like a fish to water. After a brief period of adjustment, Chaya became a star in the therapy group. She shared her feelings openly, gently challenged the other members, and increased the cohesiveness of the entire group with her refreshing sense of humor. Eventually, the group began to confront her regarding her indecisiveness. On top of the support she was receiving from me, the group added their own encouragement.

After about six months in combined group and individual therapy, Chaya came into her appointment with me one day and announced that she had decided what she wanted to do. She was going to go back to school!

With me and the group cheering her on, Chaya entered a local community college. Battling intense fears of failure, Chaya enrolled in a two-year Associate of Arts degree program.

This was enormously challenging for Chaya, who suffered much anxiety before each exam. She would come to our appointments singing the same chorus about how she was convinced this time she would definitely fail the test. And when she passed test after test with flying colors, she still saw each one as an aberration which would never be repeated. Chaya graduated after two years, proudly bringing her children to the ceremony and basking in the well-deserved glory.

Graduating junior college, however, brought a new, even greater dilemma: what to do next? In much less time than it took her to decide about going back to school, Chaya decided on what career to pursue. Using her seminary credits, Chaya parlayed her Associate of Arts degree into a Bachelor of Arts degree, which enabled her to apply to graduate school in social work.

To her utter amazement, Chaya was accepted. Before she began her first semester, however, Shloimy was rushed to the emergency room after a drug overdose. Dutifully, Chaya ran to be with him. And on the way home, she found the strength to decide that, for her, the marriage was over.

She waited until Shloimy fully recovered and came home from the hospital. And the day he returned to work, Chaya informed him that he had to move out of the house. As in the past, Shloimy pleaded with Chaya to give him one more chance. This time, however, Chaya was resolute and firm. She did not raise her voice and she was not overly emotional. In clear, unequivocal terms, she informed Shloimy that the marriage was over. She wanted a divorce.

In reporting all of this to me two days later, Chaya expressed amazement that she had been so confident in conveying her feelings to Shloimy. Then she acknowledged that she never would have been able to come this far had it not been for the work she had done with me and with the group.

Chaya eventually completed her degree in social work and went on to work for a well-respected and highly professional mental health agency. She continued seeing me until after the divorce was finalized and she settled into the joint custody arrangement worked out by the *beis din* which handled her *get.*

During and after her divorce, Chaya suffered deep feelings of sadness that her marriage of over twenty years had ended the way it did. And like the Mizbei'ach in the Beis HaMikdash which shed tears over each divorce (*Gittin* 90a), my eyes were not dry when Chaya shared her feelings with me. Nevertheless, she experienced no regrets or doubts about the decision she had made. And three years after she ended her therapy with me, she called to share the good news that she was getting remarried to a gentle, stable, and very caring divorcee whose children were all married and out of the house.

Looking back now on the more than three years of work I did with Chaya, her story highlights for me how one can succeed in overcoming feelings of helpless indecision by learning to repair his or her damaged self-image, building self-confidence, and taking the necessary risks to fulfill one's potential.

CHAPTER 6

Peeling Away Perfectionism

— Ari

Chaya was gripped with indecision regarding whether or not to end her marriage. Many more people by far, however, are indecisive about whether or not to get engaged in the first place. While I have seen many young people who could not make up their minds about a particular *shidduch*, one of the most memorable was Ari.

Ari was a clean-cut, clean-shaven young man in his late twenties. He dressed in the typical yeshivah style of black suit and white shirt. He was polite and mild mannered. From this description, he certainly does not sound out of the ordinary. What made him so unforgettable, however, was the fact that he traveled all the way from England to consult with me, and no one had ever come so far for that before.

In those days, there was no caller ID. I did not know until Ari told me that he was calling from overseas. He had read one of my articles in *The Jewish Observer*, and based on that, he decided that only I could help him. During our initial phone conversation, I discouraged him from coming to New York just to meet with me. "Therapy takes time," I explained. "Whatever you want to discuss will probably not be resolved in one visit."

Ari replied that he was prepared to stay for a few days, and he was willing to meet with me as many times as necessary. He begged me for an appointment, and I relented with considerable reservation.

At our first meeting, Ari got right to the point. He was seeing a young woman in London for *shidduchim* purposes. She was ready to get engaged and had made that very clear to him. He, on the other hand, was extremely uncertain. He was consulting with me, therefore, to help him make up his mind.

"How long have you been seeing her?" I asked.

"Well, that depends on which time you are referring to," Ari replied, letting me know that this relationship was much more complicated than it initially sounded.

"Let's start at the beginning," I suggested. "How long ago did you first meet her?"

"I first met her four years ago," Ari confessed with a deep sigh. "We went out the usual six or eight times. I liked her a lot. But I didn't feel ready to get engaged, so we broke it off."

"Do you mean it was mutual?" I asked. "Or was it your decision?"

"Well, I wouldn't say it was my decision," Ari corrected me. "I would have continued to see her. But since she wanted me to decide one way or the other and I wasn't ready to get engaged, I ended it."

"Tell me about the next time," I prompted.

"The next time was about eight months later. I kept thinking about her. As I said, I liked her a lot. And even though I did go out with other girls after we broke up, I just could not get her out of my mind. So after eight months, I called the original shadchan and said that if the girl would be willing, I would like to try again.

"The shadchan got back to me with a yes and we started seeing each other again. After about seven or eight meetings, we reached the same stand-off. She was ready to get engaged, but I wasn't. I was willing to continue seeing her, but she wasn't. Then she told me that if we broke up again, it would be final. I begged her for a little more time and she consented. But when the deadline came, I was no closer to being able to decide. So she broke it off and we both began seeing other people."

"I take it you have been seeing her recently," I conjectured out loud. "How did that come about?"

"Well, I really tried to forget about her," Ari said earnestly. "I tried to get her out of my mind because she had said that if we broke up again, it would be permanent. But I just kept thinking that I had made a terrible mistake. I was convinced she was the right one for me, and I felt very guilty that I had been so foolish. I knew she would never agree to see me again, but I finally decided I would try and see what happened. It was extremely difficult for me to call the shadchan once again, so instead, I called the girl directly three weeks ago.

"I must have called her at the just the right time, when she was feeling discouraged about *shidduchim*. She wasn't seeing anyone else then and she agreed to meet me. But she warned me before we went out that she was not willing to see me for another eight times. She said she would see me for another three or four times. But if I could not decide after that, she was not willing to prolong the agony any further.

"We've gone out twice so far in this current round, and I don't see myself any closer to deciding than before we started. So I asked her if we could 'stop the clock' while I consult with someone overseas. She agreed, so that's why I'm here."

Ari slumped down in his chair with a defeated expression on his face. He shook his head and stared at the floor. Then he looked up at me and asked me what I thought.

"You haven't told me yet what your reservations are," I pointed out. "You obviously see a lot of positives in this girl. Tell me what you think is holding you back."

"It really isn't anything specific," Ari acknowledged. "It's more of a feeling."

"What's the negative feeling you have about her?" I asked.

"No, it's not a feeling I *have*," Ari corrected me. "It's a feeling I *don't* have."

"Please tell me what you mean by that."

"I think I should be feeling more excitement about getting engaged," Ari said. "After all, this is supposed to be for life. If I'm getting engaged, I should be feeling happy about it, not tense and anxious. And since I don't feel the way I should, it makes me suspect that maybe she's not the right one."

"After you broke up, however, you didn't feel that way," I observed. "When she's not available to you, she looks perfect. It's only when she becomes available that you have second thoughts. Maybe you are seeing her accurately after each break-up. And then when she agrees to see you again, you start doubting your perceptions."

"Well, how do I know when I'm seeing things accurately? Maybe I'm seeing things accurately when we're dating. How can I be sure?"

"Speaking of being sure, how do you know that you would feel excited with *any* girl? Maybe you are not capable of having those feelings."

Ari sat up straight in his chair. "What are you trying to tell me?" he asked.

"I'm getting the impression that you are a perfectionist, Ari. Only a therapist from America can help you. Only when you feel a high level of excitement and happiness, without any anxiety whatsoever, can you be sure you are getting engaged to the right girl. I'm sure this girl has much of what you are looking for; otherwise you would not have seen her so many times."

Then I shared with Ari the following story I had heard about the Steipler Gaon, Rav Yaakov Yisrael Kanievsky, *ztz"l*. A distraught father once met with the Steipler, complaining that his daughter was hopelessly indecisive about getting engaged to a particular young man.

"Tell me," the Steipler asked, "when your daughter shops for shoes, does she decide right away or is it difficult for her to make up her mind?”

“Oh,” the man laughed, “it can take her all day! And even after she decides, she is still unsure about the purchase.”

“Then what do you expect?” asked the Steipler. “Should deciding about marriage be an easier decision for her? If she is so particular about a pair of shoes, she will be even more so when it comes to deciding about a *shidduch*!”

Ari was somewhat taken aback by what I had to say. He sat silently as he absorbed my assessment of what was behind his dilemma. Then he asked, “So let’s say I am perfectionistic. What do you propose I do about it?”

“I recommend that you meet with a therapist in London who you can see for more than one or two visits, and I suggest you work together to figure out how you came to be this way and then what you can do to overcome it. This process will probably take longer than this particular young lady will have the patience to endure. And this may not help you feel ready to get engaged to her. But at least it will help for the next one, so you won’t have to keep riding this same roller-coaster every time you find someone who comes close to what you are looking for.”

Ari accepted my recommendation. Nevertheless, he still requested that we meet again before he returned to London. In fact, we met twice more before he left New York. During those two sessions, we basically went over what I had told him the first time we met. By the end of our third session, I had the feeling that Ari was really ready to focus more on his own perfectionism than how the young woman he had been seeing made him feel.

Although we did not succeed in resolving his dilemma, I felt we had made good use of the time we spent together. Ari also confirmed this at the end of our last session by telling me he was glad he had made the trip to meet me.

CHAPTER 7

Peeling Away Perfectionism, Part II
— Moish

Another young man who felt crippled with indecision about a *shidduch* was Moish, an affable *yeshivah bachur* in his mid-twenties. He experienced the same back and forth ambivalence that Ari went through, albeit in a more condensed manner.

Moish had dated approximately a dozen girls until he met Shoshana, a fine Bais Yaakov girl from Brooklyn. Moish felt that Shoshana had everything he was looking for in a *shidduch*. When it came time to get engaged, however, he felt he could not go through with it. In fact, he felt so stressed by the internal pressure to make up his mind that he began experiencing physical symptoms.

Moish's mouth was constantly dry. He had a nagging headache that did not respond to Tylenol. He lost his appetite. He could not concentrate during *seder*. And he was not sleeping through the night. In short, Moish was a nervous wreck.

All day long, Moish kept going back and forth in his mind about Shoshana. One minute he thought he was ready to get engaged and the next minute he was convinced that would be a catastrophic error. On the other hand, breaking off with her might also be a tragic mistake.

Moish's parents tried to help by encouraging him to overlook his concerns. When they saw that their approach was not effective, they took the opposite position and encouraged him to break it off. If he was feeling so miserable, they reasoned, perhaps that was a clear indication that Shoshana was simply not the right one for him. When their encouragement seemed to make Moish feel worse, they finally recommended that he consult with me.

I could see how uptight Moish was right away. He sat on the edge of his chair and began wringing his hands. He filled me in on his dating history with Shoshana and then declared in a pleading voice, "I don't know what to do!"

Trying to help Moish sort out his dilemma, I said, "Tell me what bothers you about Shoshana."

Moish seemed to appreciate my question. At the same time, however, he appeared reluctant to answer it. Hesitatingly and with a note of shame, he said, "Sometimes I think the bump on the bridge of her nose is too big. I know I really shouldn't be bothered by something like that, but I can't help it. It does bother me...at times."

"When does it bother you?" I asked. "And when does it not seem to matter?"

"Well," Moish began, "I really didn't notice it on our first date. On the second date, I had a chance to see her profile. That's when it really hit me. I thought to myself, *I don't think I could marry someone with such a nose.* The shadchan was a little pushy after that date and I felt I had to agree to a third date.

"The third date went really well. Instead of sitting in a lounge like we did the first two times, we went to play miniature golf. That's actually what the shadchan suggested. Well, we both had a really good time. And when I came home, I realized that I hadn't thought about her nose even once.

"So on the next date, our fourth, I decided to pay careful attention to her nose to see how I felt about it, and I saw that it was still bothering me. At that point, I wasn't sure about continuing. But the shadchan got pushy again and I felt I couldn't say no.

"On the fifth date, I realized that her nose really bothered me. And I felt I just had to break things off. So as soon as I got home, I called the shadchan and said it was over. The shadchan didn't argue with me at all and said she would let Shoshana know right away.

"That night, I couldn't sleep. I thought that I had made a terrible mistake. I called the shadchan the first thing in the morning and asked her if she had called Shoshana. She said she had and asked why. I then told her I had second thoughts about having broken it off and wanted to continue. She said she would call Shoshana and get back to me.

"I was a nervous wreck until the shadchan called back that night to tell me that Shoshana was willing to go out again. While I was relieved, I was also worried that maybe her nose would still be an issue.

"Last week we went out for the sixth time and my worst fears were realized. Shoshana's nose still bothered me. At the end of the date, Shoshana asked that we not go through the shadchan anymore. Instead, we should discuss with each other when to meet again. I couldn't bring myself to tell her about my doubts. So I made up an excuse that I am busy this week and cannot go out again until next week.

"When I came home, I discussed all of this with my parents for almost two hours. And they saw how upset and tense I have been about all of this. At the end of our discussion, I think they lost patience with me. And that's when they suggested I meet with you.

"Now, I'm not asking you if I should get engaged, because I know telling me to go ahead or to break it off won't help. My parents already tried both. I guess what I'm really asking is what you think about what I've told you.

"I think you have been suffering terribly through all of this," I replied, trying to help Moish feel that he had been heard.

Moish appeared slightly calmed by my response. "But what do you think about my fears that Shoshana may not be the right one?" Moish persisted.

"I'm not sure there ever will be a right one for you," I said. "Of course, I cannot say for sure. But I'm not convinced yet that any girl would be right for you."

"Why not?" Moish asked as he sat up in his chair.

"Look," I said, leaning forward, "this is not about Shoshana at all. It's about *you*. You are too much of a perfectionist. You would find something wrong with any girl. Shoshana's nose is not the issue here. The issue is that you believe any imperfection is an indication that the girl is not right. And since no one is perfect, that means no one is for you."

"How can you be so sure?" Moish challenged.

"I'll tell you," I said. "According to your account, Shoshana's nose bothered you on some dates and not on others. Now certainly you don't think the shape of her nose changed from one date to the next, do you? Therefore, your feelings about the relationship affected your feelings about her nose. When you felt threatened with making a commitment, her nose was unacceptable. Then when you felt less threatened, either because you were enjoying yourself or because the *shidduch* had been broken, you were free to see the minor flaw for what is really is — a minor flaw. And I'm sure Shoshana has everything else you want in a *shidduch*; otherwise you never would have agreed to see her for a second date."

It looked as if my words had hit him like a cement truck. Moish was stunned. After a brief silence, he asked rhetorically, "So you really think I'm too much of a perfectionist and would not be happy with any girl?"

I just smiled, nodding gently.

"And you think her nose will not bother me if we do get engaged?" Moish wanted to know.

"I didn't say that," I corrected. "You may very well be bothered by her nose if you do get engaged. That's what makes this decision so difficult for you. All I'm saying is that I think it would be a shame if your search for perfection prevents you from ever getting married."

I then went on to share with Moish what Chazal have to say about this. "There are three [types of people] whose life is not worth living: those who are compassionate, those who are short-tempered, and those who are finicky" (*Pesachim* 113b). And as the Maharsha adds, this refers to those who are *overly* compassionate, short-tempered, or finicky.

"Why is an overly finicky man's life not worth living?" I asked rhetorically. "It's because that he can never be happy. He is such a perfectionist that he always finds something wrong, missing, or inadequate. So it stands to reason that no woman can ever satisfy or please a man like that."

Moish left, saying he would have to mull over what I had said to him. A few days later, he met Shoshana for their seventh date. And by the next date, they were engaged. A few years later, I met Moish at a simchah, and he informed me that he had married Shoshana and has never regretted it. Then he thanked me for helping him before the engagement.

CHAPTER 8

Peeling Away Perfectionism, Part III

— Tzvi

If there was ever an Olympic competition in perfectionism, I have no doubt that Tzvi would win the gold medal. He really took perfectionism to a whole new level. And while this created enormous difficulties for him when he entered *shidduchim*, he worked on and eventually overcame this disability. But we are getting ahead of ourselves. So let's start at the beginning.

After completing high school, Tzvi entered a prestigious out-of-town yeshivah and quickly earned a reputation as a serious learner. He succeeded in getting top *chavrusos* each *zeman*, and all of his rebbeim recognized that he was dedicated and goal-oriented.

Three years later, many of Tzvi's friends left the yeshivah to spend a year or two learning in Eretz Yisrael. Tzvi felt that the change in venue would detract from his mission to excel in his learning. He opted instead to remain for a fourth year along with a small group of his like-minded friends. At the end of his fourth year and in consultation with his rebbeim, Tzvi decided to begin the *parshah* of *shidduchim.*

Dating was a challenge for which Tzvi was not fully prepared. He was personable and an excellent conversationalist. What he found to be difficult, however, was the decision-making aspect of *shidduchim.* He knew what he wanted in a *shidduch.* That was not the problem. What was stressful for Tzvi, however, was deciding whether the girl adequately fit the bill for him.

Because of his respect for *daas Torah*, Tzvi never made these decisions by himself. Rather, he discussed each *shidduch* and even each date with at least one of his rebbeim. At times, he even consulted more than one. In fact, Tzvi never saw himself as someone who had trouble making decisions, because he always followed the guidance offered by his rebbeim.

Then Tzvi met Raizy, the daughter of a prominent *rosh yeshivah*, and Tzvi felt strongly that she was his *bashert.* The couple went out five times and Tzvi felt he was about ready to get engaged. They were discussing serious topics and Tzvi got the strong impression that Raizy was also ready. Tzvi was getting clear encouragement from his rebbeim to go ahead, and Tzvi's parents were both fully on board with his getting engaged. Everything was falling into place when Tzvi and Raizy went out for their sixth date.

In fact, Tzvi had privately decided that he would "unofficially propose" on the sixth date. By "unofficially," Tzvi meant that he wasn't ready for a full commitment because he wasn't "100 percent ready." Just to be sure, however, that Raizy really shared his values, Tzvi came to the date with a list of thirty-five *chumras* in halachah that he kept, wanted kept in his home, and hoped his future wife would accept as well.

Raizy took one look at Tzvi's list and realized at once that she wanted no part of such a life. She came home in tears and immediately broke off the *shidduch.*

Tzvi was totally clueless about what had happened. He thought he was just being on the safe side by sharing the list with Raizy. These were not demands or standards written in stone. In fact, Tzvi expected that the list could and would be discussed and even negotiated if necessary. He never expected that Raizy would run for the hills upon seeing it.

Tzvi was crushed by the sudden, unexpected breakup of what he thought was already a committed relationship with his life partner. He became depressed, confused, and could not concentrate at all on his learning. When Tzvi reviewed the fiasco of his sixth date together with his *rosh yeshivah*, the *rosh yeshivah* advised Tzvi to take a break. Instead of remaining in *beis midrash* during the approaching *bein hazemanim* as he usually did, the *rosh yeshivah* suggested that he return home, rest up, and...see me.

When I met Tzvi, he was very discouraged and disheartened by the unexpected turn of events with Raizy. His initial agenda at our first meeting was to find out if I felt there was any chance he could rekindle their relationship.

I told Tzvi that I doubted it, but it certainly would not hurt to try. Either he would succeed, which was obviously his first choice, or even if he would not succeed, the failed attempt would help him bring closure to the whole episode which was still very much on his mind.

"How would you suggest I go about trying?" Tzvi asked.

"You should write her a letter of apology," I recommended. "Before you send it, however, you should review it with me to be sure it says exactly what you want it to convey."

Tzvi was very compliant and wrote the letter immediately, bringing it with him to our next session. When I heard what he had written, I realized that we had considerable work to do. The letter was defensive, a bit accusatory, and in no way acknowledged how inappropriate his presentation of the list had been. I helped Tzvi revise the letter, which he mailed the same day.

A week later, the shadchan called and conveyed Raizy's firm

conviction not to resume their relationship. At that point, Tzvi asked me, "What's next?"

I pointed out the perfectionistic nature of his list and the manner in which he had presented it to Raizy. In order to feel secure in his decision to marry her, he had the unrealistic expectation that Raizy would either accept or calmly negotiate with him every last detail of his extreme personal standards. To my surprise, Tzvi accepted my observation and then asked, "So how can I overcome that? I certainly don't want this to happen again."

I suggested that we first needed to explore the roots of his perfectionism by reviewing his early childhood experiences. Tzvi was skeptical, but nonetheless willing to cooperate.

Over the next few sessions, I learned that Tzvi's parents were both highly educated high-level achievers. His father, a successful corporate lawyer, had been somewhat critical and demanding at home with Tzvi and his siblings. Nothing ever seemed good enough for Tzvi's father, who was difficult to please. Tzvi learned early on that only achieving perfection would elicit approval from either parent. Since this had always been the way he and his siblings were raised, he had difficulty seeing how destructive his parents' excessively high standards were on them. Eventually he came to accept that his excessive demands on himself were harmful and the root cause of his fiasco with Raizy.

At that point, he felt ready to return to yeshivah for the new *zeman* with the new personal goal of learning to be less perfect. We agreed to meet periodically whenever he came home for an "off Shabbos" or *bein hazemanim* break.

Tzvi kept a notebook to record his questions for me in between sessions, since we were not meeting on a weekly basis. He also used this notebook to record examples of his progress that he wanted to share with me. Each time we met, Tzvi would present incidents of when he would wrestle with and overcome his perfectionistic nature. Even his rebbeim noticed and commented on his progress.

During this time, Tzvi also shared with me some disturbing thoughts that he had never shared with anyone. These were obsessive thoughts which fit in with his perfectionistic personality. Overcoming these intrusive and anxiety-provoking thoughts was not a simple task. Nevertheless, Tzvi applied himself to this goal with the same zeal with which he approached everything else. Eventually we succeeded in reducing his preoccupation with them.

Tzvi reentered the *shidduchim* market shortly after returning to yeshivah. He had a number of long-term dating relationships. In each case, his perfectionism resurfaced and needed to be restrained. With each successive *shidduch*, however, Tzvi gained greater and greater mastery over his perfectionistic tendencies. And in each case, Tzvi learned how to differentiate between his parents' unrealistic standards, which he had internalized, and the more realistic expectations he was learning to adopt for himself.

Finally, Tzvi called to share the good news that he was engaged. He did not even have to consult with me before making the final decision for himself. Given his history, of course, I was somewhat apprehensive about his handling of the engagement period and marriage.

My qualms were quieted, however, when Tzvi called me after the week of his *sheva berachos* to report that he was happy, learning better than ever, and extremely grateful to me for all of the hard work we had done together. In fact, he even called me about a year later on *erev Rosh Hashanah* to thank me again and to let me know that he was still very happy with his wife and his decision to marry her.

CHAPTER 9

Sorting Out Feelings
— *Shea*

By now, some readers may be getting the mistaken impression that it always takes months or years of therapy for people to resolve indecision. Nothing could be further from the truth. The examples presented above represent illustrations of people who were pathologically stuck and unable to move forward. Most of the time, people are able to resolve their dilemmas simply by sorting out their feelings on their own or with the help of close friends or relatives. Shea's case illustrates this process.

Shea is now a grandfather and serving as the *rav* of a large, devoted congregation. He is an accomplished *talmid chacham, marbitz Torah,* and confident communal leader overseas. Many years ago, however, on the eve of his engagement, he suffered a brief bout of intense anxiety and indecision.

Shea grew up in the United States and always expected that he would marry an American girl. When a *shidduch* was proposed for him with the daughter of a prominent *rav* from Europe, Shea's parents encouraged him not to reject it out of hand. Shea accepted his parents' guidance, giving them the go-ahead to look further into it.

To everyone's surprise, the more Shea's parents learned about the girl and her family, the more interested they became in the *shidduch.* A few weeks later, Shea and his parents found themselves on an airplane headed for a meeting with the girl and her parents.

When Shea and his parents arrived, they checked into a local hotel, settled in, and prepared for their meeting the next day. The meeting between the two families went well. Then the couple spent some time alone in private conversation. Reactions to the one-on-one meeting were positive on both sides. The two sets of parents met again to discuss more practical matters, and the *l'chaim* was scheduled for the following evening at the girl's home.

Shea and his parents returned to the hotel to relax and prepare for the simchah the next night. It was then that Shea's mother noticed that he did not appear to be himself. At first, he denied that anything was wrong. When pressed, however, he acknowledged nagging doubts about going ahead with the engagement.

Shea's parents were supportive, encouraging him not to feel forced into anything. If he wanted to break it off for any reason, they told him, they were fully behind him. He should only get engaged if he felt ready to do so.

Shea told his parents that he was still undecided. He saw many positives in the girl and her family, and he did not want to cancel the engagement scheduled for the next night. At the same time, he felt very worried and anxious about getting engaged, and he was afraid of making a mistake either way.

Shea's parents had never encountered anything like this before with any of their older, already married, children. They wanted very much to help their son and they didn't know what they should do. In desperation, Shea's mother decided to reach out to me over the phone for guidance. As the family knew me socially, they had my home phone number. Even though it was the middle of the night where they were because of the time difference, it was still a reasonable hour in New York.

After filling me in, Shea's mother posed her question to me. "Based on your clinical experience, would you say this is a case of cold feet, where Shea just needs a little push to make it over this hurdle? Or could this be more serious, in which case we should break it off now to prevent a catastrophe later?"

My mind raced as I considered how much money the call was costing them during those pre-cell phone days, when overseas calls were astronomically expensive. Not knowing Shea very well, I felt at a severe disadvantage. At the same time, I empathized with their dilemma and wanted to help in the most concise fashion possible.

After a brief pause, I replied, "It is difficult for me to answer without meeting with Shea. What I can tell you is that there are two basic reasons why young people sometimes have difficulty finalizing an engagement. Some are fearful of the separation from parents and/or the change inherent in getting married. Others find something in the prospective fiancé which is objectionable and with which they cannot reconcile themselves. If it is the former, encouraging going ahead is helpful. If it is the latter, a postponement would definitely be indicated."

"How can we know," Shea's mother asked, "to which group Shea belongs?"

"Ask him if there is anything specific about the girl that bothers him," I advised. "If the answer is yes, he may belong in the second category. If he answers no, he probably belongs in the first."

Shea's parents thanked me profusely. A few days later after they returned to New York, I learned that the engagement went ahead as planned. "We spoke with Shea as you advised," Shea's mother reported over the phone during a local call, "and he was extremely relieved when we told him we had spoken with you."

Although Shea is now living overseas, our paths have crossed a few times since he married. Each time we meet, he thanks me again for the assistance I gave to him through his parents when he was gripped with indecision.

"When my parents asked me that question," Shea shared with me, "I thought, *No, there really is nothing about the girl that bothers me.* Then I realized that it was just the whole idea of getting married that made me nervous. Once I got in touch with that, I was ready to go ahead with the engagement. And looking back now, I'm really glad I did!"

FEAR OF FAILURE AND/OR OF MAKING MISTAKES

CHAPTER 10

Good Decisions Versus Right Decisions

— Dov

O nkelos is the Aramaic translation of the Chumash, and almost always the translation is literal. On very rare occasions, however, Onkelos veers from the literal interpretation in order to teach an important lesson.

One such *pasuk* is, "And you shall remember the L-rd, your G-d, that He is the One Who gives you the strength to make wealth" (*Devarim* 8:18). The Hebrew word for strength is *koach*, which is the word used in this *pasuk*. Onkelos, however, renders *koach* as *eitzah*, which means "counsel" or "advice." What Onkelos is teaching us, therefore, is that HaKadosh Baruch Hu not only controls all of the events in our lives (for better or worse), but He is responsible for some of our thoughts and decisions as well. Of course, our will and desire to do good or bad is still under our control. And that is why we are considered to have free will.

Someone who struggled with accepting some of his decisions was Dov, an athletic day trader in his mid-thirties. Dov initially consulted me regarding some marital issues. After a few sessions, however, the focus of our attention soon shifted to more personal matters.

At the time, I did not even know what a day trader does, and Dov was happy to enlighten me. A day trader is somewhat akin to a stockbroker. A day trader differs, however, in that he buys and sells stocks for very short periods of time, hence the term "day trader." And while days and weeks of research may precede a purchase, the stock is often bought and sold the same day.

Dov was bright and well educated, with an MBA. And while he was well trained for his work in the financial world, he was not at all emotionally well suited for his job. He was extremely self-critical. Even though he earned a comfortable income from his work, he beat himself up so badly after any trading mistakes he made that he was seriously considering making a career change.

In sharing his dilemma, Dov put it this way, "I put in hours of research online, checking into a company before I make a purchase. I know what to look for and usually pick up-and-coming, strong stocks. I do not make impulsive buys. And I usually pick winners. That's why I'm doing so well financially. But when I come into the office in the morning and check the Dow Jones, if I see that the stock I sold yesterday went up or the one I held onto went down, I just cannot forgive myself and I feel down for the rest of the day. The stress is eating me up and I don't think I can take it anymore."

It did not take us long to identify the source of Dov's self-critical nature. Dov, an only child, was raised by an extremely authoritarian, demanding mother and a workaholic, absentee father. Dov's mother insisted on absolute obedience and tolerated nothing less. One graphic example will suffice to describe the conditions under which Dov grew up.

Dov's mother was not a very good cook. Many of the meals she prepared for Dov were less than appetizing. In fact, they were often overcooked, tasteless, or worse. Regardless of the condition of the food she prepared, Dov's mother insisted that he not only eat it, but also *finish* everything on the plate she set before him. His protests and objections were never accepted. Dov quickly learned that he had better comply with his mother's demands "or else."

As a result of the harsh parenting he received as a child, Dov internalized his mother's unforgiving nature, and whenever he made a decision at the office that did not work out as planned, he was relentless in his self-criticism. He would become preoccupied with that "failure," and he was helpless to stop the flood of guilt feelings for having made the "wrong" decision that threatened to drown him.

Dov was highly intelligent and very insightful. Nevertheless, connecting his self-critical nature with his difficult childhood made no dent in his self-flagellation whenever he purchased the wrong stock or sold one too early. I realized, therefore, that some other intervention would be needed to rescue Dov from himself.

One day, as Dov was launching into another bout of self-incrimination following the sale of a stock he felt he should have held onto, I thought of a graphic metaphor that might help him. "Have you ever driven down Ocean Parkway, going to Manhattan?" I asked.

"Sure," Dov replied, clearly curious as to where I was headed with that question.

"Then you are familiar with the extension of Ocean Parkway called the Prospect Expressway?" I asked rhetorically.

"Of course," Dov said. "I've driven that way many times. What's your point?"

"Well, as you approach the end of the Prospect Expressway, you have to decide whether to take the ramp leading up to the elevated Gawanus Expressway or the exit leading down below to Hamilton Avenue," I explained, trying to paint the word picture as graphically as possible.

"Now, suppose you reach that crest in the Prospect Expressway from where you can see the traffic conditions on both the Gawanus

Expressway and Hamilton Avenue. And it looks like the Gawanus is packed with crawling traffic, while Hamilton Avenue looks clear. Which route do you choose?" I asked a very confused looking Dov.

"That's a no-brainer. I go with Hamilton Avenue, of course," Dov said, shrugging his shoulders.

"Okay. Now let's suppose you sail along Hamilton Avenue, which is free of traffic, and then you come to flashing red lights that mean the drawbridge is going up over the Gawanus Canal. Has that ever happened to you?" I asked.

"No, it never did. But I know what you're talking about because it happened to my brother once," Dov replied.

"And suppose you have to sit and wait for the full ten or twelve minutes it takes for the barge to pass through the canal before the drawbridge comes back down and you can proceed. Meanwhile, the creeping traffic up on the Gawanus Expressway is moving faster than you are at the moment. So how do you feel about the decision you made to take Hamilton Avenue now?" I asked.

"That it was a bad decision," Dov responded with a chuckle.

"That's exactly what I thought you'd say," I noted. "But was it really a bad decision?"

Now Dov was confused and asked me to explain.

"You see, Dov, there's a big difference between a bad decision and a wrong decision," I said.

"There is?" he asked. "What is the difference?"

"Good and bad decisions are judgments made based on the information available at the time," I said. "Right and wrong decisions are judgments made after the fact, based on the *outcome* of those decisions."

"Let's go back to my example," I continued. "When you approached the end of the Prospect Expressway and saw the Gawanus backed up while Hamilton Avenue was clear, it would have been a bad decision to take the Gawanus. Based on the information you had at the time, Hamilton Avenue was, without a doubt, the better option. That is the route you chose. So you made a good decision."

"But the drawbridge went up," Dov protested. "So it turned out not to be a good decision."

"No, that's not correct," I countered. "It was a good decision because there was no way you could have known that the drawbridge would be raised, blocking your way. As it turned out, it was a wrong decision because you were delayed much longer than you would have been had you chosen the Gawanus Expressway. So the outcome proved that the other route would have been faster. But there was no way you could have anticipated that at the time you made your decision."

Dov pondered what I had said and drank it in like a life-sustaining elixir. "So what you are trying to tell me is that if I do my research and decide to buy or sell a stock, I should evaluate my decision later on based on the quality of my research and not the ultimate outcome," he said in a reflective tone of voice.

"Exactly!" I exclaimed. "You hit the bull's eye! You can criticize yourself if you make an impulsive purchase without doing proper research. But if everything you know tells you the stock will go down and you sell it, and then the next day you see it went up, there's no reason to be angry at yourself. You made a perfectly good decision even though it turned out to be the wrong decision."

Dov reflected back what I said in his own words before the session ended so that he was confident he had it straight. The next week, he came in and reported that he had reviewed with himself the distinction between a good decision and a right decision many times at work. And as a result, he had succeeded in lowering his stress level and was beginning to feel he could continue practicing the same line of work.

A few weeks later, Dov informed me that he was offered a higher-level position at an out-of-town financial firm. "It's an offer that's too good to refuse," Dov explained. Then he added, "But I don't think I ever would have considered it if you hadn't helped me to deal differently with my decisions at work."

Dov accepted the new position and eventually moved his family to where his new job was located. By the time he left New York, his progress in overcoming his self-critical nature appeared to be permanent and not temporary. I was fully convinced of this a year later when Dov called on *erev Rosh Hashanah* to wish me a *shanah tovah.* At that time, he thanked me for our work and once again mentioned how helpful the distinction between a good decision and a right decision had been for him, especially in his new position.

CHAPTER 11

My Bowling Triumph

— Motti

If self-esteem was measured vertically, I would have to say that Motti's self-esteem hovered somewhere near his ankles. He appeared so beaten down by life that he could barely lift his head to make eye contact when we first met.

Motti was in his early thirties when he was referred to me by the mashgiach of the kollel in which he learned. Perhaps it would be more correct to say in which he was registered, because at the time, he was not showing up regularly for *seder*. In spite of his poor attendance, however, that was not the reason for the referral.

The mashgiach referred Motti for therapy because Motti's wife, Faigy, had informed the mashgiach that she wanted a divorce. After nine years of marriage, Faigy felt she could no longer tolerate Motti's irresponsibility and unreliability. Almost nothing she asked of him was ever accomplished in a timely fashion. He was either late or incomplete in tending to the smallest household chores. At times, he forgot about them altogether. And even when Faigy took care of running the house herself, she saw that Motti was unable to maintain his own personal responsibilities. He missed *sedarim*, lost *chavrusos* due to lateness, and often was caught napping in the middle of the day.

Faigy was more than willing to sacrifice financial security in order to support her husband's full-time learning. If he was not really learning, however, she felt he should be working to help her support their growing family. After a few months of inactivity, which Motti called "looking for work," Faigy was ready to throw in the towel. That was when she met with the mashgiach, requesting his help in arranging for a divorce. And that was when the mashgiach convinced Faigy to hold off on ending the marriage while Motti got help.

When I first met Motti, he expressed eagerness to do whatever it took to save his marriage. Faigy was unwilling to participate in couples counseling. Either Motti would shape up or she would ship out. No ifs, ands, or buts.

Motti desperately wanted to save his marriage, although he worried that Faigy already had reached the end of her rope. While not suffering from clinical depression, Motti was certainly depressed about the state in which he found himself. He clearly illustrated the wisdom of Chazal, who understood that "idleness leads to depression" (*Kesubos* 59b).

Motti acknowledged that it was time for him to move into the work force. He even praised his wife for putting up with him as long as she had. He truly wanted to help support his family. Unfortunately, he could not think of any line of work he could reasonably hope to find. It was not that Motti lacked marketable skills. Rather, he had such a defeatist attitude that he was convinced he would fail at any job that would be offered to him.

Motti blamed only himself for his failures in life. When asked about his childhood, he described his upbringing in glowing, unrealistic terms. It was clear that he did not want to shift the blame onto anyone other than himself. As we built a relationship of trust, however, Motti gradually grew more willing to acknowledge the reality of his past.

Both of Motti's parents had been very critical, although his father was especially harsh, which profoundly wounded his self-image. Motti had been compared unfavorably to his more accomplished siblings, which further knocked down his self-esteem. By the time Motti reached adulthood, all that he had been told about his failings became self-fulfilling prophecies.

Motti's self-defeating attitudes accompanied him into my office and threatened our work as well. For example, Motti often showed up late for his appointments. At times, he forgot or missed sessions completely. Each time, he expected me to reject him as summarily as he had been at home as a child. It took a long time and hard work on my part to convince him that I was nonjudgmental and supportive.

A few months into our work, Motti came in and reported that the mashgiach had found a part-time teaching job for him at a local *yeshivah ketanah*. Faigy very much wanted him to accept this position and the mashgiach was pushing him to take it as well. Motti, however, was nothing less than terrified.

"I know that if I take the job," Motti shared with me, "I'll just end up getting fired. I have to show up on time for a teaching job, and getting up on time is something I'm struggling with right now. But even if I do manage to show up on time, I'm not sure I'll be able to handle the class. I just don't think I'm cut out for teaching. I don't dislike children. I have four of my own. But I'm not especially good with kids."

"Do you feel you would do better with a different kind of job?" I asked.

"Yes," Motti responded ruefully. "Only, I really can't say what kind of job I would prefer."

"If you don't think the teaching job is for you," I suggested, "you don't have to take it."

"I know," Motti answered with a sigh. "But I feel like I *have* to. I'm sure it wasn't so easy for the mashgiach to get it for me. He probably had to work at convincing the *menahel*. And my track record hasn't been so great, so I feel it would be a lack of *hakaras hatov* if I turned it down. Also I'm afraid that if I don't take it, Faigy will leave me."

Once he put it that way, I realized Motti really did have no choice. He *had* to take the job. But how on earth could he avoid the self-fulfilling prophecy that he would fail?

Just then I thought of an approach that could help Motti in his struggle to overcome his own defeatist attitude.

"Motti, have you ever gone bowling?" I asked.

"I'm not really very athletic," Motti said with a smirk as he patted his more than ample stomach.

"Well, I'm not that athletic myself," I confessed. "But a few years ago, a close friend and colleague of mine called and invited me to join him in a game of bowling.

"'I haven't been bowling in years,' I told him. 'Not since the days when it was considered clever marketing to advertise that bowling is fun.'

"We both had a good laugh. And since we both were not as busy as we are today, we had enough time in the middle of the day to take in a trip to the local bowling alley. It took a bit of convincing, but I finally agreed. And a few minutes later, my friend drove by to pick me up.

"The alley was practically empty in the middle of a weekday, and the proprietor seemed both happy and surprised to see us. We rented shoes, selected balls, and went over to our lane.

"'Let's bet on the game,' my friend suggested.

"I told him I wasn't much of a gambler. Then I asked how much he wanted to bet. He proposed we bet the price of the game. Foolishly, I consented and then we began to play.

"As out of shape as my friend was, I was in worse shape. We both scored in the double digits. But as poorly as my friend bowled, I scored lower. He won and I had to pay for his game.

"'Let's bowl another game,' he suggested. 'Double or nothing.'

"I was already tired and I knew I could never overcome the gap between our scores. But I was having such a good time that I did not want to leave. So against my better judgment, I accepted the challenge.

"During the second game," I lamented, "I did not do any better than I did during the first game, and most of my balls were ending up in the gutter. Also, I was beginning to feel a bit embarrassed by my poor showing."

At this point, I could see that Motti was nodding gently, appearing to identify with my feelings of failure and shame.

"Then," I continued, "as I stood at the foul line, about to bowl the first ball of the last frame of that second game, I remembered an article I had read in a magazine about sports psychology. I had not even known there was such a specialty.

"Since professional sports are such a lucrative field today, literally millions of dollars can be made or lost depending on whether a particular team wins or loses a game. As a result, an athlete's performance has major financial consequences. Sports psychologists, therefore, are hired to help the players overcome any hurdles preventing them from optimum performance.

"One of the most common barriers to peak performance is a 'slump,' which is a series of failures or errors during recent games. When a player falls into a slump, the sports psychologists discovered, the fear of another poor performance becomes a self-fulfilling prophecy. But more than that, it becomes a mental *rehearsal* of the failures during the game, practically guaranteeing a continuation of the slump.

"The solution, the sports psychologists learned, is to help the athlete visualize a successful performance. By concentrating only on the winning play and/or game, the athlete engages in a mental rehearsal of peak performance. Later, in the actual game, he simply follows the pattern that he practiced in his mind. This technique has shown significantly positive results and has helped many multimillion dollar athletes break out of debilitating and discouraging slumps.

"*If this technique can work for professional athletes*, I reasoned to myself, *then it can help me save face here in the bowling alley.* So I closed my eyes and concentrated on picturing my ball rolling down the alley along the strike path, knocking down all ten pins.

"'Hey, Wikler,' my friend called out, 'just bowl already. What's taking you so long?'

"I told him to leave me alone. I was simply concentrating before bowling my last frame. Then I returned to my mental exercise. I recall now how difficult it was for me to hold the positive picture of the strike in my mind. Images of my ball rolling into the gutter kept interfering with my concentration. But after a minute or two, I succeeded. Then I took a deep breath and bowled my ball.

"I stood at the foul line and watched in amazement as my ball followed the path I had visualized. It continued along the strike path all the way down the lane and knocked down all ten pins! My friend could not believe his eyes. I too was truly in shock.

"'How did you do that?' my friend asked in amazement.

"I simply shrugged, keeping my strategy to myself.

"'You know, now you get two more balls,' my friend said, reminding me of the scoring rules.

"When I stepped up to the foul line to bowl the first of my last two balls, I thought to myself that there was no way I, a complete novice, would bowl two strikes in a row. Nevertheless, I reasoned, maybe it was possible. After all, if I did it once, I suppose I could do it again. I stood at the foul line, repeating the same procedure that had enabled me to bowl the first strike.

"'Come on, Wikler,' my friend urged. 'Just bowl already so we can finish the game and go home.'

"'Just chill,' I teased him. 'I'm concentrating again.'

"And that is exactly what I did. Then I took another deep breath and bowled my ball. My jaw dropped as I saw it follow the same path as the previous one. And when all ten pins were knocked down again, my friend jumped up from his seat.

"'Wikler, how did you do that?' he shouted. 'I cannot believe you just bowled two strikes in a row. Don't forget, you still get one more shot. Let's see what you do with that one.'

"Now, to say the pressure was on would be putting it mildly. I certainly did not expect to do so well with my last ball. After all, many better bowlers have never managed to score two strikes in a row. Three strikes in a row would be practically unheard of. Nevertheless, if I had done it twice just now, it *was* technically possible for me to do it again. Even if you flip a coin ninety-nine times and it comes up heads, the chances of it coming up heads on the one-hundredth time are still fifty-fifty.

"By this time, my friend was no longer leisurely lounging on the bench behind me. He was standing off to the side, staring straight at me. 'Take your time, Meir,' he coached.

"I felt as if I were up at bat at the bottom of the ninth inning of the seventh game of the World Series, with a full count of three balls and two strikes. No one else was in the bowling alley at the time, but I felt as if the whole world were watching me.

"I just kept repeating to myself that if I did it once, I could do it again. Then I followed the same successful strategy that produced the previous two strikes. I took two deep breaths and bowled my last ball. My friend and I just stared as it looked guided by some remote control device, rolling straight for the 'strike pocket.' When all ten pins dropped, my friend and I could not believe our eyes.

"I was speechless. My friend just kept shaking his head and muttering, 'Unbelievable! Unbelievable!'

"When we tallied my score, I still lost the second game because I had been so far behind to begin with. Nevertheless, my friend added icing to my cake by commenting, 'Meir, you may have lost the game, but you won the day. I have never seen anyone bowl three strikes in a row. What a finale to a great outing. We really have to do this again sometime.'

"Oddly enough, neither one of us has been bowling since. But my purpose in telling you this somewhat long-winded story is to demonstrate for you what I feel you have to do before you enter that classroom on Monday."

I then walked Motti through the way he could apply the positive thinking approach to his upcoming first day as a sixth-grade rebbi. Needless to say, Motti was extremely skeptical that he could "bowl three strikes in a row." Nevertheless, he did agree to try, and he proceeded to verbalize the mental image of him succeeding on his first day in front of the class.

Motti came the following week for his appointment with a faint smile on his face.

"*Nu*, so tell me what happened on Monday," I blurted out even before Motti sat down. "Don't keep me in suspense."

"I guess it went better than I expected," Motti reported almost reluctantly. He then went on to describe all of the mistakes in classroom management that he made on his first day. In spite of those missteps, however, he acknowledged that he had made a good start and he was beginning to entertain the idea that he could succeed as a classroom teacher after all.

Following his description of each mishandled rebbi/*talmid* interaction, Motti turned to me and asked, "Wasn't that a mistake?" It was as if he was trying to get me to confirm his negative self-image. While I could not deny that he had used poor judgment, I did not want to add to his self-incriminations. I taught him, therefore, how to say to himself, "I may not have done that as well as I would have liked, but next time I'll do it better, *b'ezras Hashem*."

Motti's career in *chinuch* was not nearly as positive as his first day had been. While he definitely connected with his class, Motti was still shooting himself in the foot, so to speak, continuing some of the self-destructive behaviors that brought him to see me initially.

The yeshivah where Motti was teaching was located twenty-five minutes from his home by car, and Motti found it difficult to arrive on time on a consistent basis. At first he came only a few minutes late once in a while. Eventually, the frequency of his tardiness increased and lengthened. The *menahel* was incredibly forgiving and understanding. Nevertheless, as the school year was coming to a close, the *menahel* informed Motti that he could not in good conscience rehire him for the next year.

Motti was not angry with anyone but himself. He did not blame the *menahel*, his wife, or even me for his failure. While Motti had an excuse for each time he was late, he could not deny that they added up to being sufficient grounds for his not being rehired for the coming year.

At that point, I feared that Motti might regress. This was just the kind of rejection that could topple all of the hard work we had done together to overcome his low self-esteem, feelings of inadequacy, and self-denigration. To my great surprise, however, Motti's self-image withstood the blow.

"What do you think you'll do instead of teaching?" I asked, not even expecting a reply.

"I really don't know," Motti answered in the way I would have expected. But then, uncharacteristically, he added, "But I know what I'd *like* to do."

"Really?" I asked rhetorically, feeling very caught off-guard. "Tell me, what would you like to do?"

"I'd like to go back to school," Motti replied with a confidence I had never seen before. "I'd like to get an MBA and become an accountant. I've always liked working with numbers, and I think working as an accountant would help me feel better about myself. After all, it is considered a respectable occupation, and it usually provides a *bekavodig* income."

"Do you have a bachelor's degree?" I asked, still stunned by Motti's newfound sureness.

"No, I don't," Motti said. "But I think the mashgiach can help me get a BHL (Bachelors of Hebrew Letters) degree from the yeshivah. And with that I can apply to a special MBA program I've heard of that caters to *kollel yungerleit*."

My first thought was that Motti had as much chance of getting an MBA as he did of getting a medical degree. Nevertheless, I was mindful of how much criticism he had been subjected to growing up and I did not want to dampen his spirit in any way. *Even if he fails*, I thought, *he should be congratulated for trying.*

"Motti, that sounds like a terrific plan," I said after pulling myself together.

As predicted, the mashgiach did help Motti obtain a BHL from the yeshivah. And unlike his past failures, he succeeded in submitting his application on time for the MBA program. Well, almost on time. He was actually a day late. But the school processed it anyway, and two weeks later, Motti reported that he had gone for his interview, and completed his scholarship and student loan applications.

Waiting to hear the results of his efforts was nothing less than excruciating for Motti. He tried not to get his hopes up in order to minimize the possible disappointment. He was, however, wholly unsuccessful. The longer he waited, the higher his stress level rose. With each passing day, he wanted to be accepted into the MBA program more and more. He became increasingly convinced that becoming an accountant was the only viable plan for him. And at the same time, he became increasingly convinced that this latest attempt to improve his life would simply add another failure to the long list of failures that characterized his adult life.

Motti was no longer seeing me regularly; he was only coming in on an as-needed basis. As a result, it was not in person that Motti told me the good news that he had been accepted into the MBA program. His scholarship and loan applications were also accepted. He was due to begin classes at the end of the next month.

However, the two-year program was not all smooth sailing for him. He had issues with some of his classes. For example, he received some grades that were lower than he felt he deserved, and the confrontational manner in which he initially planned to speak with his professors would have been clearly self-destructive. To his credit, however, Motti had the good sense to discuss these meetings with me in advance, which gave me the opportunity to help him adopt a more conciliatory, effective strategy for dealing with them.

We officially ended our work on the eve of Motti's graduation. In our final meeting, Motti expressed his appreciation for the successful outcome of our work. He also confided that he never really believed he would ever reach the milestone he had achieved. And although she never voiced any doubts, Motti was convinced that Faigy shared similar feelings of skepticism.

However, now that he was poised to enter the field of professional accounting, Faigy no longer looked down on her husband, and she no longer spoke of wanting a divorce. In fact, Motti reported that his overall *shalom bayis* had improved dramatically since he first entered the MBA program.

I did not meet with Motti anymore after our final session, and I wondered from time to time how he was doing. Earlier this year, however, I ran into him outside of shul one night after *maariv*, after davening somewhere I seldom go.

Motti approached me and greeted me warmly. I asked how he was doing, and he filled me in on his progress since we last met. It had taken a while until he found his first job at a public accounting firm. After a few years in that entry-level position, Motti was hired as the CFO of a small mental health agency providing low-cost therapy to the *frum* community where he lives.

"I guess I've kind of come full circle," Motti told me with obvious pride. "Instead of needing therapy like I did when I first met you, I'm now sort of helping others get the help they need to improve their lives."

FEELINGS OF WORTHLESSNESS AND INADEQUACY

CHAPTER 12

Creating the Self-Esteem Log

— Baruch

*O*rchos Tzaddikim discusses the importance of wearing clean clothes, eating clean food, and maintaining proper personal hygiene. It then concludes, "Even though these things could appear to be similar to arrogance and conceit, since their purpose is for the sake of Heaven, they are mitzvos [to conduct oneself that way]" (*Shaar Rishon, Shaar HaGaavah*).

More recently, Rabbi Dr. Abraham Twerski put it this way, "Commenting on a *pasuk* in *Tehillim* (118:13), [Rav Simcha Zissel Ziv] says that every person has a *yetzer hara* that tries to disable him by crushing him and deluding him into thinking of himself as inferior, unlikable, and unworthy."[1]

---

1. *Hamodia Weekly Magazine, Inyan*, June 14, 2017, 42—43.

In spite of the fact that maintaining proper self-esteem is necessary for fulfilling *ratzon Hashem*, many people struggle to achieve a healthy level of self-respect. Whether they were put down by misguided, critical parents and teachers or whether they were bullied by cruel peers and classmates, these people find it difficult to give themselves the inner support and self-confidence needed for success in life.

One such individual was Baruch, a sandy-haired entrepreneur in his late twenties. Baruch had a boyish smile and a charming personality that made him easy to like. He was soft-spoken, kindhearted, and extremely devoted to his wife and children. The major stumbling block in his life was his consistent failure to follow through on any of the myriad projects he started, but never managed to complete. After his umpteenth disappointment with himself for not reaching the finish line, he finally sought professional help from a close friend and colleague of mine, Rabbi Yaakov Salomon, LCSW.

Baruch's presenting problems were his feelings of discouragement and depression. Eager to climb out of the hole in which he found himself, Baruch committed to working with Rabbi Salomon on a regular weekly basis.

After a few months of intense psychotherapy, both Rabbi Salomon and Baruch felt they had reached an impasse. Baruch felt he liked Rabbi Salomon and wanted to continue working with him, and the feeling was mutual. Nevertheless, in spite of the mountains of encouragement and support Rabbi Salomon provided each week, they had not succeeded in budging Baruch any farther along the path toward achieving his ultimate goal of feeling better about himself.

At that point, Rabbi Salomon made the following proposal to Baruch. "I have a close friend and colleague," he began. "His name is Dr. Meir Wikler, and we often consult each other regarding our more challenging cases. Sometimes, only with the patient's permission of course, we conduct in-person consultations, where one of us will come and sit in on a therapy session the other is conducting, in order to offer insights and suggestions for improving the treatment."

Baruch perked up at the suggestion and appeared intrigued by the idea.

"Lately, I've been thinking about the work we are doing," continued Rabbi Salomon, "and I think we're both feeling kind of stuck. So I was wondering how you would feel if I invited Dr. Wikler to join us next week for an in-person consultation?"

"Thank you so much," Baruch gushed. "I'm flattered that you would go to all that trouble for me. I hope he'll be able to come."

"I cannot promise anything," Rabbi Salomon cautioned, "but I'll call him as soon as we're finished today and try to set it up for next week."

When Rabbi Salomon called and invited me to consult with him and Baruch, I accepted immediately. "I'll certainly try my best," I said. "I hope you both won't be disappointed."

The following week, at the appointed time, I arrived at Rabbi Salomon's Brooklyn office. I met privately with Rabbi Salomon for a few minutes, during which time he filled me in on Baruch's treatment history. Then Rabbi Salomon stepped out into his waiting room to invite Baruch in to meet with us.

As we had decided in our brief preconsultation meeting, Rabbi Salomon began conducting the session as if I were not present. "Tell me how your week went, Baruch," Rabbi Salomon said.

"I've actually been quite busy this past week," Baruch related proudly. "I'm looking into a new venture." Looking at me and then turning back to Rabbi Salomon, he asked, "Everything I say here will be kept confidential, right?"

"Baruch, the same privacy rules apply today as when we meet alone," Rabbi Salomon replied.

"Someone asked me to become his partner in developing a chain of fitness centers catering to the *frum* community," Baruch enthused. "You know, separate hours for men and women and things like that. We've been meeting with real estate people and discussing possible locations for Boro Park and Flatbush to start with. I'm really excited about this because it could turn out to be really big."

"Just what are you expecting?" Rabbi Salomon asked, tilting his chair back.

"This could be the break I've been looking for," Baruch explained. "We could really make a bundle on this operation. Then I'll finally be able to be in the big leagues like I've always wanted."

"You know, Baruch, that's exactly what you told me about the *chasunah* hall you were going to build last year," Rabbi Salomon gently observed. "I certainly hope this new venture is successful. But could it be that you are engaging in some wishful thinking? After all, most businesses grow incrementally and are not overnight successes."

"The *chasunah* hall project only fell through because I made some foolish mistakes in negotiating on the property," Baruch offered in his own defense. "I wasn't as firm and forceful as I should have been. I won't make those same mistakes again."

"What does your wife think of this project?" Rabbi Salomon asked.

"Oh, she's even more skeptical than you are," Baruch acknowledged. "But when this takes off, she's going to look at me very differently. You'll see. She'll finally respect me when I become rich. And there are no fitness centers in Boro Park or Flatbush now, so how can we not succeed?"

"Baruch, I'm not telling you to abandon this project," Rabbi Salomon clarified. "I'm just suggesting that you not raise your expectations too high. I remember how crushed you were the last time when things did not work out as you had planned."

During the natural pause at that point in the session, I shared my observations. "Baruch, Rabbi Salomon shared with me a bit of the history of his work with you before our meeting today."

Baruch nodded knowingly, looking eager to hear what I would contribute.

"It seems to me that you have been making a critical mistake in your thinking. You have taken the wagon of your self-esteem, your entire self-image, and hitched it to your next business venture. The only problem with that arrangement is that you lack the confidence to follow through and succeed each time. So you are in a Catch-22 situation. In order to build your self-esteem, you need to succeed in business. And in order to succeed in business, you need the confidence which comes from having a positive self-image."

Baruch was nodding in agreement as I was talking. When I finished, he heaved a big sigh and asked, "So what would you recommend?"

"I'll tell you what I think you need to change," I said, facing Baruch. "Instead of looking forward to solve your self-esteem problem, you need to look back. Instead of looking to the future, you need to look into the past."

"I don't really understand," Baruch said with a furrowed brow.

"Look, you and Rabbi Salomon have known each other for quite some time. Correct?"

"Sure. It must be close to a year by now," Baruch said, glancing over at Rabbi Salomon.

"Okay. So together you need to examine some of the things you have *already* done that have been successful. The future is unreliable. The past is irrefutable. Only by reviewing your past achievements can you ever hope to repair your self-image. That is something I believe Rabbi Salomon can help you with. And I am convinced that if you stick to that plan, you will learn to feel better about yourself, which will boost your confidence in all the areas of your life."

Baruch and Rabbi Salomon thanked me for my contribution and then concluded the session with each other.

After I left, I thought of all the people I had worked with and was currently working with who shared Baruch's feelings of inadequacy and lack of confidence, causing them to guarantee their own failure by inflating their expectations of themselves with wishful thinking. As I continued to develop the germ of the idea first uncovered in Rabbi Salomon's office, I came up with the cognitive exercise I call the Self-Esteem Log, which is described in the next chapter.

CHAPTER 13

Using the Self-Esteem Log
— *Yossi*

Hesitant to start *shidduchim*, Yossi first came to see me when he was twenty-two years old. Many of his friends were already going out and he felt he should be joining them. In addition, Yossi's parents were eager for him to get into the *parshah*, as he had younger siblings who would not marry out of order before him. Nevertheless, Yossi just did not feel ready. When his parents suggested speaking to someone about it, Yossi readily agreed.

It did not take long for us to uncover what was holding Yossi back. He feared rejection and failure to such an extent that he was trying to avoid the whole process. Yossi was thoroughly convinced that no decent girl would be interested in him. Firstly, he did not feel good about the way he looked. He had gained weight recently and was not happy about it. Moreover, he did not dress well and wanted to change that. Finally, he suffered frequent acne breakouts and wanted to consult a dermatologist to see if anything could be done about it.

Besides his appearance, Yossi also did not feel he had much to offer in other areas. His family was neither wealthy nor *meyuchasdig*. He was not a top learner in yeshivah. And he was not a very good conversationalist. With all of these liabilities, therefore, he could not imagine that any good girl would agree to meet him.

Scratching a bit further beneath the surface, I learned that his parents had not been very supportive as he was growing up. While he blamed himself for his poor self-image, he eventually acknowledged that his father's indirect criticism had impacted him negatively.

Yossi's father had not been abusive physically or verbally. But through his advice and suggestions, as well meaning as they might have been, Yossi's father conveyed his negative opinion on a regular basis. "Why don't you do it this way?" his father would say. Or, "Let me do it for you. I can do it better." In short, Yossi learned to distrust himself and his judgment on just about everything.

"So even if my upbringing affected the way I feel about myself," Yossi challenged, "at the end of the day, I still have low self-esteem. Since it's up to me to change that, what can I do to learn to feel better about myself?"

A perfect candidate for the Self-Esteem Log, I thought. Then I launched into my usual introduction for whenever I recommend this exercise.

"Yossi, do you consider yourself fluent in English?"

"Well, my grammar is not that great. But, yeah, I guess I speak English okay."

"All right, now how did you learn to speak English?"

"I heard it as I was growing up, I suppose."

"Wrong. That is not how children acquire language proficiency. If hearing a language was all one needed in order to learn it, I would be fluent in Hungarian by now because I live here in Boro Park, where Hungarian is spoken extensively. But I cannot speak one word of Hungarian."

"Okay, then how do children learn to speak a language?" Yossi wanted to know.

"They hear it spoken *to them*," I explained. "Studies have shown that only through face-to-face communication can children acquire language proficiency. And the same is true for adults."

"What does that have to do with self-esteem?"

"You see, Yossi, self-esteem is a form of language that someone with confidence speaks to himself. For example, 'I did that well.' 'I'm good at this.' 'That didn't go as well as I would have wanted. But I'll do it better next time.' These are the self-affirmations of someone with a good self-image.

"On the other hand, assertions such as: 'I'm no good at this,' 'I'll never succeed at this,' and 'Everyone else is better than me' are the words of someone with a poor self-image.

"You only learn how to talk to yourself in a self-affirming way, Yossi, if that's how you were spoken to when you were growing up. So what can you do if you reached adulthood without a positive self-image? Is it too late? Of course not!

"Think, what would you do if you worked for a company that had a branch office in Japan and the boss needed to send you there for ten days? You don't speak any Japanese, so how would you be able to work?"

"I don't know. I'd ask the boss to send someone else."

"No you wouldn't! You'd go to a crash course in conversational Japanese. And you can do the same to learn how to speak to yourself in the language of self-esteem. The crash course I'm going to give you is called the Self-Esteem Log. It's a ten-minute cognitive exercise I've developed to help people just like you. Are you willing to try it?"

"I don't know. Tell me what's involved," Yossi said cautiously.

"First, you have to buy yourself a spiral notebook. Any size will do. Then you write in the notebook for ten minutes a day, not more and not less. If the ten minutes are up and you haven't completed all the parts, you stop. The assignment is to write for only ten minutes. Once you do that, you have completed the assignment regardless of where you are up to."

"Why exactly ten minutes?" Yossi wanted to know.

"If you put in less than ten minutes," I explained, "you will not make significant progress. And if you work on this for any longer than ten minutes, the exercise will become too burdensome and you will not be able to keep on with it long enough to achieve real change."

"What do I write in the log?"

"Each entry consists of four parts. Part 1 is easy. That's the date of each entry. That's important because you need to be able to look back and know when you wrote each one.

"Part 2 is for you to describe a *machshavah, dibbur*, or a *maaseh* — a thought, something you said, or something you did during the previous twenty-four hours only, about which you feel good or proud. You cannot write about anything that took place more than twenty-four hours earlier. You need not write a whole megillah of background information. All that is necessary are a few sentences describing what you thought, said, or did that was good. You only need to include enough details so that you can look back at the entry in six months and remember the incident clearly.

"Part 3 is an itemized list, like a shopping list. There you write as many reasons as you can think of as to why what you did was good. Usually anything that is good is good for more than one reason, and your job is to list as many reasons as you can. Now most things are not completely good or bad. Rather, they are a combination of both. For the purposes of this exercise, however, you are only to list the reasons it is good.

"For example, let's say you wrote down in the previous part something you did that was good, but you think you don't do it nearly as often as you should. Then in this part, you should simply list why it was good that you did it, but leave off the thought that you should do it more often. The goal here is strictly to practice giving yourself credit for something you've done that is praiseworthy.

"Part 4 is also an itemized list. This time, however, you list the ways in which the thought, words, or deed you wrote about in the second part reflect positively on you.

"I'd like to give you now an example of just the opposite. Suppose you attended a meeting and said something stupid. Afterwards, you'd be busy beating yourself up for what you said."

"And how!" Yossi chimed in, nodding his head in agreement.

"And not only would you be regretting what you said," I continued, "but you'd also be looking at the whole incident from the angle of how poorly that comment reflected on you. For example, you'd suppose, *Now they probably think I'm an impulsive guy who speaks without thinking, that I have poor judgment, and that I'm lacking in basic common sense.*

"But in a similar vein, if you've done something good, it should reflect positively on you in multiple ways. And that is your task in the last part — to list as many of those ways as you can. Do you think you can do that?"

Yossi shrugged his shoulders and answered softly, "I'll try."

"Good. Be sure to bring your log with you when you come next time, because I'll want you to read one of your entries. When we review some of your entries together, I'll be able to give you suggestions about how to tweak the exercise to make it more effective."

Yossi had a hard time getting started. At first, we spent time working on his Self-Esteem Log in my office. Even when he graduated to doing it at home, he needed a lot of coaxing and encouragement to work on it more than once or twice a week.

"To his credit, though, he did not give up; he doggedly stuck to it. Over time, he became more and more proficient and comfortable with this exercise. Eventually, he even reported that it was making him feel better about himself. And at the point where he felt ready to enter *shidduchim*, he chose to end his weekly meetings with me.

CHAPTER 14

The Toolbox
— *Minna*

Whenever I work with someone using the Self-Esteem Log, I always ask him to keep a separate section of his notebook for recording the suggestions I give him for improving his entries. This section is called The Toolbox because it includes all the tools he needs to get the most out of this log writing exercise.

Below are the best tools I have developed and refined over the years, using them with people such as Minna, a middle-aged housewife and child of Holocaust survivors, who struggled her whole life with feelings of guilt, inadequacy, and low self-esteem.

TOOL #1

Part 1, the date of the entry, is so simple that no tools are needed to improve it.

Part 2, writing about a good thought or something good, said or done, however, is much more challenging. Many people are simply incapable of considering that anything they thought, said, or did in the last twenty-four hours is worthy of writing about. In fact, the reason they have difficulty with it is the very reason why they need to work on their self-esteem in the first place.

Tool #1 helps people find something to write about by offering four levels for completing Part 2. They are all totally acceptable, although the highest level is preferable.

> **Level 1** — writing something about which the person feels good or proud. If he cannot think of anything that qualifies for this level, he should then go down to the next level.

> **Level 2** — writing something about which the person feels uncertain whether it belongs in the log or not. It is a doubtful case. Maybe it is good. But then again, maybe it is not that good. Writing about something on this level allows a person the freedom to *begin* to think positively about himself without fearing that he is deluding himself in any way.

> **Level 3** — for this level, the person should think of me like I am a fly on the wall. What does this mean?

> The expression "fly on the wall" refers to someone who wishes he could be present, but not seen, at a private meeting. Just as a fly could easily gain access to a clandestine rendezvous, this person wishes he could eavesdrop on a confidential conversation without anyone knowing about it.

> "For the Self-Esteem Log," I explained to Minna, "assume I was a fly on the wall wherever you went during the past twenty-four hours. Not only did I hear everything you said, and see everything you did, but I also was able to read all of your thoughts. So when you sit down to write in your log, assume that you hear me saying to you, 'I cannot believe you are not writing about ________! I think that was good and you certainly should

write about it.' In other words, since you know me, you should imagine what I would tell you to write about even though you don't think it was anything special."

Level 4 — this is like a "doubtful 3." In other words, if the person is not sure whether even I, as a fly on the wall, would see something as good, he should go ahead and write about it because *maybe* I would. I instructed Minna to write about this sort of instance too.

TOOL #2

Most of the tools I offer are designed to help people complete Part 3, which is the list of reasons why what they wrote about in Part 2 is good. These are all preceded by a metaphor that I use to introduce and explain a tool, but which does not have to be written down. At this point, I told it to Minna.

"Suppose on Sunday a poor man comes to your home in the middle of the winter. He complains that he is freezing in his home and has no heat. He does, however, have a wood burning stove, and he asks you to give him a log, which he can use to warm himself. Then you go into your backyard and get him one.

"The next day, another poor man comes to your door. He tells you that he, his wife, and his eight children are suffering from the cold. He also has a wood burning stove in his home and he also asks for a donation of wood. You retrieve a log from your yard and give it to him.

"Do we say that what you did on Sunday is the same as what you did on Monday?" I ask.

"Of course," Minna replied.

"Okay. But did you *accomplish* the same thing on Sunday as on Monday?" I ask, rephrasing my question.

"Sure," Minna responded. "I don't see what you are driving at."

"On Sunday, you warmed up one cold person. On Monday, however, you provided warmth for ten people."

"Okay, I see your point," Minna conceded.

"Good. Now here's the tool: In order to fully evaluate any thought, speech, or action, it is necessary to consider not only all the people who benefited, but also the ways in which each one benefited. Each benefit for each person needs to be listed separately.

TOOL #3

At another session, I said to Minna, "Suppose someone asks you to go to Boston for a *dvar mitzvah*. You get in your car and start driving. After three hours, you've reached Hartford, Connecticut. Would we say that you've accomplished anything?"

"Well, I'm more than halfway to my destination," Minna answered. "So, I suppose I'm that much closer to Boston, where I can fulfill my mission."

"Exactly correct!" I enthused. "Even though you have not even begun to accomplish the *dvar mitzvah*, by getting closer to your destination, you have definitely made progress.

"So here's Tool #3: If your thought, speech, or action brings you any closer to a larger, long-term goal, then that becomes a separate reason why what you thought, said, or did is good, and it must be listed separately in your log."

TOOL #4

At another session, I gave Minna the following *mashal*. "Suppose you are walking along the sidewalk, approaching a front yard where some children are playing ball. Suddenly, their ball rolls down the lawn and into the street. From your vantage point, you see a car barreling down the road, heading straight for the ball. One of the children takes off after the ball and starts running between two parked cars. There is no way the car's driver will see the child, and the child is totally oblivious to the oncoming car. You are too far away from the child to grab him and prevent the inevitable tragedy unfolding before your eyes. Your only recourse is to shout at the child, which you do. The child stops in his tracks. The car whizzes by and the calamity is averted. The child's mother, who has been watching from the window of her home, rushes out and calls you a hero. Is her praise justified?"

"Of course," Minna answers matter-of-factly.

"But all you did was shout," I counter, playing devil's advocate. "Anyone can do that. Why is that such a big deal?"

"Well, according to your *mashal*," Minna replied, "I saved someone's life. I would certainly say that is worthy of praise."

"Exactly!" I confirmed enthusiastically. "Now here's the next tool for your toolbox. In order to fully evaluate any thought, speech, or action, you need to consider any and all negative consequences which may have been prevented by what you wrote in Part 2. In my *mashal*, you prevented a tragedy from taking place. That is certainly a major accomplishment.

"Also, if as a result of your thought, speech, or action, you prevented yourself from feeling guilty, inadequate, or depressed, then that is yet another reason why what you thought, said, or did was noteworthy. And that additional reason needs to be added to your entry in Part 3, which lists the reasons why what you did was good."

TOOL #5

Another time, while reviewing Minna's log, I told her the following *mashal.* "Suppose you had a friend who taught the fifth grade," I began. "And suppose she had to leave town to care for an ailing parent out of town. In order to hold onto her job for an indefinite period of time, her *menaheles* told her she would have to find a long-term substitute for her class. So she asks if you will do her the favor of covering for her, and you agree.

"Your friend gives you all of the teaching materials and lesson plans, and she instructs you to give written homework every night and collect it from your students every morning. Now, out of the twenty-five girls in the class, twenty-four do the homework every night and hand it in the next morning. One girl, however, never brings in her homework.

"At first, you warn her. Then you threaten her. Finally, you consult with the *menaheles* about this particular student. The *menaheles* calls the parents and really puts her foot down. Then she calls a meeting at school for the parents, you, the school guidance counselor, and herself. All of this is to no avail. The girl is not a behavioral problem. She listens and participates in class. And she passes all of her tests. Nevertheless, she stubbornly resists doing any homework.

"Now it is five months into the school year. You walk down the aisles of the classroom in the morning, collecting the girls' homework. And when you get to this girl's desk, she hands you her homework for the first time all year! How do you react? What do you say to this girl?"

Minna looked puzzled. "I'm really not sure," she mumbled. "I don't know what I should say. On the one hand, she should be praised, I suppose. But on the other hand, she really should have been doing the homework all year long."

"I would say that you should praise her profusely for doing her homework," I answered. "After all, you would want her to continue, wouldn't you?"

"I guess so," Minna acquiesced.

"Now let's continue the *mashal*," I said. "Let's suppose that later in the day, another girl in the class asks to speak with you during recess. She comes to you and asks the obvious question, '*Morah*, how come you made such a fuss when she gave in her homework today? I've been doing the homework all year and haven't missed even once, yet you never said anything like that to me.' How would you answer her?"

"That's a good question," Minna replied. "How should I answer her?"

"Perhaps you could tell the second girl," I suggested, "that apparently the first girl had a harder time doing her homework. And since homework was more challenging for her, she was entitled to more acknowledgment for overcoming that challenge. Now if you stop talking in class, which is something you are struggling with, then I would also make a fuss over it. What do you think about that answer?"

"Gee, I wouldn't have thought of that," Minna admitted. "But I agree that would be the right thing to say."

"Okay, now here's Tool #5 for your toolbox, based on that *mashal*," I said. "If any thought, speech, or action is more difficult for a particular person for any reason, then if he succeeds in thinking, saying, or doing it, he deserves more credit. And he is entitled to additional credit for each additional reason it was more challenging. For example, if he was in a similar circumstance in the past and was not able to do what he did this time, then that is an additional reason to note in Part 3 why what he wrote about in Part 2 was good."

TOOL #6

Sometimes people have a difficult time understanding what they are supposed to write in Part 4. Minna was no exception as she asked me one day, "Isn't Part 4 just a repetition of Part 3?"

"It's not a repetition," I explained. "It's a restatement. In Part 3 you list the reasons why what you wrote about in Part 2 was good. In Part 4, however, you list the ways in which what you did reflect positively on you. In fact, you really need to have at least one item in Part 4 that corresponds with each item in Part 3.

"To make it easier to complete Part 4, let me give you the following formula which you can use to complete Parts 3 and 4. Each item in Part 3 can begin as follows: 'It (what you wrote in Part 2) was good because ________.' And each item in Part 4 can begin like this: 'It (what you wrote in Part 2) shows that I am someone who can ________.' Or, 'It shows that I am someone who is ________.'"

Minna diligently worked on her Self-Esteem Log for five months. During that time, she reported a slight improvement in all of her presenting problems. She did not, however, reach the level of self-confidence she had hoped to achieve, and she opted to terminate our work together while continuing to work on her Self-Esteem Log at home.

CHAPTER 15

A Success Story
— *Heshy and Perel*

Heshy and Perel initially consulted me for couple's therapy. Heshy was learning full time in a small kollel and Perel was a receptionist at a doctor's office. They had been married for less than a year, but already things were going in the wrong direction and rapidly deteriorating.

Perel had a hard time articulating her feelings during our initial joint meeting. She was very concerned about not hurting Heshy. After I gently explained to her that I would be unable to help them overcome the stresses in their marriage unless she was more forthcoming, Perel agreed to tell me what was bothering her.

"I always wanted to marry someone who was confident and self-assured," Perel haltingly revealed, choking back tears. "I wanted a real man. And that's what I thought Heshy was when we were dating. But since we've been married, I see he is not that way at all. He is constantly asking me for reassurance about everything. It has gotten to the point where I think I might have, uh, I might have…made a terrible mistake."

In his defense, Heshy pointed to what he saw as Perel's somewhat critical nature and his sincere desire to please her. At the same time, however, Heshy did acknowledge that self-esteem was a problem for him and it was something on which he was willing to work.

Perel really was not interested in couple's therapy. She saw the problem as Heshy's and his alone. At my coaxing, however, she reluctantly consented to a brief round of therapy sessions.

After a few weeks, we had not gotten very far. Perel was unwilling to accept any responsibility for the stress in her marriage. She firmly rejected any suggestion that she was overly critical and/or that finding fault with Heshy should have any impact on his self-confidence. And Heshy, for his part, was increasingly willing to pursue individual therapy to work on his self-esteem. By mutual consent, therefore, we shifted gears by terminating the marriage counseling and beginning individual therapy with Heshy.

Heshy proved to be a very willing and cooperative patient, preparing for each session by making notes during the week about what he wanted to discuss. As his presenting problem was low self-esteem and low self-confidence, we launched into working on the Self-Esteem Log after the second or third session of his individual treatment.

Heshy was extremely diligent about making his entries, and in a very short time, he had built up to writing every night. Each time I introduced a new tool for him to add to his toolbox, I noticed he was successfully able to incorporate that tool into all of his future entries.

After a couple of months, Heshy reported that he felt better about himself and noticed that his level of self-confidence had also risen. He even reported that Perel had noticed and complimented him on a few occasions. Finally, he was able to give me concrete examples of when he had successfully asserted himself in situations where he had previously been unable to do so.

I congratulated Heshy on his personal growth and supported his decision to terminate the therapy. We had one final session and then I did not see him anymore.

Three years later, after having received a printed invitation, I decided to attend a *hachnasas sefer Torah.* I arrived early so that I could participate in the *kesivas ha'osios.* I entered the large room where the final *osios* were being written and took my place at the end of the long line that had formed alongside the table where the *sefer Torah* lay open.

The line proceeded slowly and I made small talk with the other men on line near me. As I approached the table with the *sefer Torah*, I got a glimpse of the *sofer* who was working there. It was Heshy!

I was sure that he had not been a *sofer* when I had worked with him, and I was very curious to find out what had happened. I did not want to make Heshy uncomfortable, however. So, as I usually do in such situations, I decided to take my cue from him.

When my turn came to write an *os*, I simply smiled at Heshy in a noncommittal fashion. In return, however, he smiled broadly and unabashedly exclaimed, "Oh, Dr. Wikler, so nice to see you! How have you been?"

I do not know if I was more surprised by Heshy's self-assured greeting or by his new profession. "*Baruch Hashem*," I stammered. "It's great to see you too. Tell me, I didn't know that you were a *sofer.* When did this happen?"

"You're right," Heshy replied. "I wasn't. About two years ago, I decided that I wanted to learn *safrus*, and I decided that the best place to learn it was Eretz Yisrael. So Perel and I agreed to spend one *zeman* in Yerushalayim so I could. I started with megillos and mezuzos. And a little over a year ago, I started working on this *sefer Torah*. So this is a really big simchah for me. I'm so glad you are here to see it, because I don't think I could have ever done it if not for our work together a few years ago."

"Believe me, Heshy, this is a really big simchah for me too," I said, holding back tears of joy. "Now show me, which *os* should I fill in?"

SECTION V

ANGER MANAGEMENT

CHAPTER 16

Reaching the Repressed Rage

— *Luzer*

In the famous *Iggeres HaRamban,* Ramban wrote to his son that anger, "is an evil trait that causes people to sin. And as Chazal have said, 'Whoever gets angry, all types of Gehinnom rule over him.'" Moreover, he instructed his son to reread the letter once a week and to teach others to do so as well. Finally, he promised that anyone who reads the letter regularly will be saved from all calamities and will be guaranteed to be a *ben Olam Haba.*

Aside from the individual's spiritual fallout resulting from poor anger management, the emotional and psychological collateral damage to his family members is clearly evident to any mental health practitioner. The benefits of helping people gain control of their tempers cannot be overemphasized, all of which are illustrated by the next case example.

Luzer and his wife, Goldie, came together for the first appointment.

Both in their mid-forties, they had a long history of ups and downs in their marriage, and I was not the first therapist they had seen. Apparently they had not been satisfied with the work they had done with their previous therapists and both were willing to give it another try.

Initially, I mistakenly assumed they were coming for marital counseling. Goldie set me straight right away. "Luzer has an anger management problem," she told me with a no-nonsense look on her face. "And I want you to work with him so he can learn how to act more like a mensch at home."

"If you want me to work one-on-one with Luzer," I innocently asked, "then why did you come today?"

"I want to make sure you get the picture straight," she shot back. "I simply don't trust that he will be honest with you about how he acts."

"Okay," I said, not wanting to be confrontational, "then why don't you give me an example?"

Goldie took a deep breath and launched into the story she was clearly prepared to tell me. "Last week," she began, "we had a disagreement about something. To tell you the truth, right now I cannot even recall what it was about. We find ourselves fighting so often these days that I cannot seem to remember all of the points of friction between us.

"Anyway, as I was saying, we had a disagreement while we were both in sitting in the kitchen. In the middle of our quarrel, Luzer just picked himself up and walked over to the stove where I had a pot of some noodles cooking. Luzer lifted the lid and looked inside the pot. Then he went over to the sink and took the bottle of dishwashing liquid. He coolly and calmly walked back to the stove and emptied the dishwashing liquid into the pot of noodles. Then he walked out without saying another word.

"I was so disgusted by what he did that I decided then and there that we have to meet with someone. And that's when I called you to make this appointment."

Luzer had a smug look on his face. "Do I get a chance to speak too?" he asked impatiently.

"Of course," I said. "Now it's your turn."

"Goldie very conveniently left out a few significant details," Luzer said in his defense. "She didn't tell you how she always criticizes everything I do and how she often does so in front of the children."

"I'm sure all of that is very annoying for you," I said to Luzer, "but are you saying that would justify what you did to the pot on the stove?"

"Maybe not *justify*," Luzer replied sheepishly. "But it would *explain* it."

"Goldie wants you to come for individual therapy," I said to Luzer. "How do you feel about that?"

I expected Luzer to object to being identified as the source of the problems they were having at home. To my surprise, he responded, "I have no problem meeting with you alone. In fact, I think I would prefer it."

I then turned to Goldie and explained, "If I do begin to work with Luzer, I will then be his therapist. That means that I will not meet or speak with you again unless Luzer approves. Are you all right with that?"

"Sure," Goldie said. "I want you to work with him. But does that mean that I cannot even speak with you over the phone if I have to tell you something about Luzer that I feel you need to know?"

"That's right," I said.

"I think I'm going to like this arrangement," Luzer chuckled.

"And why won't I be able to speak with you?" Goldie protested.

"Because in order for my work with Luzer to have the greatest chance of being successful," I said, "he has to know that I am not being influenced by anyone else and that whatever we discuss is kept absolutely confidential. If I am speaking with you without his permission, he will not be able to trust me or feel safe talking with me. And then I will not be able to help him, which will not be in either of your best interests."

Goldie reluctantly accepted my explanation and I began seeing Luzer individually.

"Where would you like to start?" I asked Luzer at his first individual session.

"You heard Goldie last week," Luzer retorted. "She already gave us our marching orders. She feels I need anger management."

"I know what she wants," I countered. "But she's not coming anymore. This is for and about you. So you get to decide what we should work on, not anyone else."

"Well, I suppose I do lose my temper too often," Luzer confessed. "So I guess I would like to learn how to control myself better when I get upset."

"Fine," I said. "So the first step would be to identify what triggers you. In other words, we need to learn what sets you off each time."

"Oh, that's easy," Luzer snickered. "It's Goldie. She's what sets me off each time."

I smiled, appreciating Luzer's sense of humor. As a wholesale stationery salesman, Luzer had a pleasant, jocular personality, and I could imagine how much his customers appreciated his phone calls. *Funny how many people with anger management issues at home are so personable with others outside,* I thought.

"I don't mean which events trigger your eruptions," I clarified. "Rather, we need to identify what thoughts and feelings fuel each outburst. In other words, what *about* Goldie's behavior gets you so upset?

"I'm not sure what you're looking for," Label said.

"Okay, here's what I want you to do," I advised. "During the upcoming week, look for incidents that fall into the following three categories: those where you felt angry but did not lose your temper, those where you were upset and did blow up, and those where you did not feel angry, although in similar situations in the past you might have exploded. Then try to record what you were thinking and feeling in each case so we can discuss all of this next time."

At our next session, Luzer came in with his notes written on the back of a damaged envelope. "I don't have any examples of category #2," he said with a smile. "But I don't imagine you're disappointed to hear that."

"Not at all," I beamed approvingly. Then we reviewed the incidents he shared from the previous week.

"It seems to me that all of these situations are examples of when you feel that you are not being treated with the proper respect," I concluded. "Would you agree?"

"Absolutely!" Luzer roared. "I think you have it straight."

"Not so fast," I cautioned. "Tell me how you feel you should have been treated in each case."

"Look," Luzer said in a more serious, reflective tone, "I'm the husband and the father. I believe I'm entitled to being treated with more respect, more deference. When I was growing up, and still today, my father was king in our home. No one disagreed with him about anything. I know I can't expect that nowadays, but I don't think I should have to put up with so much disrespect."

"No," I agreed, "no one should have to tolerate disrespect. But the examples you brought today indicate more disregard than disrespect. This seems to be a loaded issue for you. In order to sort this all out, we're probably going to have to talk more about what things were like for you when you were growing up."

Over the next few weeks, we did just that. At first, Luzer described everything as "wonderful," "normal," and "unremarkable." Exploring his past in greater detail, however, revealed that things were not as picture-perfect as he initially presented them. And once Luzer opened up fully, a much clearer rendering emerged.

"If the term 'kids at risk' had been around when I was growing up," Luzer shared with me one day, "it certainly would have applied to me. I guess I was kind of rebellious as a teenager. I didn't really have a head for learning. So I guess I was looking for other outlets. I recall, for example, that I once stole a car and took it for a joy ride...when I was fourteen. I cannot imagine what I was thinking at the time, other than that it seemed like fun. I could have been in a serious accident, gotten arrested, or both. *Baruch Hashem*, neither happened. But that will give you an idea of what kind of a kid I was back then."

"Fourteen-year-old *bachurim* who are not learning certainly do look for other outlets," I confirmed. "But not all of them steal cars. There must have been more going on at that time. I'm wondering why you were not learning well."

We then focused more on Luzer's learning difficulties as a child. "I still have trouble with it," Luzer added parenthetically. "It's not that I don't believe it's important. I know it is. After all, my father is a prominent *chassidishe rebbe.* But whenever I open a *sefer,* I fall asleep. I cannot keep a *chavrusa.* And whenever I try to attend a *shiur,* my mind always wanders. Believe me, I'm not proud that I don't learn. In fact, I'm very embarrassed about it. All of my brothers are *talmidei chachamim,* either *klei kodesh* or at least *kovei'a ittim.* I feel like the black sheep of the family, though no one says anything about it."

I suggested that we make it a treatment goal to help Luzer overcome his mental block against learning. He was very receptive and highly motivated.

Over the next few weeks we set up short-term and long-term rewards in a behavioral plan to get Luzer back into a realistic, modified learning schedule. At first, there appeared to be some signs of progress. Eventually, all of our efforts proved futile. Luzer's mental block against learning was much more stubborn than either of us realized.

Then Luzer came in one day eager to share a recent incident with me. "I was visiting my parents in their home over the weekend," he began, "and I don't know what possessed me; I decided to go up to their attic, something I rarely ever do. I started rummaging around there, not looking for anything in particular. Then I came across a small cardboard box with some papers inside. I opened it and looked through it. It contained some of my papers from elementary school. I picked one up and noticed it was a *Gemara bechinah* with my name on it, and I couldn't believe my eyes. It had the grade of one hundred written in red on it. Then I found another one that had a ninety-five written on it.

"I went downstairs with both test papers and walked into my

father's study. 'Hey, Ta, look what I found,' I said to him. Then I showed him both tests.

"He looked at both and was silent for a few moments. Then he looked up and asked, 'How come you only got a ninety-five on this one?' I didn't respond. But on my way home, I was thinking about what I felt like saying.

"I felt like saying, 'You know, Ta, that's probably what you said to me when I first brought these tests home when I was a kid.'"

Luzer went on to describe how he felt he could never satisfy his father's unrealistic expectations of him. He also spoke about how much he yearned for his father's approval, which was never forthcoming, and how he eventually gave up trying to earn it.

With this missing piece, the picture puzzle was now complete. Luzer understood that his mental block against learning was connected to his buried resentment toward his father. And his overreactions at home were a result of his chronic denial of those hostile feelings.

Armed with these new insights, Luzer was now able to defuse the types of situations at home which used to trigger his loss of control. That success, together with a new schedule at work that prevented him from keeping our daytime appointment, prompted Luzer to terminate his therapy with me.

Many years later, Luzer called. He was not trying to make an appointment. Rather, he wanted to share some good news.

"I get two mazal tovs," he began. "My son just had his bar mitzvah."

"Oh, mazal tov," I said. "May you and Goldie see much *Yiddishe nachas* from him always."

"But that's not all," Luzer continued. "I get another mazal tov. At the *seudas bar mitzvah*, my son made a *siyum* on the *Shishah Sidrei Mishnah*… that he learned together with *me*!"

"Wow, that's an even bigger mazal tov!" I exclaimed.

"Yes," Luzer added. "And I don't think it would have been possible had it not been for the work that we did years ago. So I'm also calling to thank you.

CHAPTER 17

Reclaiming Self-Respect
— Yechiel

Yechiel was a tall, lanky *kollel yungerman* in his late twenties who wore a rumpled black suit, creased open-necked white shirt, no tie, and a dusty black fedora. He rarely made eye contact with anyone and had a very defeated attitude about him. Even before we both sat down at our initial meeting, he began speaking.

"I just want you to know something before we start," Yechiel warned me.

"What's that?" I asked, wondering what he was preparing me for.

"I don't believe in therapy," he said haltingly, in a most nonconfrontational manner.

That's the first time anyone ever started that way, I said to myself. Instead of debating the issue with Yechiel, I chose to follow his gambit. "And why don't you believe in therapy?" I asked, genuinely curious as to where this would lead us.

"Look," Yechiel said with a didactic tone to his voice, "we believe that all wisdom can be found in the Torah. Right?"

"Sure," I confirmed. "I'm with you on that."

"Okay," Yechiel continued. "And we believe that the greatest Torah scholars today are the *roshei yeshivah*."

"I agree with that too," I said. "But what does that have to do with therapy?"

"Well, I've consulted some of the biggest *roshei yeshivah* today about my problem, and they have been unable to help me. So if they can't help me with their greater *daas Torah*, then it stands to reason that you won't be able to help me with your lesser knowledge of Torah. Uh, now I don't mean to disparage your learning, but you must admit that your level of scholarship is not anywhere near theirs."

"I don't disagree with anything you've said so far," I conceded. "I just have one question for you. If you feel that way, then why did you make this appointment to see me?"

"My *rosh yeshivah* sent me," Yechiel confessed sheepishly.

"How did he convince you to come?" I wondered out loud.

"He gave me two *mashalim*," Yechiel replied. "First, he said that sometimes you will find in the *sefarim* of *Acharonim* that they argue with a *Rishon*. How is it possible for an *Acharon* to take issue with a *Rishon* on any aspect of the Torah? he asked. Then he answered that while the *Rishonim* were well-versed in *kol haTorah kulo*, sometimes an *Acharon* would specialize in one area and therefore have a better grasp of that area than the *Rishon*. Similarly, he pointed out that while *roshei yeshivah* counsel people with problems, that is certainly not all that they do. Therapists, however, spend all day doing nothing else. It is possible, therefore, that a therapist might be able to help someone overcome a problem with which even *roshei yeshivah* were unsuccessful.

"The second *mashal* he gave me was comparing *roshei yeshivah* to eagles, the strongest birds that fly higher and see farther than any other fowl. Because they fly so high, however, they might not be able to see a tiny crumb of bread that a sparrow can see because the sparrow flies so close to the ground. Similarly, he said, therapists might be able to find solutions that *roshei yeshivah* cannot."

Once Yechiel fully expressed his ambivalence about therapy, he was ready to reveal the issue which had prompted him to come in the first place. "I'm ashamed to admit it," he began, "but...sometimes...I lose my temper.

"I'm not talking about just raising my voice, although that would certainly be bad enough. I'm talking about really losing control. I even use language that is totally unbefitting a *ben Torah.* Every time this happens, I am totally ashamed of myself and I promise myself that I will never allow it to happen again. Unfortunately, though, it always does happen again, and that's why I'm here."

Now if you put Yechiel together with another ninety-nine men and had to pick, based on appearance alone, the one in a hundred who had an anger management problem, he would be the last one you would suspect. He was so mild-mannered and soft- spoken, I sometimes had to strain to catch every word. His whole deportment was so passive and unassuming that I struggled to reconcile what Yechiel was saying with the way in which he presented himself. Yechiel gave new meaning to the expression, "Looks are deceiving."

"With whom do you lose your temper?" I asked.

"My wife, my kids," Yechiel replied, with guilt dripping from every pore on his face.

"I see this bothers you very much," I reflected.

"Are you kidding?" Yechiel asked rhetorically. "Most people hate the winter and look forward to the summer. I am just the opposite and I'll tell you why. In the winter, everyone closes their windows. In the summer, most windows are open. When windows are closed, I can comfort myself with the thought that maybe the neighbors didn't hear me screaming at home. Then I can walk down the street without feeling embarrassed. But in the summer, I know all the neighbors hear me when I lose control, and then it is difficult for me to face them the next day.

"Also, most people prefer Sukkos over Yom Kippur. Again, I am just the opposite. On Yom Kippur, I know that the *eimas hadin* will protect me for twenty-five hours. I am reassured that at least for one day a year I am safe and do not have to fear losing control. But on Sukkos, everyone is eating outside. And at least once during that week I'm bound to lose my temper. Then I know all the neighbors are being treated to the show. I can just imagine them sitting in their sukkahs, smirking and giggling to each other, 'There goes Yechiel again.' And when I see them in shul or on the street, I can't help imagining what they are thinking: *Wow, he really gave it to them last night!*"

Yechiel went on to recount his unsuccessful efforts to lick his anger management problem by meeting with various *roshei yeshivah.* The list of those he had consulted sounded like a Who's Who of the yeshivah world. He really went all the way to the top. In each case, the *roshei yeshivah* offered *chizuk* and encouragement. When he returned to report his lack of success, each time he was told to try someone else.

As I had done with Luzer, I instructed Yechiel to look for and bring back to me examples of incidents at home which fell into three categories: those in which he lost his temper, those in which he controlled his temper, and those in which he did not even feel angry, but in the past, he would have.

The next week Yechiel returned with examples of only the first two categories. After going through them carefully together, it became quite clear that the common denominator in all the cases was that Yechiel did not feel he was being treated with proper deference and respect. One example will suffice to illustrate this theme.

Yechiel came home at the end of the day, expecting to eat supper. His wife was busy with the children and asked him to wait. He had a narrow window of time in which to eat before he had to leave the house. As time dragged on, he felt his wife was ignoring him and his need to eat.

"Did you remind your wife that you needed to leave at a certain time?" I asked.

"She knows my schedule," Yechiel said. "And besides, I didn't want to appear as if I was disparaging her taking care of the children. But then I couldn't take it anymore and exploded."

"What would you have expected your wife to do differently?" I asked.

"Well, she could have stopped for a second and told me how much longer she would be," Yechiel said. "Then I would know if I should serve myself or wait for her to serve me."

"Did you go without supper that night?" I asked.

"No," Yechiel explained. "As I was standing around waiting, I took some of what was cooking on the stove."

"Do you mean that you ate your supper standing?" I asked.

"Yes," Yechiel confirmed, almost surprised at my question.

"Why didn't you eat sitting down?" I asked, not suspecting the answer I would receive.

"Well, I couldn't sit down," Yechiel said, aware that I needed more information. "You see, after my wife does the laundry, she has nowhere else to put it besides on the kitchen table. So at that time there was no room at the table for me to sit. But that is often the case. I'm used to eating standing up. I have to do it more often than not, because my wife doesn't always get to put the laundry away the same day it's washed."

Yechiel was beginning to perspire, and the air-conditioning in my office was not working that day. So I invited him to make himself more comfortable by taking off his suit jacket.

"I, uh, prefer to keep it on," Yechiel said sheepishly.

"Would you mind telling me why?" I gently inquired.

"Well, I, uh, don't always have time to shower," Yechiel explained. "And if I remove my jacket, there might be an odor. So I prefer to keep it on for *kavod habrios*."

"I thank you for respecting me," I said. "But it seems that you are not really showing yourself much self-respect."

Yechiel said that was an issue for him. He felt so badly about himself that he literally did not feel entitled to better treatment.

I then pointed out to Yechiel that this might be the root of his anger management challenge.

"How so?" Yechiel asked, truly confused by my interpretation.

"You see," I said, leaning forward, "if you mistreat yourself, then you are more desperate for others to treat you with even more respect than is normal, in order to compensate. And then, when they do not live up to your expectations, you become enraged. If you could learn to treat yourself with more self-respect, you would be less demanding of others."

"That sounds good in theory," Yechiel protested. "But how can I treat myself better if I don't feel worthy of better treatment?"

"That's a good question," I affirmed. "And I believe Chazal have the answer."

I then quoted what the *Sefer HaChinuch* (*parshas Bo*, mitzvah 16) has to say about the subject, "Know that man is influenced by his actions. And his heart [and mind] and all his thoughts are constantly [influenced] by his deeds, whether good or bad.... Because hearts [and minds] are drawn after actions."

I also pointed to what the Ramchal says in *Mesillas Yesharim* (chap. 7), "External movements [of a person] awaken internal ones. And certainly, [a person] has more control of his external [actions] than his internal [thoughts and feelings]. But if [a person] will use what is under his control, he will eventually be able to procure that which is not [currently] under his control."

Yechiel was convinced, and he wholeheartedly agreed to try to implement my behavioral strategy.

My first step was to get Yechiel to treat himself with more self-respect at dinnertime. "Push the laundry to the side or remove some from the kitchen table. Put down a place mat. Take a paper napkin for yourself and set down the cutlery. If your wife is not ready to serve you when you come home, serve yourself and sit down and eat like a mensch."

Yechiel struggled with this assignment. He was not able to complete it all right away. I praised him, however, for even partial successes. Eventually, he reported that he managed to do it all the way, and the satisfaction he experienced infused him with the optimism to continue.

Next, we worked on Yechiel showering on a daily basis. This was more difficult to accomplish, as his daily routine was somewhat disorganized. Nevertheless, with mutual persistence, we cleared that hurdle as well.

The last goal we set was for Yechiel to take better care of his wardrobe. More specifically, he took his shabby suit to the cleaners and dusted off his hat.

Without our having addressed Yechiel's temper per se, he volunteered one day that he had seen a marked improvement in that area.

"Has your wife noticed the change?" I asked, trying to test the validity of his report.

"Oh yes, she has," Yechiel assured me.

"How do you know?" I asked, wanting to be certain he was not simply telling me what I wanted to hear.

"She mentioned it herself without my asking," Yechiel said proudly. "Just yesterday, when I mentioned that I have an appointment to see you today, she said, 'I really owe him a tremendous debt of gratitude. He's helped you so much.'"

"Don't let her give me all the credit, Yechiel," I cautioned. "You did a lot of hard work here and at home. And only you know how difficult that work was. She may be able to see the results, but she cannot know how much effort you put in to get to where you are today unless you tell her."

Over the years, I have bumped into Yechiel occasionally at simchahs. Whenever we meet, I see he is not comfortable engaging me in conversation and I respect his preference for maintaining that distance. Of course, I would like to ask him how he is doing, but since it might embarrass him if I were to initiate conversation, I restrain myself. The warm smile on his face, however, says more to me than words could ever express.

NEGATIVE ASSOCIATIONS

What Are Negative Associations?

My First Day in High School

The term "associations" refers to emotional states that are linked or associated with particular life experiences. We all have associations. Some are positive. Some are negative. Our ability to make these connections is similar to our imagination, which Rambam refers to as the *koach hamedameh* in his *Shemoneh Perakim* (1:9). Our most powerful associations are those connected with sensory perceptions.

For example, suppose your late, beloved *bubby, a"h*, had a wonderful recipe for chicken soup that you have not tasted for years. Now your aunt found the recipe and serves you a piping hot bowl of that heavenly broth. As the tantalizing aroma wafts up into your nostrils, you sigh and observe, "This smells just like the soup *Bubby* used to make!" And at that moment, the cozy, warm, and yummy feeling you always had whenever you visited your grandparents washes over you like a large, fluffy feather quilt.

Your *bubby* is no longer here, having passed on to the *olam ha'emes* many years ago. Nevertheless, you associated the good feeling you always had in her home with the smell and taste of her scrumptious chicken soup. And now that you are tasting her soup in your aunt's home, you are reexperiencing that same good feeling. This is a positive association.

Here is another example: Suppose you had one best friend in kindergarten. This friend lived around the corner as you were both growing up and you played together every day. This friend attended the same elementary school as you and remained your best friend throughout.

When it came time for high school, you both attended the same school and even deepened your friendship. Then, at the end of tenth grade, your friend's family moved out of state, severing this priceless relationship.

During the final few weeks before your friend moved away, a popular new Jewish song was topping all of the charts. You heard that song played at every simchah. It was playing on every stereo of every car in which you traveled. And practically every chazzan in shul used that niggun on Shabbos for "*Lechah Dodi,*" "*Keil Adon,*" or Kedushah. Now, many years later, whenever you hear that melody, feelings of sadness and longing are evoked, which bring you back to those stressful days in tenth grade when you were struggling with the pain of separation from your first best friend. Those gloomy feelings would be considered a negative association.

Finally, one more example — a personal one — should suffice. I attended the same yeshivah for elementary school for nine years. No, I was not left back. The yeshivah I attended was very progressive and had its own kindergarten. When I entered high school, therefore, it was the first time I was going to school at a new location, in a new building, with new classmates.

To say I was a bit anxious would be putting it mildly. I was eager and excited, but also somewhat uncomfortable with all of the new adjustments I was making.

When we all arrived on the first day, all ninth graders were assigned lockers and given the combination numbers for the padlocks. I never had a locker in elementary school. The whole idea of having my own private space at school really appealed to me. When we were instructed not to share our combination numbers with anyone else, I made a silent commitment to myself to follow that advice.

I then put my coat and all of the books I did not need into my locker and proceeded to my first class. *I'll get the books I need for the rest of the classes*, I thought, *during the short breaks between classes throughout the day.* After my first class, I ran down to the basement where the lockers were located to retrieve my books for the next class. To my dismay and utter frustration, I was unable to unlock the padlock.

Not wanting to be late for class, especially on the first day of school, I ran back up the stairs without my books. My stress level rose considerably as I suffered some embarrassment in that class because I did not have my books, notebook, or even a pencil with me.

At the next break, I ran down to the basement and again tried to open my lock. And once more, I could not.

By midday, I had not managed to open my locker. But I'd had no trouble opening it in the morning. For some reason, whatever I tried after the first time did not work. Finally, in desperation, I shared my combination with a friend and asked him to try to help me. "I guess I'm not very experienced with these kinds of locks," I told him in my defense.

To my surprise, even my friend could not get my lock to open. After each afternoon class, I kept trying to open that stubborn lock. By midafternoon, I was beginning to entertain the thought that I might have to go home without my coat and books. What a horrible start to my first day in ninth grade.

With no other choice available, I approached another friend and gave him my combination, asking him to try to open my uncooperative lock. When he, too, failed to get it open, I began to see the prospect of returning home empty-handed as no longer a possibility, but as a probability.

Shortly before the buses were scheduled to leave, I decided to give it one more try. I approached a classmate whose last name began with *w*, (and who was therefore assigned to the locker almost next to mine), who was standing nearby me, getting his coat from his locker, and I asked him for help.

Instead of asking me to point out which locker was mine, as my two friends had done earlier in the day, he asked me what my locker number was. I told him. He then went over and opened the lock on the first try! Apparently I had been attempting to open the *wrong* lock all day long. I then grabbed my coat and books, catching my bus just as it was about to leave.

To say it had been a stressful day would be putting it mildly. In my mind, those anxious feelings were not associated with books or locks. Rather, they were connected with the strong smell of paint that permeated the basement halls on that first day of high school. In preparation for the new school year, the interior of the school had been painted. While the paint had dried on all the upper floors, the paint in the basement was still wet. They must have used a lead-based paint at that time because I haven't come across that distinct paint odor in a while.

But for many years afterwards, whenever I passed a house, apartment, or room that was freshly painted, I was gripped with unexplained feelings of anxiety. And then, as soon as I passed beyond the smell of the paint, the feelings dissipated. I found this extremely puzzling. After all, why should I be experiencing that queasy feeling in the pit of my stomach just because I smelled fresh paint? I could never figure it out.

It was not until I entered graduate school and learned about associations that I discovered what the reader has already grasped. I had associated intense feelings of anxiety with the smell of fresh, lead-based paint. As a result, I felt anxious regardless of what was going on in my life at the time. As soon as I made this connection, the association did not disappear. I was able, however, to whittle away at the anxiety by reminding myself that I was no longer in high school, trying unsuccessfully to open the wrong combination lock.

Over time and drawing on my clinical training and experience, I was able to develop a useful therapeutic tool to help others overcome negative associations that interfered with their functioning and/or compromised some of their significant relationships. That tool is described in the next chapter.

CHAPTER 19

The Five-Step Exercise

— Yankel

Yankel was a life insurance salesman in his late thirties when I first began working with him. He was personable, well-liked in his community, and successful at work, having earned entry into the prestigious Director's Roundtable — an employee incentive program at his company which recognizes the achievement of the most successful salesmen — for two years in a row. He was also married to a well-known and respected *sheitel macher* and had four beautiful children who were all excelling in school.

What, one might wonder, would propel someone like Yankel, with so much going for him, to enter therapy? The answer was that he simply could not enjoy any of the good fortune with which he was blessed, and that gnawed at him every day like a festering wound that would not heal.

In short, Yankel suffered from chronic feelings of depression ever since adolescence, and I was not the first therapist he had seen. In fact, he had worked for almost four years with his former therapist, making considerable progress with him. Yankel felt, however, that he had accomplished as much as he could with that therapist, and he wanted to see if he could get even further working with someone else.

As a result of the work he had done in his previous therapy, Yankel had a very clear understanding of the source of his depression. Yankel was the oldest of three brothers, and their father was a well-known and well-respected *chassidishe dayan* and *rav* of a large, well-attended shul in the community. As *rav,* their father demanded high standards of *hasmadah* and *dikduk b'mitzvos* from his *mispallelim.* This resulted in attracting high caliber *bnei Torah* and earning a reputation of excellence for the shul.

But his father's applying the same demanding, perfectionistic standards to his own children yielded disastrous results. Yankel's younger brother became a drug addict in high school and landed in jail before his twentieth birthday. And his youngest brother went through a messy divorce, after which he became totally estranged from the family.

Yankel felt he could never do enough to please his father no matter how hard he tried. While he was growing up, he believed he had to be at the top of his class every year. Getting perfect scores on all his tests was not his only goal. He had to also get all the extra credit points on each and every quiz. And while his rebbeim all considered Yankel to be a *masmid* and an *illui,* he never experienced any feelings of satisfaction or accomplishment because he never received any approval for his efforts from the one whose opinion meant the most to him, his father.

Whenever Yankel attempted to enjoy or appreciate his successes, he was constantly plagued by self-critical thoughts: *I could do better. Others do more.*

During the course of our work together, Yankel shared many areas of life where self-doubt and self-criticism literally robbed him of the joy and satisfaction he otherwise might have enjoyed. One session, he focused on his job, and he specifically zeroed in on his relationship with his manager, Phil.

"Every morning when I come into the office," Yankel began, "I'm always nervous that Phil is watching what time I'm arriving. If I'm a couple of minutes late, I'm sure he's noticing and thinking that I don't deserve to be included in the Director's Roundtable. In fact, I feel he's watching me even if the door to his office is closed. And the stress this causes me stays with me the entire day. I also feel he's thinking that I'm not selling enough policies, even though I know that I'm selling more than anyone else in the office."

"Has Phil ever said anything to you about your performance?" I asked.

"Rarely," Yankel replied. "He works mostly with the newer guys, training them. But the funny thing is that on the few occasions when he has commented, he has always had something positive to say. And when the monthly statistical reports come out, he always makes a point of congratulating me on my sales record. I know it makes no sense, but I simply cannot shake the conviction that, on the inside, he's critical of me, really disappointed in my performance, and his praise is insincere. I feel such stress about this that it is a big struggle for me to come into work every day. Even before I walk in the door, I feel this pressure to perform that makes me so insecure about my job that I even worry about how I would support my family if Phil asked me to leave."

"Yankel, would consider your emotional reaction to Phil inappropriate?" I asked.

"Definitely!" Yankel shot back. "I just don't know what I can do to shake this nagging feeling that Phil disapproves of me and is within a hairsbreadth of firing me all the time."

I then explained the concept of negative associations to Yankel and he was easily able to relate to it. "I also have an exercise I've developed to help people overcome their negative associations," I added. "Would you like to try it?"

"Sure," Yankel answered eagerly. Then he took out his phone on which to make notes.

"I call this The Five Steps," I began. "It's for any time you catch yourself having an emotional reaction to a situation which you feel is inappropriate in any way. The first step is to write down what you are feeling. Let's do this right now, together, so you'll get a better idea of how this works."

"Okay," Yankel agreed. "So I should write down what I'm feeling at this moment?"

"No," I corrected. "Write down what you feel when you walk into your office every morning."

"Oh, I get it," Yankel said. "Well, let's see. I feel threatened, insecure, and about to be fired, as if I'm not maintaining even minimal performance standards."

"Good," I commented. "Now let's move on to Step 2, which is to write down the situation or circumstances that triggered the emotions you wrote about in Step 1."

"Do you mean what is making me feel so insecure?" Yankel asked.

"Yes, exactly," I confirmed.

"But I don't really know that," Yankel said. "That's why this is so confusing for me."

"Yankel, I don't mean that you should write down *why* you are feeling insecure. That is the purpose of doing this exercise. What I mean is for you to write down *what* happened that precipitated your emotional reaction."

"Okay," Yankel said, nodding his head. "I suppose you mean that I'm entering a situation where my performance is being monitored by someone who could either promote or fire me if he wanted to."

"That's it," I encouraged. "Now you're ready for Step 3, which is to write down a situation, circumstance, or episode from the past in which you felt the same way as you described in Step 1."

"You mean insecure and threatened?" Yankel asked.

"Yes," I confirmed. "Try to think of something from when you were a child."

"Well, that's easy," Yankel said as his face lit up with a flash of insight and awareness. "I felt the same way whenever I walked into yeshivah. I was always afraid of disappointing my father because however well I did academically, it was never good enough for him."

"That's what this is aiming for," I encouraged. "But it's more effective if you can focus on a specific episode or incident."

"Okay," Yankel said, scratching his head and scanning his memory for a clear example. "Well, I remember once showing my father a test on which I had received a ninety-five. I still can see the look of disappointment on his face as he frowned and shook his head in disapproval."

"Great," I said. "That's a perfect example. Now you're ready for Step 4, which is to make an itemized list of the similarities between the situations you described in Steps 2 and 3."

"You just lost me," Yankel said with a look of confusion on his face. "The two situations are very different."

"Yes, they are," I confirmed. "But they are also similar in some ways. Here, I'll help you. In both cases, you were dealing with an authority figure. In both cases, your performance was being scrutinized by someone who had the power to hurt you in some way. And finally, if you failed to satisfy the authority figure, you would be helpless to do anything about it. There was no court of appeals."

"Okay," Yankel conceded as he rapidly typed what I had said into his phone. "Now I understand what you meant."

"Good," I said. "Now let's move on to Step 5. Here is where you write down the differences between the two situations described in Steps 2 and 3. You begin, and if you have trouble, I'll help you."

"Uh, let's see," Yankel said, pursing his lips in concentration. "I suppose even if I get fired, I could find another job; whereas when I was growing up, I couldn't exactly find another set of parents."

"Excellent, Yankel," I said. "What else can you think of?"

"Uh, there's more?" Yankel asked.

"Much more," I replied.

"Okay," Yankel said, chewing the top of his pen. "Phil is not really critical of me like my father was. With Phil, it's just a fear. But with my father, it was a reality I lived with every day."

"Excellent," I cheered. "But there's still more."

"Really?" Yankel wondered. "Now I need your help. What other differences are there?"

"The biggest difference is *you*," I pointed out. "In other words, in the situation described in Step 3, you were a helpless, young child. In the case you wrote about in Step 2, you are a mature, independent adult."

Yankel just sat there absorbing the impact of this exercise. Then he asked, "So how is this supposed to work exactly?"

I took a Chumash off the bookshelf and said, "Let me give you a *mashal.* When *klal Yisrael* were trapped between the Yam Suf, the mountains, and the Mitzrim, what did Moshe *Rabbeinu* say to calm them down? He said, 'As you see Mitzrayim today, you will never again see them' (*Shemos* 14:13). Rashi says this means that Moshe was hinting that the Mitzrim you see today will not remain alive beyond today. But one could also say that after the about-to-happen *Kri'as Yam Suf,* the way *klal Yisrael* will look at and feel about this nation of former tormentors will never be the same.

"Similarly, if you repeatedly go through this exercise whenever you catch yourself overreacting, it can help you detach yourself from the negative associations which interfere in your life. Yes, there are similarities between the current and former circumstances. That is what forms the basis of the association. But there are also significant differences. And reminding yourself of those can help you to react more appropriately to the current situation."

Yankel tried working on the Five-Step Exercise at home, and he came in the following week and reported that he could already see some improvement. He still felt somewhat anxious and uncomfortable when he entered his office each morning, but the intense insecurity and almost paranoia were no longer there. He could see how continued use of this exercise might help him even further.

There were many other issues we addressed during our work together. Yankel's therapy lasted over two years until we achieved the results he was looking for, to be able to enjoy the many blessings in his life without feeling guilty, inadequate, or like a failure.

CHAPTER 20

The Five-Step Exercise, Part II

— *Yonah*

Most of the time, I am consulted about emotional challenges or family conflicts. Less often, however, people seek help for dealing with concrete issues impacting their lives. At such times, I usually feel less able to effect change, because there is little I can do to alter the situation. All I can offer is to help people cope with the difficult circumstances in which they find themselves.

Yonah certainly fell into the latter category. His wife was diagnosed with a life-threatening illness six weeks prior to his coming to see me. Although Yonah, a tall, clean-shaven man in his early forties, was the major breadwinner in the family, his wife, Shiffy, was the emotional backbone of the family. She was the doer, go-getter, and go-to person whenever Yonah or one of his four children had any kind of crisis. Whether business was temporarily slow at Yonah's *sefarim* and Judaica store, one of the children had a falling out with a best friend, or there was any kind of financial crisis in the family, it was always Shiffy who knew just what to do and what to say to make everyone feel better.

The fact that Shiffy was the one who was incapacitated by the debilitating side effects of the aggressive treatments she was receiving was too much for Yonah to handle. When he broke down in tears one day while giving his brother an update on Shiffy's medical condition, Yonah realized he needed help to get him through the trials and tribulations that lay ahead. It was at that point that his brother recommended that Yonah meet with me.

"I'm not really sure what you can do for me," Yonah confessed at our first meeting. "My older brother thought it would be a good idea, and I always take his advice."

"Tell me," I probed, "what about the whole *parshah* with Shiffy is the hardest for you to handle?"

Yonah initially focused on the crippling anxiety he experienced every time Shiffy had any diagnostic test, scan, or procedure. And during the course of her illness, there were many. Immediately, Yonah would picture the worst-case scenario. And then he would consider the *possible* negative results as if they were *probable.*

This type of catastrophic thinking will be discussed in depth in chapter 29. One of the most helpful tools in managing the concomitant excessive anxiety is the split-screen technique. Needless to say, I taught Yonah this approach, which he used extensively and successfully during the course of Shiffy's illness.

After working with Yonah for about five months, he asked if we could shift our focus to something that was weighing heavily on him, and for which he felt the split-screen method was ineffective. Shiffy's illness was not responding to the treatments as well as her doctors had hoped, and a dangerous, potentially life-threatening procedure was now being considered. Her doctors had hoped this would not be necessary. Now, however, they saw no other alternative. This posed a new threat to Shiffy's life, and Yonah was contemplating the unthinkable.

"There is something I've been thinking about," Yonah began and then cleared his throat, "which I don't feel I can discuss with anyone else."

I had no idea what was coming. One thing was clear though. Whatever it was, it was not going to be easy for me to hear.

"I think I have to be realistic," Yonah said. "I don't think I'm engaging in catastrophic thinking when I say that Shiffy might not make it, *chas veshalom.* I mean I'm hopeful and I'm davening harder than ever before in my life. But I cannot pretend that there is no risk involved in this procedure."

I gulped hard and nodded. *Could Yonah really be about to discuss the unspeakable?* I wondered as I marveled at Yonah's courage. At the same time, I could not believe how much progress he had made in managing his own anxiety to have reached the point where he could even bring up this delicate and terrifying subject. I shared my feelings of admiration with him and then encouraged him to continue.

"When I allow myself to consider even the possibility of the worst-case scenario," Yonah almost whispered, "then I see myself as totally lost, hopeless, and alone. Of course, I know I would not really be alone because I have a loving, supportive family and extended family. And I really would not be lost and hopeless. Nevertheless, whenever I contemplate this worst-case scenario, that's the feeling that overwhelms me. I understand it would be appropriate to feel sad and even depressed. I suppose that would be normal. But I don't think it would be expected for someone else in my situation to feel so lost, helpless, and alone. I mean, in every marriage, one spouse passes on before the other. And, as devastating as that is for the surviving spouses, I don't believe they all feel as alone as I imagine I would feel."

Once again, I praised Yonah for his courage in broaching this topic with me, and I cited it as an indication of how much progress he had made. Then I briefly presented to him the phenomenon of negative associations as discussed above. I went on to explain the Five-Step Exercise and asked if he would be willing to use it now in my office.

Yonah was very receptive to the idea. He took out a pen and paper and asked me to repeat the instructions for Step 1, which I did. Then he wrote, "I am feeling hopeless, helpless, lost, and all alone."

"Good," I said. "Now write what situation or scenario has triggered those feelings."

"My wife will most likely need the procedure the doctors were trying to avoid, but now see as necessary," Yonah said slowly while writing in his notebook. "As a result, I could end up as a single parent to my children. Contemplating this possibility is what has triggered those feelings."

"Now here is the hard part," I cautioned. "Try to think of a situation or scenario from your past in which you experienced the same feelings as you described in Step 1."

Yonah furrowed his brow. Then he stared at the floor. I could not tell whether he was trying to think of something or whether he had thought of something and was wrestling with himself as to whether or not he should share it with me. After a few moments of silence, he spoke.

"This isn't something I generally publicize," Yonah said with a note of embarrassment, "but I guess it's all right if I mention it to you."

"Yonah," I advised, "you know that everything you tell me is kept strictly confidential. I've already explained to you that you are protected by law. I am even required by law to explain to you your rights to privacy, which I did at our first meeting."

"Yes, I remember." Yonah reassured me with a weak smile. "Well, I already told you that I didn't have an easy childhood. But I never went into much detail about it. I suppose now, perhaps, there would be a *toeles* for me to tell you more about it."

"Whatever you tell me in therapy is for *toeles*," I pointed out. "Besides, if there is anything negative that you tell me about someone, I am not listening to be *mekabel*, but only in order to understand you better."

"Well, my father, *a"h*, was not an emotionally healthy man. He suffered from depression and perhaps had other issues as well. I know he was on medication and had seen a psychiatrist, although I never learned the full extent of his challenges. Anyway, one day when I was about nine years old, he up and abandoned our family. I don't know where he went or why, and I never saw him again after that. I don't know if it was too painful for my mother or if she was trying to shield me and my siblings. But either way, she never spoke about him after that. And even if we asked, she always tried to change the subject.

"As a result of my father abandoning our family, my mother had a very difficult time making ends meet. She worked. But I don't believe we lived on her income alone. She must have gotten some help from someone or somewhere. More than the financial limitations, however, my mother's inability to really tend to our emotional needs was the worst consequence for us. She was either too emotionally hurt or simply overwhelmed. Either way, after my father left, she was just not there for us anymore.

"There were nights when there wasn't any supper prepared for us. We certainly didn't starve; we always had food. But we often had to take whatever we could find by ourselves. Our mother simply wasn't able to be there for us — emotionally and sometimes physically.

"So when you ask me for a situation in which I felt alone, helpless, and frightened, my father's walking out on us is what comes to mind."

"I'm sure that's putting it mildly!" I exclaimed. "What a horrible thing for a nine-year-old to have to go through. It must have been terrifying."

"Other people have it worse," Yonah said, trying to minimize his childhood trauma. "After all, it was not as if I was physically abused or anything. That's certainly much worse. I can't imagine how children deal with that."

"Yes, child abuse *is* terrible," I concurred. "But this is not a competition for whose suffering is greater. And what happened to you certainly would cause any child to feel insecure. After all, your entire support system was suddenly pulled out from under you at such a tender age."

"Okay," Yonah said, although I could tell he was not fully convinced.

"Remind me again, what's the next step?"

"The next step is Step 4," I said, leaving the issue partially unresolved. "In Step 4, you make a list of the similarities between the situations described in Steps 2 and 3."

"Well, in both cases," Yonah began, "I'm being left by someone very important to me. With my wife, she is not choosing to leave me. But I am nonetheless being left by her. And in my father's case, I wasn't the only one left. But I was left too."

"Exactly," I said. "But there are many more similarities. See if you can come up with them. If you have trouble, I'll help you."

"Okay," Yonah said. "Um, well, in both cases, the consequences of my being left are very serious and dramatically impact my life for the present and the future."

"Very good," I said. "But there are still more."

"Wow," Yonah sighed, "this is harder than I thought. Uh, in both cases the one who is leaving is a very close family member. And in both cases, there is nothing I can do to prevent being left. It is totally beyond my control."

"Yes, indeed," I affirmed enthusiastically. "I think you got them all there. I can't think of any more myself. And now it should be clear to you as to why the current situation should evoke such feelings from your past. We have compiled a long list of significant similarities. Now let's try to finish this before we run out of time for today. The final step, Step 5, is to list the differences between the situations you described in Steps 2 and 3. You can start that yourself now."

Yonah studied the floor again. After a considerable silence, he wrote, "In one case it was my father, a parent, and in the other case, Shiffy is my wife. In one case, the separation was caused by reasons which I still don't fully understand. And in the other case, the separation would be caused by a clear medical problem. In one case, there was always the hope of reunion, which never happened and caused me additional disappointment. In the other case, the separation would be final, until Mashiach comes, that is. I think I got them all. Do you see any that I missed?”

“That’s an impressively long list,” I observed, complimenting Yonah. “But there is one major area of difference that you omitted.”

“Really?” Yonah asked, looking perplexed.

“Yes,” I said. “You left out all of the differences in *you*.”

“Oh,” Yonah said, nodding his head. “Do you mean that when my father left, I was a child, and now I am an adult?”

“Exactly correct,” I emphasized. “Yes, not only were you a child, but you were also immature, helpless, and totally dependent on your parents for all of your emotional and physical needs. Today you are not only an adult, but you are also an independent, mature adult who maintains his own successful business. And you have resources in your life now that you did not have when you were a child.”

“Resources?” Yonah asked. “What resources are you referring to?”

“You have people to turn to for support if you need it, who were not available to you when you were nine years old,” I said.

“You mean like you,” Yonah asked.

“Yes,” I said. “But not only me. You also have friends, your *rav*, and your older brother, who you said you are closer with now than you were as children. Because of the similarities, it is understandable that you would associate the loss of your father when you were a child with the possible loss of your wife now. Considering the differences between those two situations, however, can help you to feel less alone, insecure, and helpless.”

Before we ended the session, I recommended that Yonah take out and review the answers he had written to the Five-Step questions whenever he catches himself feeling overwhelmed during the coming week.

As her doctors had warned, Shiffy did need to undergo the dreaded procedure. *Baruch Hashem,* she survived it. Due to complications, however, she needed to remain in the hospital for another three weeks, during which her parents pitched in by taking the children to temporarily live with them. And even when she was able to go home, her weakened immune system did not allow her to bring the children back home until another three weeks had passed. Eventually, Yonah, Shiffy, and their children were fully reunited at home and began the pleasant task of returning, gradually, to normal life.

As Shiffy's condition improved, Yonah no longer felt the need to meet with me on a regular basis. We tapered down our meetings until we had our final session, where we reviewed our work together.

At that termination session, Yonah reported to me that he felt very hopeful and positive about Shiffy's prospects for a healthy future. Of course, nothing was certain. But from the reports they had received from her doctors, there was more than ample reason for optimism.

"And even if something unexpected comes up, *chalilah*," Yonah added, "I feel much better equipped to deal with it than I did when we first started."

"Tell me," I asked, "what did you find most helpful in getting you to where you are today?"

"There really were many things," Yonah replied. "It's hard for me to pinpoint them all. But what does stand out for me, looking back, are those two exercises you taught me. More specifically, what I'm referring to are the split-screen technique and the Five-Step Exercise. I found that I used both quite a bit, especially during Shiffy's most recent hospitalization. That was a real challenge for me. And I felt I was tested as never before. *Baruch Hashem,* I got through it better than some of the lesser setbacks we encountered at the outset of our journey."

As I always do at a termination session, I offered Yonah the option of returning in three months for a follow-up appointment, which he gladly accepted.

Three months later, when Yonah came in for his follow-up appointment, I was delighted to learn that Shiffy had fully recuperated and had already returned to her part-time teaching job. So we spent most of the session discussing his recent, exciting plans to open up a branch of his store at a new location across town.

EXCESSIVE ANXIETY

CHAPTER 21

What Is Anxiety?

— *Reuven*

According to the National Institute of Mental Health, approximately forty million adults between the ages of eighteen and fifty-four suffer from some sort of anxiety disorder. Exactly what is excessive anxiety and what are its symptoms?

Anxiety is another term for fear and worry. Most anxiety is reality-based and appropriate for the circumstances that trigger it. For instance, if we hear an intruder in the middle of the night, *chas veshalom*, or if our brakes fail on the highway, it is normal to experience intense fear. And if we have to give a model lesson or go on a job interview, it is natural to feel some less intense worry and tension. While these situations generate some anxiety, for most people the *level* of anxiety is clearly appropriate.

Some individuals, however, at times experience levels of anxiety that are excessive and inappropriate. These people can feel worry, fear, and even panic. They may feel lightheaded, dizzy, and unable to concentrate. In more extreme cases, they may experience heart palpitations and shortness of breath. They even may fear blushing, fainting, vomiting, having a heart attack, losing control, or "going crazy." The physical symptoms are real and not "just in their mind." And there may be some legitimacy to the danger they perceive. The *extent* of the danger, however, is clearly blown out of proportion.

Typically, anxiety sufferers are tormented by their obsessive preoccupation with their worries and concerns. They also engage in what is called "catastrophic thinking." In other words, they believe that the worst possible outcome of any situation is what is most likely to happen. While this worst-case scenario is a possibility, it may only be a remote possibility. But anxiety sufferers treat this negative possibility as a *probability*, and then they go on to act as if this worst-case scenario has already taken place.

The Torah refers to excessive anxiety in *parshas Bechukosai*: "They will be chased by the sound of a rustling leaf. They will run away [in fear] as one runs from a sword. And they will fall, but no one is chasing them" (*Vayikra* 26:36).

For the one suffering from excessive anxiety, the danger appears all too real. To them, all their worry and concern is appropriate. In fact, they often feel intense frustration and completely misunderstood by friends and relatives who encourage them not to worry.

One of the best examples I ever encountered of someone suffering from excessive anxiety was Reuven, a twenty-something, wiry *yeshivah bachur* I worked with almost forty-five years ago. Reuven was plagued by all sorts of anxieties. He was obsessively preoccupied with his standing in the yeshivah where he learned. He was convinced that his peers looked down on him. He felt intense pressure to compete with others in order to improve his status and image in other people's eyes. And he never felt any satisfaction or sense of accomplishment in spite of his intense investment of time and effort in the *beis midrash.*

One of Reuven's many concerns was his deeply held conviction that he would never be able to find a suitable *shidduch.* And even if he did manage to find a girl willing to marry him, he feared that he would be unable to support a family. His parents had struggled financially while he was growing up, and he did not want to have to go through a repeat of the family tension that economic stress caused his parents. He recalled, for example, that his parents often quarreled openly in his presence regarding financial matters. At times, these altercations were so intense that Reuven feared his parents might even get a divorce.

Reuven was a very private person, and it was excruciatingly difficult for him to come to talk with me. On occasion, I would see him from the window as he came for his weekly appointment. He would walk quickly, repeatedly glancing over his shoulder to check if anyone he knew was watching him as he approached my office. And when he finally arrived and sat down, he was always out of breath.

Reuven spoke quickly, trying to get as much said in the allotted time as he could, as if the more information he gave me, the quicker he would find relief. At the time, I mistakenly assumed that Reuven would be helped by getting his worries off his chest and out onto the table. As I listened empathically, however, I noticed that his tension only mounted. By the end of each session, Reuven was even more wound up than when we started. Even though he never seemed to come up for air and spoke a mile a minute, Reuven always expressed disappointment and frustration with me when the session was over, complaining that I had not helped him.

Reuven clearly needed to talk, and I believed he could be helped by my supportive listening. What I did not understand at the time was that my nondirective, laid-back approach was exacerbating his condition. Then, when I started engaging him more actively by interrupting him with my questions and comments, I saw that he still felt frustrated and tense. My approaches just were not helping, and so Reuven terminated the therapy.

Had I known then what I know now, I would have explained to Reuven that the goal of therapy for excessive anxiety is not the elimination of all anxiety. That is not realistic or even necessary.

The goal, rather, is to learn to *control* the anxiety so that it does not interfere with or impede healthy functioning. I then would have offered him one or more of the following techniques for managing anxiety that I have taught other anxiety sufferers with much success.

CHAPTER 22

Charting Anxiety

— *Shimon*

While anxiety sufferers often feel as if their entire day is one continuous state of high-level anxiety, in reality, the degree of their tension wanes and waxes. Like a stock market chart or a graph showing opinion poll results, one's level of anxiousness rises and falls many times during the day. It can be extremely helpful, therefore, to chart both the highs and lows one is experiencing each day. In other words, what events, feelings, or thoughts trigger the most intense levels of anxiety? Also, what experiences, interactions, or ideas tend to relieve at least some of the anxiety or generate calm feelings of safety and security?

Often people are not even aware that they are saying things to themselves that are helpful. They tend to overlook this strategy because they have an all-or-nothing attitude. In other words, they are of the opinion that if it does not eliminate their anxiety completely, then it really is not helpful. This is, of course, completely inaccurate.

Any reduction in anxiety is a success that can be built upon to achieve even greater results.

Once someone has even a week's worth of notes on his high and low anxiety episodes, he is then in a position to use the information gathered. Regarding the high-anxiety episodes, what is the common thread? Is there a pattern here? How can these situations be dealt with more successfully? And regarding the low-anxiety episodes, exactly what succeeded in reducing the anxiety, however little? Then a list of these helpful strategies should be compiled so they can be utilized again in the future when high anxiety strikes.

One person may discover, for example, that he becomes more anxious when he is farther from home. Another person may learn that his anxiety is triggered whenever he feels exposed to the judgment of others, while a third person learns that his anxiety peaks whenever he suspects the possibility of physical injury or a possible medical problem. Once the theme or unifying factor of one's anxiety is identified, he is then able to look for the source of his anxiety in his past.

Returning to Reuven, for example, it is clear to me in retrospect that his anxiety originated in the marital tension he witnessed between his parents at home when he was younger. Nothing plants anxiety into the life of a child like the fear that his parents may divorce. Even more than death, children are terrified of the prospect of their family falling apart. Normally, children do not even consider such a frightening scenario. When they hear their parents arguing openly with raised voices, as Reuven did, they then are forced to contemplate the unthinkable — a divorce.

Once someone identifies the source of his anxiety, he is in a much better position to separate his past from his present using the techniques that will be described later. But even if the source of his anxiety is never discovered, the charting exercise is still helpful because it begins the process of compiling a list of effective strategies for managing anxiety.

Consider, for example, Shimon, an eleven-year-old boy I worked with more recently. He was terrified he might vomit in public whenever he was in a new or unexpected social situation. As a result of his charting, he learned the following steps he could take to reduce his anxiety and therefore reduce the chances that he would, in fact, regurgitate.

He carried an improvised air sickness bag in his pocket made from a plastic food storage bag inserted in a small brown paper bag. So if he did vomit under stress, he would at least be spared the added shame of soiling himself and/or his surroundings.

He even practiced throwing up in between parked cars for the times he was on the street on Shabbos, when he could not carry his air sickness bag. He did this during the week by taking a swig from a water bottle, holding the water in his mouth, pretending he needed to vomit, and then expectorating it between parked cars. This got him used to how he would vomit, if necessary, in the least obtrusive manner possible.

He also learned to remind himself that even though he might feel nauseous, it would not necessarily lead to his having to vomit. Only a small fraction of the times he became nervous triggered feelings of nausea and then actually led to vomiting. Focusing on this fact that he was more likely not to end up vomiting served to calm him during times of stress.

In addition, he learned that he could explain away the vomiting by telling others that he had a stomach virus, which carries no stigma. This was a helpful strategy in situations where he imagined others might suspect that he was really vomiting due to his skyrocketing level of anxiety.

Finally, he realized that people sometimes throw up from indigestion after eating something that does not agree with them. Those who might see him vomiting, therefore, would not automatically assume it was a result of anxiety.

CHAPTER 23

Systematic Desensitization

— *Levy*

When we are frightened by something, the very thought of it generates snowballing anxiety. And just as that is true for adults, it applies even more so to children, who generally tend to be more anxious than adults. At such times, it often seems as if one has only two options: 1) avoid the situation arousing the anxiety, or 2) face what feels like overwhelming fear. Given these two options, most choose the former.

There is, however, a third, more therapeutic option — namely, systematic desensitization. This approach entails introducing the patient to gradually increasing levels of exposure to the object of his or her fear. In this way, the anxious person deals with his fear in bite-size pieces that he is able to handle. As Chazal have taught, "*Tafasta merubah, lo tafasta. Tafasta mu'at, tafasta* — If you try to accomplish too much, you will fail. However, if you attempt to achieve just a little, you will succeed" (*Rosh Hashanah* 4b). This need not be done in a therapist's office and can be even more effective if done in the comfort of one's home.

Consider, for example, Levy, a cherubic nine-year-old who developed a pathological fear of going to the dentist. His mother, practically in tears, reported to me that during his most recent trip to the dentist to get a cavity filled, Levy carried on so violently that the dentist resorted to putting Levy in a straitjacket. After the dental work was completed, the shell-shocked dentist told Levy's mother that he was unwilling to ever do it again. He recommended that she make arrangements for her son to be admitted to the hospital the next time he needed dental work, so that he could be sedated.

Desperate to avoid the hospitalization, Levy's parents consulted with me and I suggested a course of systematic desensitization.

"How do we break down going to the dentist into graduated steps?" Levy's mom asked.

I then instructed her to recreate a visit to the dentist at home, where the negative associations Levy had could be replaced with positive ones. "Pick a time when you, your husband, Levy, and his younger sister are all at home," I began, "and inform Levy that you are going to 'play dentist' with him. Then, at the appointed time, have your husband put on his *kittel* to simulate a dentist's white coat. Have Levy sit in a recliner and drape a sheet over him. Then let your husband place whole wheat crackers in Levy's mouth to simulate taking X-rays of his teeth. (When the 'X-rays' are finished, you can let him eat the crackers.) After the 'X-rays,' have your husband simulate drilling by brushing Levy's teeth with an electric toothbrush.

"The key to the success of this charade is for the atmosphere to be lighthearted and fun. Feign seriousness throughout the 'visit.' For example, tell your daughter that she cannot take a turn sitting in the 'dentist's chair' because she does not have an appointment for that day. And Mom should be hovering over Levy in an exaggerated display of concern that everything should be proceeding properly.

"If you are successful, both children will start giggling and the whole affair will be so much fun that both children will ask you to repeat it."

The following week, Levy's parents returned to report a resounding success. As I predicted, both children absolutely loved the rehearsal and begged for an encore.

"Now what?" Levy's mom asked.

"Repeat it," I advised. "Only this time make it even more serious and dramatic. That way it will be even more fun. Then discuss with Levy what he would want as a prize if he lets the dentist work on him next time without putting up any resistance. Hopefully, the combination of the positive associations from the rehearsals, coupled with the prospect of earning a meaningful reward, will help Levy overcome his excessive anxiety.

Three weeks later, Levy's parents returned and proudly reported that Levy was so well behaved at the dentist's office that the dentist simply could not get over the change since Levy's last visit. Then they laughingly described the look of horror on the dentist's face when he first saw Levy walk into his office. In fact, Levy not only allowed the dentist to clean, examine, and X-ray his teeth, but he even sat still while the dentist drilled and filled another cavity!

Chalk up one more success for systematic desensitization.

CHAPTER 24

Systematic Desensitization, Part II
— Feivel

This technique can help adults as well as children. I recall, for example, a *chassidishe bachur*, Feivel, who was in his early twenties when he came to see me about his fear of flying in an airplane.

"Why don't you just travel by car, bus, or train?" I asked, playing devil's advocate.

"I was just *redt* a *shidduch* from Europe," Feivel explained, "and I will have to go for the *beshow* in three weeks. This is just the *shidduch* I have been hoping for. I can't let this go. Do you think you can help me get on the plane in three weeks?"

"I certainly do not offer guarantees," I replied. "But I am willing to work with you to try to make this happen."

We then began an intensive program of systematic desensitization. In my office, I used guided imagery to help Feivel visualize himself first boarding the plane and eventually flying calmly. This was combined with excursions to the airport, where Feivel was instructed to watch planes taking off and landing. He was instructed to sit in the waiting area and imagine himself boarding and eventually actually flying in a plane.

All of these steps were challenging for Feivel. He resisted all of them at first. His strong motivation, however, propelled him forward each time, enabling him to conquer each step until the day of his departure.

To help insure a successful flight, at our final session before leaving for the airport, I told Feivel to take a candy from my office and keep it in his pocket. If he would feel totally panicked and desperate during the flight, he was instructed to suck on the candy. "But this is only for an absolute emergency," I counseled.

Two weeks later, Feivel returned with a huge smile on his face. "Mazal tov," he announced as he entered my office. "I'm a *chasan!*" Feivel went on to fill me in on the details.

The flight had been difficult for him. He perspired a lot, especially upon takeoff. He never really felt at ease during the flight either way. "But I did it," he said proudly. And then with a wry grin, he added, "And I never had to take out the sucking candy you gave me. In fact, I still have it with me. Then he reached into his pocket and retrieved it to show me as he beamed with satisfaction.

CHAPTER 25

Social Phobia
— Nachy

Systematic desensitization is also an effective strategy for dealing with a common excessive anxiety condition called social phobia. Those with social phobia experience excessive, and at times crippling, anxiety triggered specifically by certain social situations. Outside of those situations, these people act appropriately and are totally in-distinguishable from anyone else. Placed in one of the situations that triggers their anxiety, however, and they experience fear and panic which completely immobilizes them, causing them added embarrass-ment and shame.

Take Nachy, for example. He was a yeshivish, unmarried man in his early twenties when I met with him. He was working for a software company, earning a good living. He had plenty of friends and a disarming, delightful sense of humor. And in spite of his disability, he was still able to make jokes about his severe social phobia.

Nachy had no difficulty socializing one-on-one. But in a group of even three or more, he was completely unable to participate in conversation. It was not that he did not want to contribute or that he had nothing to say. Rather, he was so gripped with fear that he was incapable of opening his mouth. All of his friends understood Nachy's situation and fully accepted him. They never teased him or pressured him to speak in a group. In fact, they generously covered for him whenever necessary. Nachy himself, however, could not tolerate the frustration he felt whenever his twosome became a threesome. And at one point, he felt he could take it no longer. It was then that he consulted with me.

Nachy's social phobia was not limited to social gatherings and group discussions. He also found it extremely difficult to make phone calls to strangers and to leave messages on answering machines. "Whenever I hear the beep tone and know I have to speak," he explained, "I freeze. I cannot even leave my name. I feel such intense pressure that I prefer to hang up and call back later."

One of the most unusual manifestations of Nachy's social phobia was his inability to recite *kiddush levanah* with a minyan.

"But everyone is saying it to himself," I pointed out. "Why should that be a problem?"

"That's true," Nachy conceded. "But when it comes to the '*shalom aleichem*' part, however, I have a problem. I cannot answer, '*aleichem shalom.*' You see, whenever I feel I have to respond on the spot, I get tongue-tied and cannot speak at all. So instead of embarrassing myself each month, I just say it *b'yechidus.*"

After I explained the systematic desensitization process to Nachy, he said he was willing to try it. First, we tackled his fear of leaving messages on answering machines. I had him rehearse in my office the way he would leave his name and phone number. Once he was able to practice this easily, I had him call my office phone from my house phone. And then I assigned him the homework of calling my answering machine every day until our next appointment.

Nachy voiced skepticism. He was not sure he could do the homework

I assigned. Nevertheless, he agreed to try. And when I walked into my office the next day and found his message waiting for me on my answering machine, I knew we were making progress.

Next, I had him make calls to 800 numbers, asking for information. He used my phone and made these calls from my office.

Nachy was extremely resistant at first. With each call, however, it became slightly easier for him. After a few weeks of that, he reported he was finding it possible, although not easy by any means, to make necessary phone calls. He still resisted calling. But the resistance was not nearly as strong as it had been.

Finally, I had Nachy practice saying *kiddush levanah* in my office. I recall him laughing at the absurdity of our saying it inside my office during the day. We both realized, however, that it was a huge step to go from saying it with me in the security of my office to saying it outside of his shul on a *motza'ei Shabbos*. In order for this to work, we needed an in-between or halfway step for him to take. For this, we used guided imagery in which I asked him to visualize himself standing outside of his shul, reciting *kiddush levanah* with everyone else. He practiced this visualization in my office. Then, for homework, I asked him to set aside time at home to conduct similar visualization sessions.

We worked on these visualization sessions for a couple of weeks leading up to the next time *kiddush levanah* would be recited. I can still remember the tone of satisfaction and pride in Nachy's voice when he told me he had said the *tefillah* with a minyan. And, as if that was not enough, I heard about Nachy's success in a voice message he had left on my answering machine!

Social Phobia, Part II
— *Berel*

Kiddush of the weekly variety also posed a similar problem for Berel, a middle-aged electrician with nine children. When his oldest was engaged, Berel came to see me for help with his social anxiety.

Berel was a very happy-go-lucky person who experienced intense anxiety whenever he had to recite Kiddush at home if anyone other than his immediate family was present at his Shabbos table. For twenty years, his family understood that someone else would have to make Kiddush if anyone outside of the family was there. Even the presence of his parents, brothers-in-law, or sisters-in-law would prevent Berel from being able to get through Kiddush without stammering uncontrollably. The fact was, he also stumbled over those familiar words each week even when only his immediate family was present. Nevertheless, the stuttering was less severe when only his family was listening, and they were used to it already.

"And so am I," Berel confessed with a chuckle during the initial consultation.

"Then what prompted you to make this appointment?" I asked.

Berel cleared his throat and sat up in his chair. "As I told you, my daughter has recently become a *kallah*," he began. "And although the *chasunah* will not be for another two-and-a-half months, I'm already thinking ahead to the *Shabbos sheva berachos.* My *mechutan* will be there for the whole Shabbos. And I don't know how I'm going to get through it."

"Why not have someone else make Kiddush, like you do at home whenever someone else is there?" I asked.

"That's what I plan on doing," Berel replied, shaking his head, which indicated that I was not grasping his dilemma. "It's not the Kiddush that I'm worried about. I certainly know how to get out of that. I can suggest that the *chasan* make Kiddush for everyone. What I am worried about are the *bentshing* and *sheva berachos.* I cannot see how I will be able to get out of reciting at least one of the *sheva berachos* at one of the three *Shabbos seudos.* And most likely, the *mechutan* will insist that I say the *berachah acharisa*, the longest one! With both families there, I will embarrass myself and my daughter when I stumble over the words. So I came to you to see if there is anything I can do to prevent that catastrophe."

"Would you consider taking medication?" I asked gently.

"I'm really against taking any kind of medication," Berel insisted. "I usually avoid even taking Tylenol. So if there's any other way of working on this, I prefer to try that method."

I assured Berel that the medications for social anxiety are safe and side-effect free. In addition, the medication would work quicker than therapy. If, however, he still refused to consider that option, I was willing to work with him without his taking medication. I then went on to explain to Berel the way systematic desensitization works.

Berel was eager to get started. So I had him recite all seven *sheva berachos* in my office. In the privacy and security of that venue, however, Berel still stammered over the familiar words. *This is not going to be easy*, I thought while we were scheduling his next appointment.

As with Nachy, I put Berel through a couple of sessions of rehearsals in my office. First he read the *berachos.* Each time I coached and encouraged him. Then I suggested he sing them with the familiar tune.

It did not take long for Berel to get to the point where he could recite the *berachos* smoothly. To make it more challenging, I would describe the scene at the *Shabbos sheva berachos* so he could acclimate himself to the visual image of "performing" in front of others.

After two perfect recitations, I congratulated Berel.

"But there's a big difference between saying the *berachos* here and my saying them at the *Shabbos sheva berachos*, where there will be so many strange people around," Berel protested.

Reluctantly, I agreed. "In order to build up to the real event," I thought out loud, "we would need some stranger to sit in on these rehearsals. How would you feel about that?"

Berel was willing to give it a try. But he could not think of how we could get a stranger to sit in on his therapy session. Then it struck me that we might be able to enlist my wife, Malka. I proposed this to Berel. As long as she wouldn't tell anyone about it, he replied, he would be willing to try.

After briefing my wife, I invited her into the consultation room and introduced her to Berel. Then Berel took the siddur and went through the *sheva berachos.* He was so anxious about it that his throat became dry and he asked for some water. A couple of sips later, he tried again and got through the *berachos* with only minor hitches. Then I asked my wife to give Berel feedback. She was very supportive and encouraging.

Berel had a hard time accepting Malka's praise at first. After a few more rehearsals, however, he began to feel more comfortable. With the increased comfort came increased confidence. And as his confidence rose, his anxiety receded.

Malka joined us for part of the next couple of sessions. To make it all more realistic for Berel, I brought out grape juice and a *becher* at the final session before the *chasunah.* Then I wished him *hatzlachah* and figuratively held my breath until I saw him again two weeks later.

Berel walked in for his first session after *Shabbos sheva berachos* beaming with such pride that I knew right away he had succeeded. He gave me a detailed report of the Friday night *bentsh*ing, at which his *mechutan* insisted Berel recite the *berachah acharisa*. He described how his heart was pounding as he lifted the *kos*. To his great relief, however, he recited the *berachah* almost flawlessly. And the minor hitch he encountered was so negligible that he realized no one noticed. Berel was so grateful to me, and he also asked that I thank my wife on his behalf.

Subsequently, we went on to tackle his Kiddush anxiety as well, using the same systematic desensitization approach which had conquered his *sheva berachos* anxiety. And when we concluded our work a few months later, Berel presented me with a beautiful *birkas habayis* mirror, which adorns my home to this day.

Globalizing/Partializing

— *Suri*

Anxious people sometimes involuntarily elevate their own level of anxiety by lumping all of their problems together, making them feel stuck, helpless, and overwhelmed. This unhealthy mental process is called globalizing. And it can completely immobilize people, preventing them from moving forward.

Take Suri, for example. When she first walked into my office, she began speaking even before she sat down. And she spoke so quickly that I felt out of breath just listening to her as she ticked off her long list of challenges.

Being a single mother, Suri felt the extra burden of parenting her two elementary school-age sons, one of whom seemed to be adjusting poorly to her recent divorce. Her ex-husband was not paying the child support the *beis din* had imposed and she felt pressured to find work quickly. While she had a degree in accounting, she could not find a position that would enable her to be home when her children got off the school bus. In addition, Suri felt she had been so hurt recently by her best friend that the relationship could not continue to be the source of support it had been until now. Finally, her father, who had been emotionally abusive to her when she was growing up, was now terminally ill and living out of town. Should she be visiting him now out of respect? she wondered out loud. While she never fully forgave him for his mistreatment of her, she nevertheless felt she had a Torah obligation to put that aside and make the trip to fulfill *kibbud av.*

"You've certainly got a lot on your plate," I observed when Suri finally came up for air. "Were you expecting to deal with all of that today?"

Suri went on to explain why she needed to address all of these issues as early as yesterday. Her previously studious son was already beginning to fail in yeshivah and his rebbi had already called Suri to report this sudden downturn. Her finances were extremely limited and she felt the need to secure employment ASAP. And her father's condition was deteriorating rapidly, forcing her to make a decision one way or the other very soon about traveling to see him.

I validated the pressure Suri was experiencing. I also empathized with the need she felt to resolve all of her problems immediately. Nevertheless, I gently pointed out to her that she was clearly globalizing, and it was totally unrealistic for us to address all of the items on her long list of presenting problems in the short time left in that session.

For the first time since she began the session, Suri leaned back in her chair. She silently nodded as I continued speaking.

I then explained that the antidote for globalizing is partializing. As long as she lumps all of her problems together, I pointed out, she will feel them all weighing down on her. On the other hand, if she can separate them and then prioritize them, she will be in a better position to accomplish something and move forward. Before we ended, I gave her the homework of selecting one of her concerns to focus on for the next session.

Suri was very dissatisfied with me and my recommendation. She told me bluntly that I had not been helpful and she felt as overwhelmed as she did when she first walked in the door. Begrudgingly, however, she did agree to consider what I had asked her to do.

When Suri came in for her next session, she was much more focused and also much less anxious. She acknowledged that she had reflected on my explanation of globalizing, and she reluctantly admitted that it had helped her to put her situation in a better perspective.

We then went on to discuss the issue she had selected for that day's session. Her son was not doing that badly. Her father's condition had improved slightly. And she had partially repaired the breach in her relationship with her best friend. What she wanted to speak about first, therefore, was her uncertainty about accepting a recent offer of employment that seemed to have equal pros and cons.

By the end of that session, Suri had clarified her feelings and resolved to accept the job offer she had received. She then acknowledged that my having encouraged her to be more focused on a single issue had helped her move forward.

CHAPTER 28

Globalizing/ Partializing, Part II
— My Personal Example

The technique of partializing is something I learned after I engaged in globalizing in the spring of '83, while coming down the homestretch to complete my doctoral dissertation.

I had finished all of my required course work for my doctoral degree. In addition, I had completed all of the necessary and extensive library research, endless meetings with my faculty advisors, and recruiting and interviewing the study volunteers needed for my doctoral dissertation. Finally, I had written the first draft of my dissertation and submitted copies to each of the three members of the faculty committee, who would decide whether I would earn my doctoral degree. I then met with each of them to learn what revisions they wanted me to make in order for them to accept my dissertation.

Armed with their three long lists of additions and changes each professor wanted, I had to rewrite my 386-page dissertation within a narrow window of about ten days. If it took any longer than that, there would not be enough time for my typist to retype the entire document, for me to make copies and submit them to the committee, and for them to review it and meet with me for my defense of the dissertation, all before the university's deadline for graduating in June. (Keep in mind, this all took place in '83, well before laptops and PCs and word processing. Even a single change on one page would require the retyping of an entire manuscript.)

While ten days sounds like ample time to make the necessary revisions, it should be noted that, at that time, I was working three days a week at a clinic and maintained a private practice of two days a week. I was left, therefore, with only two or three solid blocks of time during which I was able to work uninterruptedly on making all of the necessary revisions to my dissertation.

At the start of the first block of free time, I sat down at my desk with a fresh pad of yellow paper, sharpened pencils, a copy of my first draft, and the three lists of required revisions mandated by each of the members of my doctoral committee. I glanced at the clock, noting that I had slightly less than two hours before I would have to stop working and rush to my next obligation.

My heart began to pound as I considered how little time I had to accomplish so much work. I rearranged the papers on my desk, telling myself that I had better get started already. Gradually, I started to perspire as my head began to throb. My eyes darted from my papers to the clock and back to my papers. After about a half hour, I could no longer deny that I was in the throes of a full-blown anxiety attack. I was stuck and could not get past the terror of missing my self-imposed deadline to complete the revisions in order to graduate that June.

Even though I fully recognized what was happening to me, I was totally helpless to rescue myself from the quicksand of my spiraling anxiety. As Chazal understood so well, *"Ein chovesh matir atzmo mi'beis assurin* — A prisoner is never able to extricate himself from jail" (*Nedarim* 7b).

In total desperation, I reached out to my dear friend and colleague, Rabbi Yaakov Salomon. Dialing his number, I davened that he would be available to take my call.

He was! I then went on to describe what I was experiencing and why. I really could not imagine how or even if he would be able to help. At the time, calling him was all I could think of doing. Looking back, of course, I realize it was the smartest thing I could have done. At least, I thought to myself at the time, he will be sympathetic, understanding, and comforting. As it turned out, he was all of that and more.

"Tell me," he began, "is your dissertation divided into sections?"

"Of course," I replied. "There are thirteen chapters, like a book."

"Good," he continued. "Now here is what I want you to do. Take the first chapter and just work on that. Put everything else away. Try to think of the first chapter as if it is an article you are writing for a journal or a magazine. You've published articles before. So that's something you know you can do. Then, once you've finished working on the first chapter, you can go on to the next."

The advice was so simple, yet it felt so profound. What Yaakov enabled me to see — even in my state of high anxiety — was that the only path out of the morass caused by attempting to tackle too much at one time is to break the challenge down into manageable pieces that can be addressed one at a time.

Yaakov's advice hit the mark dead center. I felt the weight of fear and panic lift as soon as I got off the phone. He was absolutely right. I was trying to make all of the revisions at once, which was impossible. Once I focused only on the first chapter, I completed that in no time at all. And by the time I moved on to the second chapter, I was no longer stuck. I worked productively until the end of that block of time.

I also continued to work productively through the subsequent blocks of time, meeting all of the necessary deadlines to graduate in June of '83. At that time, I not only earned my doctorate degree, but I also acquired a valuable technique for managing the crippling anxiety of globalizing, which I have shared and used with many more people besides Suri.

CHAPTER 29

The Split-Screen Technique

— *Tammy*

Much of the excessive and inappropriate anxiety people experience is generated by the mental process known as catastrophic thinking. Faced with uncertainty, some people consider all of the possible outcomes and then conclude that the most likely outcome is the worst-case scenario. As they are dealing with prospects for the future, of course, the worst-case scenario *is* possible. What makes catastrophic thinking pathological, however, is that the one suffering from this condition sees the possible negative outcome as almost certain. So he experiences all of the pain and suffering now, as if he has already arrived at that very unwanted destination.

Tammy is a classic example of someone who engages in catastrophic thinking. As her husband, Moshe, puts it, she is always thinking negatively. As far as she is concerned, anything that could possibly go wrong probably will. Her life is one continuous string of imagined catastrophes, most of which never materialize. Of course, each time one of her expected disasters passes without incident, she never feels that her initial expectations were distorted. Rather, she feels that she somehow managed to "dodge the bullet," making her even more worried about the next time.

For example, a few months after 9/11, Tammy went out to eat with her husband to celebrate their anniversary. She had been really looking forward to this night out, as she had been especially stressed during the week as a result of some unexpected complications in her typically overpacked schedule of shopping, cooking, errands, and chauffeuring and caring for her five children.

To eliminate the stress of finding parking and to shorten the time a babysitter was needed, Tammy and her husband chose a local dairy restaurant for their dinner out. Once the couple was seated, Tammy looked around just to absorb the pleasant ambience of the eatery. It was then that Tammy noticed a lone diner at the table closest to the door.

The diner was wearing a nondescript cap and was casually dressed. As a result of his generic appearance, Tammy could not tell whether or not he was Jewish. Why is he eating out alone? Tammy wondered.

As she studied his overall appearance, her gaze lowered and then she noticed the backpack at his feet. Tammy then combined all of this "evidence" and quickly concluded that he must be a suicide bomber intent on taking all of the patrons with him when he detonated the bomb in his knapsack. He chose a table near the door so that he could prevent everyone from escaping. And also, his facial features and expression matched Tammy's mental profile of a terrorist.

In Tammy's defense, it should be stressed that many New Yorkers experienced similar hypervigilant anxieties in the months following 9/11. New York City even hired professional counselors in the aftermath of that tragedy to work with any resident suffering from elevated anxiety. In fact, had Tammy not been working with me at the time, she might have availed herself of that free service.

As Tammy sat most uncomfortably in the restaurant, she wrestled with herself. Should she mention anything about her suspicions to her husband? Should she attempt to flee the restaurant? Or was there really no danger and should she just refocus on her meal?

Tammy compromised with herself and decided not to say anything to her husband. At the same time, however, as a concession to her fears, she resolved to keep an eye on the "terrorist," to see if he made any moves that would indicate he was about to detonate his "bomb." Needless to say, the evening was anything but relaxing and pleasurable for Tammy. And she only succeeded in relaxing once she returned home and took a deep breath. A few days later, as she sat in my office, she still shuddered at the thought of what might have happened.

After the fact, I tried to help Tammy see how improbable her suspicions had been. "If he really had been a terrorist," I reasoned, "don't you think there are other locations in New York which might be more desirable targets than Hershel's Bistro?"

"Well, maybe he wanted to kill only Jews," Tammy countered. "So it would make sense to attack a kosher restaurant. And in Eretz Yisrael, the terrorists target restaurants all the time."

"That's true," I conceded. "But real terrorists who don't want to be identified usually don't dress like terrorists. They prefer to disguise themselves."

Tammy reluctantly agreed that her suspicions had been somewhat excessive. Nevertheless, this episode did little to convince her that her reasoning had been clouded by her elevated anxiety. And although she had "escaped" from the restaurant unscathed, it did little to reduce her overall level of anxiety and her pattern of catastrophic thinking.

The same thing happens to Tammy as soon as she schedules an appointment for a medical check-up. What will the doctor find? Will he send her for further testing? If so, what will the test reveal? What as yet undiagnosed condition might she have? What painful procedures might be necessary to treat that condition? And how will she be able to manage all of the complications in her life those treatments might impose? You get the idea.

Tammy then assumes that the answers to all of those questions will be horrible ones and feels as if she is already living on death row. She becomes unable to concentrate, sleep, and even eat regularly as she wallows in fear and self-pity; she is literally incapable of seeing any other outcome besides the worst-case scenario.

When asked why she is so convinced, she will cite her proof based on someone she knows or has heard of who was diagnosed with, suffers from, or died from the same or similar condition she is worried about. At times, the other person is a neighbor, a friend, the relative of an acquaintance, or even just someone mentioned in a newspaper or magazine article. Either way, Tammy overidentifies with the other unfortunate individual and acts as if she is already faced with the reality of what she fears most.

For people such as Tammy, elimination of all excessive anxiety is an unrealistic goal. They will always experience anxiety before a medical appointment or a lab test. What is a realistic goal, however, is for them to *reduce* their level of anxiety to something more manageable. One very effective method for doing that is the split-screen technique.[1]

In the split-screen technique, the anxiety sufferer is asked to write down, or at least verbally articulate, the worst-case scenario. This first step is difficult because it means one must visualize a very unpleasant, even dreaded, outcome. Nevertheless, facing a fear head-on immediately begins the process of minimizing it.

The next step is to write down or articulate an alternative positive outcome. For chronic anxiety sufferers, they are so used to negative thinking that it is often impossible for them to come up with a possible positive scenario on their own. They may need, therefore, some help from others in order to complete this step.

---

1.   I would like to thank Dr. Elin Weinstein for first introducing me to this technique.

Finally, they must list all the evidence they can to support the positive outcome. Then they must mentally visualize that they are looking at a split computer screen. The worst-case scenario appears on the left side of the screen. And the alternative, positive scenario appears on the right side of the screen together with all of the reasons to suspect that that scenario will actually ensue. Throughout the day, the anxiety sufferer must monitor how much time he is involuntarily focused on the left side of the screen. Then he must give equal time to focusing on the right side of the screen.

Again, the goal here is not the elimination of all anxiety. Rather, the purpose of this exercise is to help anxiety sufferers reduce the *level* of their anxiety.

Returning to Tammy, I was seeing her when she scheduled an appointment for a medical check-up. Right away, she began obsessing about the worst-case scenario — being diagnosed with a dreaded disease requiring extensive, debilitating treatments. She became preoccupied with fear and worry about how she would be able to cope with such a negative outcome.

However, using the split-screen technique, she wrote down what the most negative outcome could be. But she could not think of a single positive outcome, so I needed to point out the obvious. It was *possible* that the doctor would *not* find that she had any illnesses at all. I explained that since we were talking about the unknown, she could not claim that such an outcome was impossible.

Then, when it came to Step 3 — listing reasons to suspect the positive outcome — she was stumped again. "I can't think of any," she complained. "Can you help me?"

Once again, I had to point out what to me was obvious. "Are you experiencing any symptoms now?" I asked.

She shook her head, unable to even say no.

"Well, it certainly isn't proof," I continued, "but it is at least a reason to suspect that you might be well. Of course, not all people who are symptom-free are well. Nevertheless, the vast majority are. So to be symptom-free and ill, you would have to be in the minority. Probability, therefore, supports the positive outcome."

Tammy accepted what I said and wrote down that reason on the right side of her notebook.

"Try to come up with another reason," I coaxed.

Tammy shrugged her shoulders. After a few moments she surrendered again. "I can't," she pleaded.

"How many times have you had a check-up in the past?" I asked.

"I don't know," Tammy replied, shaking her head. "Maybe twenty or thirty times. I can't be sure."

"Okay. Now, how many of those times did the doctor find any condition that needed treatment of any kind?" I probed.

"Oh, I don't know," Tammy answered. "Maybe two or three. But remember, one of those times I needed surgery."

"Yes, I do remember. So, approximately 10 percent of the time, the doctor found something wrong when you went for a check-up. That means that 90 percent of the time the doctor found you to be in good health. In other words, your worst-case scenario has only a 10 percent chance of occurring, while the positive scenario has a 90 percent chance of happening. Such odds are clearly in your favor."

When we concluded that session, Tammy reported that she was still worried about the worst-case scenario because her neighbor's relative was recently diagnosed with a serious illness during a routine check-up. But when she returned the following week, she did acknowledge that the split-screen technique had helped her to be less preoccupied with the negative scenario than she would have been without the benefit of this exercise.

CHAPTER 30

The Split-Screen Technique, Part II

— *Gitty*

The split-screen technique also proved helpful to Gitty, a hard-working housewife with four children. Gitty was married to a high-powered real estate lawyer, and her no-nonsense approach to life mirrored her husband's personality. Unlike her confident husband, however, Gitty suffered at times from crippling anxiety. One example here will suffice.

Three of Gitty's children were spending the first half of the summer at sleepaway camps in the Catskills. On visiting day, therefore, Gitty, her husband, and infant daughter would have to crisscross the mountains in order to make all of the necessary stops.

Gitty was not a very good traveler. Even on good days, she would become nauseous and need to make more than the usual number of bathroom stops. Long road trips were especially challenging for her. And just anticipating one could trigger an episode of catastrophic thinking.

Gitty and I had already been working together for a while when she began one midsummer session with, "I'm worried about visiting day this year."

"Tell me about it," I instructed.

"As you know, we're going to have to make stops at three different camps, all on the same day," Gitty said, setting the table for what was to follow. "And as I've told you, I don't do well on long road trips."

I nodded knowingly, letting Gitty fill in the details of her dilemma.

"It's not going to be easy. I have no one to leave my infant with, so we'll have to bring her with us. Feeding and diapering her along the way will not be a picnic. And then we have to be careful about following each camp's rules about taking campers off-grounds; however, the only way we can satisfy each child is if we pick them all up and go out for pizza. But all three of our children at camp warned us not to come late! Our oldest reminded us how last summer on visiting day, we were one of the last sets of parents to arrive. And he was really mad at us about that. So I'm really not looking forward to all of that pressure to get out of the house early and then get to each camp on time."

Gitty was getting worked up even as she spoke. And I could see her anticipating the worst as she described her vision of that Sunday drive to the country.

"If that was all we had to deal with," Gitty continued, "I think I could handle it."

Really? I thought to myself, but did not say, as I waited to see where Gitty was headed.

"But then I listened to the five-day forecast on the radio," Gitty reported, almost in tears. "And wouldn't you know, they're predicting heavy thunderstorms for Sunday! Now, if I have to be in the car during a thunderstorm, I absolutely will not be able to handle it!"

"Exactly what is the problem with a thunderstorm?" I probed gently.

"Are you kidding?" Gitty shot back. "There are so many more accidents on the highway during thunderstorms. Don't you remember two weeks ago? There was a major three-car crash on the parkway and someone was killed. I know what it's like to be in the car during a thunderstorm. It happened a couple of years ago. There was absolutely no visibility. My husband was driving at ten miles an hour and I was petrified. We couldn't see two feet in front of the car. And we were only driving in Brooklyn, a few miles from home. If we were up in the country on the highway during a thunderstorm, I would be terrified. If it weren't for visiting day and our kids expecting us, I would tell my husband we should cancel our plans."

Gitty shook her head helplessly, announcing, "I just don't know what to do."

"You know what I'm going to recommend, don't you?"

Gitty sheepishly replied, "I should use the split-screen technique?"

I nodded affirmatively and instructed Gitty to take out her notebook. Then I told her to write down her worst-case scenario.

Gitty wrote, "There will be a major thunderstorm on Sunday while we're on the highway and we are going to get into a major accident."

"Good," I said. "Now come up with an alternative, positive outcome."

"I can't think of any," Gitty pouted.

"Do you mean that you believe it is *inevitable* that you will be involved in a traffic accident on Sunday?"

"Okay, okay," Gitty relented. Then she wrote on the right side, "We will not get into an accident."

"And you will arrive safely at all of your destinations and return home safely," I prompted. "Now list the reasons to suspect the positive outcome."

"I can't think of any," Gitty snapped. "But I can think of plenty of reasons to suspect the negative outcome."

"I'll help you," I said with a smile. "Are the weather reports always accurate?"

Reluctantly, Gitty acknowledged that the forecast could be wrong. Although, she pointed out, they are usually correct.

"You told me that your husband drove at ten miles an hour the last time you were caught in a thunderstorm," I continued. "Sounds like a pretty careful driver to me. If so, that is another reason to suspect the positive outcome."

"Accidents can be caused by the other guy," Gitty countered. "Even careful drivers have accidents. There are a lot of crazy drivers out there on the highway."

"That's true," I conceded. "But we are not trying to *prove* the positive outcome. We're just listing reasons to *suspect* the positive outcome. And your husband being a careful driver is a good reason to suspect that your trip will be uneventful.

Gitty added the second reason to her list and waited for me to suggest another.

"How many drivers do you estimate will be on the road this Sunday?" I asked.

"I don't know. Maybe fifty to a hundred thousand. I really have no idea," Gitty answered, getting visibly frustrated with me.

"Okay. And how many of those will be involved in traffic accidents even if there *is* a thunderstorm?" I challenged.

"I have no idea," Gitty replied, her voice rising with her level of frustration.

"Okay, okay," I backed off. "Well, if there are a hundred thousand drivers on the road and 1 percent are involved in accidents, that would mean a thousand people. Do you suspect a thousand people will get into accidents on Sunday?"

Gitty shook her head no.

"Probably less than a thousand?" I suggested.

Gitty nodded yes.

"So fewer than 1 percent of all drivers will get into accidents this Sunday even if there is a thunderstorm. And you are convinced you will be part of the fewer than 1 percent and not part of the over 99 percent?"

"How should I word that?" Gitty asked, acquiescing to me.

"Write, 'Since the vast majority of drivers never get into accidents, there is a far greater chance we will arrive home safely on Sunday than there is that we will get into an accident even if there is a thunderstorm.'"

I then instructed Gitty to review this list whenever she finds herself preoccupied with catastrophic thinking about her upcoming trip to the Catskills. And she should spend as much time reviewing the list of reasons to suspect the positive outcome as she spends obsessing about an accident.

The following week, Gitty came for her weekly appointment. Without my having to ask, Gitty reported on her weekend trip to the mountains. The weather report had been correct. There were massive thunderstorms. Fortunately for Gitty, however, they took place while she and her family were at the pizza shop. The pizza got a bit soggy because the rain started while they were seated at an outdoor table. But she did not have to deal with any hazardous driving conditions on the highway, and she did arrive at all of her destinations safely.

Almost begrudgingly, Gitty also reported that the split-screen technique had helped her diffuse her anxiety before the road trip. After that, Gitty experienced other episodes of catastrophic thinking with their typical elevated levels of anxiety. Each time, we worked on the split-screen technique together and each time we chipped away at the wall of her anxiety until it got down to a much lower, manageable level, where she could successfully reassure and calm herself by using this technique on her own, without any further sessions with me.

PANIC ATTACKS

CHAPTER 31

What Are Panic Attacks?

Technically, panic attacks are considered a subcategory of anxiety disorders. Because they represent significantly different challenges, however, they deserve a section all their own.

Anxiety attacks differ from panic attacks in that the former are triggered by specific fearful situations, while the latter have no identifiable precipitants. In addition, anxiety attacks will subside as soon as one feels reassured or comforted, whereas panic attacks simply run their course and subside on their own after ten, twenty, or thirty minutes. As a result, panic attacks are more difficult to treat and often require medication in order to fully control them.

During a panic attack, the sufferer experiences any or all of the following symptoms: shortness of breath, heart palpitations, headache, dizziness, nausea, fear of having a heart attack, and/or fear of going crazy. While in the throes of a panic attack, one feels as if it will never end. And this sense of helplessness often intensifies the feelings of panic.

As mentioned above, panic attacks are typically not triggered by specific stressful events. Nevertheless, once one has had his or her first panic attack, fear of a recurrence can serve to bring on additional attacks. The cycle of anxiety then becomes a self-fulfilling prophecy. The more one worries about having another panic attack, the more likely he or she is to have one.

Today there are medications available which are quite effective in reducing and eliminating the recurrence of panic attacks. Nevertheless, there are those who object to taking medication, even when indicated. And while nonmedical interventions can help, their success rate is not as high as that of medication.

Suppressed Resentment

— *Bella*

The most effective strategy for conquering panic attacks I first learned in my work with Bella, a middle-aged chassidish mother of five who initially consulted me regarding her unexplained panic attacks. Bella was vehemently opposed to taking any medication. Even though I warned her that the treatment would take longer without it, she opted for talking only.

At the initial consultation, I asked Bella to describe her most recent attack.

"I woke up in the middle of the night," she began, still traumatized by the event. "I felt tightness in my chest and I had a hard time breathing. My heart was pounding and I was afraid I was having a heart attack. I had had attacks like that before, but never as intense. My husband was asleep at the time and I really didn't want to wake him, but I felt I had no choice.

"My husband got up right away and tried to be supportive. But nothing he said or did helped at all. Eventually, the feelings of panic subsided. I went back to bed, but couldn't sleep. I think I may have dozed off for only about half an hour before I had to get up to start my day.

"Now every night I go to sleep worried that I might wake up again in the middle of the night with another panic attack. That's why I decided that I cannot put this off any longer and I had to come for help."

Exploring Bella's family structure and dynamics over the next few sessions, I learned that she was suffering from a very critical, overbearing mother-in-law who never had anything positive to say to Bella. And as a compliant, passive, and confrontation-averse daughter-in-law, Bella never defended or asserted herself in any way with her mother-in-law.

Bella had been prepared for such a relationship by having a mother who was almost as critical as her mother-in-law. And just as Bella never spoke up to her mother, she similarly sustained all of her mother-in-law's insults and innuendos without indicating in any way to anyone how hurt she really was. Even her husband was unaware of how much Bella was suffering.

One day Bella's mother-in-law complained to Bella about how infrequently she and her husband got to see their grandchildren. Why don't they visit more often? she asked rhetorically.

Later that night, Bella spoke with her husband, Label, and repeated the conversation she had had with Label's mother. "Maybe we should drive over this Sunday," Bella offered.

Label was swamped at work and had been planning to catch up on Sunday. Nevertheless, they were his parents, after all, Label reasoned. "Okay. Let's go. We'll leave right after my *shiur*."

Bella's in-laws lived approximately an hour and a half from their home. That Sunday, as planned, she, her husband, and their five children packed into their minivan to visit her in-laws. When they arrived, it was just in time for Label to catch *minchah* together with his father at the shul around the corner.

As Bella unloaded her cranky, hungry children from the minivan, her mother-in-law looked on askance, without offering any assistance. Once inside, Bella was treated to a barrage of insults and criticism.

"I see your children don't know how they should be greeting their *bubby*," Bella's mother-in-law began. "They must have been noshing in the car. I see their clothes are all dirty. If you were coming already, I would have thought you might come earlier. Half the day is already gone. Does it really bother you if Label spends a little time with his parents? Is it so terrible if he wants to fulfill his mitzvah of *kibbud av v'eim*?"

Bella's mother-in-law continued in this vein until Label and his father returned from *minchah*. All the while, Bella bit her tongue and did not respond. When Label walked in, Bella wanted to tell him she was ready to leave. She did not have the heart to do so, however, and remained until Label was ready to leave three hours later. All the way home, all Bella could think was, *Never again!*

Mindful of the laws of *shemiras halashon*, Bella never repeated to Label the dressing down she had received from her mother-in-law. In fact, she did not tell anyone about it. I had to dig deep until she reluctantly shared it with me.

"Are you experiencing any stresses in your life?" I probed during one of our earlier sessions.

"Maybe. I don't know," Bella replied softly.

"How would you describe your relationship with your husband?" I asked.

"Okay," Bella answered.

"Do you feel satisfied with the number and closeness of your friends?" I asked.

"Yes, I suppose," Bella replied with a tilt of her head.

"Is there anyone in your family who is irritating you in any way?" I asked.

"Why does that matter?" Bella wanted to know.

"Because it helps me to understand what is going on in your life now. I get a fuller picture of what your life is like and what you are dealing with," I explained. "It sounds to me like there may be someone who is upsetting you. Can you tell me about it?"

"Well if I did, wouldn't that be *lashon hara*?" Bella protested.

"No, not necessarily," I countered. "If you are telling me so that I can help you better, it would be for a *toeles*, a legitimate purpose. Then, according to my understanding, that would be permissible. Your intent is not to bad-mouth anyone. Your intent is to give me a better picture of what is going on in your life right now."

"Well," Bella began, struggling to get the words out, "I am having a hard time with my mother-in-law." Bella then went on to cite the Sunday fiasco as an illustration of the tension she was feeling in their relationship.

"How did you respond to your mother-in-law?" I asked.

"I didn't say anything," Bella reported, almost taken aback by my question. "Aren't we supposed to suffer in silence if we are mistreated by someone and not protest? Don't I have to be respectful to a mother-in-law?"

"Absolutely," I concurred. "But speaking respectfully does preclude your being able to speak up for yourself. Would you be interested in hearing what the Ramban has to say about this?"

Bella nodded affirmatively. I then reached for a *Chumash Vayikra* and read to Bella the Ramban's commentary on *Vayikra* 19:17. "The text says, 'Do not hate your brother in your heart,' when he does something against your wishes. Rather, you should rebuke him [and say], 'Why did you act that way to me?' And thereby you will not bear sin because of him by concealing your resentment of him in your heart and not telling him [about it]."

Bella was not convinced. Nevertheless, she asked where that Ramban could be found and promised to discuss it with her husband.

"Speaking of your husband," I continued, "what did you tell him about the episode?"

"Nothing," Bella replied matter-of-factly. "But he knows how his mother treats me because she has said similar things in front of him in the past."

"So what did your husband do those times when he heard his mother berating you?" I asked.

"Nothing," Bella said with a hopeless shrug. "He says she's his mother and he cannot say nor do anything because of *kibbud av v'eim*."

Bella's most recent panic attack had occurred in the middle of the night following her ill-fated visit to her in-laws. At that point, it did not take a rocket scientist to see the correlation between Bella's panic attacks and her suppressed feelings of rage.

At first I asked Bella if she could see the connection. When she shook her head no, I tentatively pointed it out to her. She gave me a look as if I had just arrived from Mars. Gradually, however, Bella seemed to accept my interpretation of her symptoms.

"So how does that help me?" Bella asked, still partially resisting my assessment.

"Well, for one thing," I pointed out, "it suggests that this situation with your mother-in-law is affecting your health, and you may not be required to continue submitting yourself to this mistreatment if it is causing you to have panic attacks. I would suggest, therefore, that you and your husband sit down with your *rav* to discuss the parameters of *kibbud av v'eim* as it applies to both of you in this situation."

"In addition," I continued, "the next time you feel a panic attack coming on, you might want to ask yourself if you are suppressing any feelings of resentment toward anyone for anything. And, if so, thinking about how you can be more proactive regarding the situation may help alleviate the underlying cause of your attacks."

Bella was extremely skeptical about my prescription for her. Nevertheless, she was desperate enough to try anything. She did, therefore, suggest to her husband that they meet with their *rav*. To Bella's surprise, her husband eagerly agreed to the meeting. And their *rav* corroborated my suspicion that Bella was not required to put her health at risk by exposing herself her mother-in-law's repeated mistreatment of her. He then went on to offer Bella's husband two options: either visit his parents alone or respectfully stick up for his wife. Bella's husband felt somewhat intimidated by his mother. As a result, he chose the *rav*'s first option, and that decision provided Bella with an enormous amount of relief from a major source of stress in her life.

Bella continued to suffer panic attacks even after the resolution described above. These attacks, however, dramatically diminished in frequency, intensity, and duration. After a few weeks, they were eliminated entirely. Of course, that did not reduce Bella's fear that they might return. But eventually this worry also receded, and in time vanished as well.

The strategy that rescued Bella from her panic attacks proved helpful to others who were similarly afflicted. One more example will illustrate its effectiveness.

CHAPTER 33

Suppressed Resentment, Part II

— Bentzy and Chavy

Bentzy is a middle-aged man with a boyish appearance. He works as a salesman for a software company that requires him to go on yearly out-of-town business trips. He needs to travel about three to four times a year, so the routine of packing kosher food and looking for minyanim near his hotel are quite familiar to him.

What Bentzy was not prepared for, however, was the wave of panic that swept over him one night in his hotel room during one of these business trips. He had been relaxing on his bed after a typical day of prescheduled meetings with customers when he first noticed his heart was racing. He had difficulty breathing. He was terrified. And he was convinced that he was either going to die of a heart attack or have a nervous breakdown. Being so far away from home made matters worse. And he remembered thinking that he did not think he would survive the episode.

Bentzy cut his trip short and came home earlier than planned. He was frightened, confused, and desperate, fearing a recurrence of the nightmarish experience that had taken place in his hotel room. Not knowing where to turn for help, he called his *rav*, Rabbi Shlomo Turner.

Rabbi Turner listened empathically, validating Bentzy's concern. Then he assured Bentzy that he would find someone who could help him.

As soon as Rabbi Turner got off the phone with Bentzy, he called me. "Have you ever heard of anything like this before?" he asked. "Do you think you can help him? He's been a *mispallel* of mine for many years and I'd really like him to get over this."

I told Rabbi Turner that it sounded like Bentzy had suffered a panic attack. In order to know whether or not I could help him, however, I would need to meet with him and evaluate him in person.

Bentzy called later the same day, asking for an appointment and he took the first slot I had available. After Bentzy described his experience in the hotel room, it was clear to me that he had, in fact, suffered a panic attack.

"Will it happen again?" Bentzy asked with trepidation in his voice.

"It could," I replied bluntly. "That's the bad news. But the good news is that it is treatable with medication and/or therapy."

Before I could say anything further, Bentzy immediately informed me that he was very opposed to taking any psychotropic medication. He was concerned about possible side effects. Whatever the therapy entailed, however, he was willing to try.

Using the formulation described above, I asked Bentzy if he could think of anyone with whom he was upset or annoyed. "Often panic attacks are brought on by stressful, conflicted relationships," I explained. "When people feel angry but cannot express such feelings, they sometimes experience panic attacks."

Bentzy assured me that his relationships with everyone were not stressful. Seeing how affable and pleasant he was to deal with, I was tempted to accept his assessment. *No one*, I thought, *would*

have a difficult time getting along with this easygoing, gentle man.
Nevertheless, I probed further, asking specifically about each member
of his immediate family and his family of origin.

Bentzy's father was no longer living. His mother lived out of state
and had almost nothing to do with Bentzy and his family. He also had
little contact with his one sibling who lived out of state. His children
were clearly the light of his life. And he described each one lovingly,
with great tenderness.

When we focused on Bentzy's wife, Chavy, he professed his deep
affection for her as well. However, when I asked about Chavy's
relationships with the children, Bentzy gave me the first indication
that everything was not as idyllic as it seemed at first.

Chavy was prone to sudden, unpredictable, and irrational outbursts
of temper, most often directed at the children. According to Bentzy,
these explosions were not at all justified. And although Chavy always
blamed the children for provoking her, it was clear from Bentzy's
description of the events which transpired that she was overreacting.
After each episode, Bentzy felt terrible for whichever child had been
targeted by her.

"Does Chavy ever scream at you?" I asked gingerly.

"Oh, all the time," Bentzy said, confirming my suspicions. He
then went on to describe the uncontrollable nature of his wife's
temper tantrums. Any effort he made to calm down his wife always
exacerbated the situation.

Bentzy then answered the question I was thinking, but did not ask.
"Divorce is out of the question," he volunteered. "I'm committed to my
wife and children, and I would never even consider leaving."

I then suggested to Bentzy that he might be harboring some
suppressed feelings of resentment toward Chavy for the way she
was treating him and their children. "You can care for someone and
still begrudge the way he or she acts toward you," I explained. Then
I helped Bentzy see the connection between his panic attack and his
suppressed feelings toward his wife.

Bentzy pondered my interpretation for a few moments in silence. "If you are correct," he began, "how does that help me?"

"The next time you feel a panic attack coming on," I instructed, "ask yourself if you are feeling any resentment toward your wife. And if the answer is yes, then try to identify what you are resentful about so we can discuss it."

Bentzy did have more panic attacks, and each time he followed my instructions. Over the next few months, the frequency, intensity, and duration of Bentzy's panic attacks diminished gradually until they stopped completely.

Chavy's outbursts, of course, did not diminish. During the course of our work, however, Bentzy learned how to deal with them so that they did not trigger any more panic attacks. Much of the focus of our meetings was on how he could offset some of the negative impact Chavy had on their children.

In follow-up meetings I periodically had with Bentzy after we ended our ongoing work together, it was clear that he was successfully overcoming his panic attacks even years after our initial meeting. Also this case proved to me, once more, how directly connected panic attacks and suppressed feelings of resentment really are.

OBSESSIVE-COMPULSIVE DISORDER

CHAPTER 34

What Is Obsessive-Compulsive Disorder?

Obsessive-compulsive disorder (OCD) is officially classified as an anxiety disorder, along with panic attacks and phobias. It encompasses intrusive, anxiety-provoking thoughts, as well as compulsive, illogical behaviors. While some can experience both symptoms, most people with OCD suffer either one or the other. In this section, therefore, they will be discussed separately.

Most people experience occasional, unwanted, intrusive thoughts. These may be mental images of fearful situations or circumstances. Or they may be unpleasant memories or ideas. Almost always, people are able to dismiss these thoughts from their minds and move on to focus their attention on other matters. For people with OCD, however, these thoughts remain, stubbornly resisting all efforts to dismiss them. Like a mouse stuck in a glue trap, these thoughts hound the

OCD sufferer with greater intensity and frequency the more he or she attempts to avoid them.

To the average observer, these people can appear completely normal. They have no idiosyncratic personality traits, for example. Nevertheless, inside they suffer constantly from the unremitting nagging of these unwanted, illogical, and obsessive thoughts.

OCD can occur as early as childhood. In fact, approximately one-third of all cases can be traced back to an onset before age eighteen. It is so easy to conceal that, at times, a child may be suffering from OCD without his parents being aware of it.

At other times, the illogical, intrusive thoughts force the person to act in strange, inappropriate, or even bizarre ways. In most cases, the individual recognizes the irrational nature of these thoughts, but feels totally helpless to ignore them. As a result, he often experiences considerable embarrassment when he shares these thoughts with others, even with his therapist.

While literally any thought can become an obsessional thought, below are a few examples I have encountered in my work with such people.

"I'm not sure I locked the door to my car."

"I may have left the oven on."

"I may have a terminal illness and be unaware of it."

"I may have had milk on my hands when I touched a *fleishig* pot."

"I may have questions about *emunah* which render me an *apikorus*."

"I may have spoken disrespectfully to that person just now and need to ask him for *mechilah*."

"I think my nose is too big and others are aware of that too."

"I may not be working efficiently enough and my boss is going to fire me."

"I may not have been concentrating properly and may have missed hearing one word of the *megillah leini*ng."

"I often have an image of a Christian symbol in my mind and I am worried that it may mean I have violated the prohibition against worshipping *avodah zarah*."

"When I asked a *shailah* just now, I may not have given over the details of the case properly and therefore the *psak* I received from my *rav* may not really apply to my situation. And then if I act on the *psak*, I may be violating the halachah."

CHAPTER 35

The Role of Medication
— Ari

One of the earliest cases of OCD that I ever encountered taught me much about both the disorder and its treatment.

Ari did not come to see me for help with his OCD, but rather for help with the devastating impact it was having on his life. He was resigned that his condition was incurable. All he wanted was some way to cope with the stranglehold it had on his life and his family's life.

Ari was married with small children at home. He worked as a computer analyst for a large Manhattan-based firm, where he was underpaid and underemployed. He desperately wanted to leave his current job and seek employment elsewhere. He was prevented from doing so, however, because of his OCD symptoms.

The thoughts that literally enslaved Ari were that he had improperly pronounced words of *Krias Shema*. As a result of these obsessive thoughts, Ari needed to daven in a special spot of a particular minyan in order to get through *shacharis* in time for him to get to work each morning. The minyan davened slowly enough for Ari to complete *Krias Shema* in time to daven *Shemoneh Esrei* with the *tzibbur.* Of course, Ari had to arrive a good half hour before the start of this minyan to allow time for him to reach the *Shemoneh Esrei* with everyone else.

If anyone davened too loudly in Ari's proximity, he could not concentrate on his davening, especially during *Krias Shema.* The advantage of this particular minyan, therefore, was that it did not include too many loud daveners. Also, the spot he chose was the farthest away from the *amud,* so that he would not be distracted by the *baal tefillah* either.

If Ari davened in this minyan, he could complete *shacharis* in approximately one-and-a-half hours and still make it on time to his job, which was a short subway ride from his home on the West Side of Manhattan. Because of that, he felt he could not even consider looking for work elsewhere. After all, if he was hired by a firm farther from his home, he might need to daven at another minyan that started earlier. Then he would not know how long it would take for him to complete his davening.

The minyan situation affected Ari's family life as well. He felt unable to go anywhere for vacation because he feared he would not find a minyan with the right conditions for him to be able to concentrate on reciting the words of *Krias Shema.* For years his wife had been begging him to go anywhere for a few days' vacation. Regrettably, Ari felt forced to refuse, as much as he wanted to please her and understood how legitimate her need was to get away. It was the fact that he felt so guilty about holding his family back from going anywhere overnight that finally brought him to see me in the first place.

"I know it makes no sense," Ari woefully admitted to me, "but I just feel I need to repeat words many times until I feel secure that I have pronounced them properly. I realize it doesn't take others as long as it takes me. But I simply cannot move on until I feel relatively secure that I have pronounced them properly."

Ari then taught me experientially an essential lesson my professors failed to impart to me didactically. Using logic and reasoning is completely useless in helping someone who suffers from OCD.

"What do you think would happen if you simply said *Krias Shema* without repeating any words?" I asked innocently.

"I'm afraid I wouldn't fulfill the mitzvah *d'Oraisa*," he replied matter-of-factly.

"Of course the words need to be pronounced properly," I continued. "The *Shulchan Aruch* is clear about that (*Orach Chaim, Hilchos Krias Shema* 61:6—9). But do you think rabbeim and *roshei yeshivah* repeat words when they say Shema?"

"No, I know they don't," he acknowledged. "But they probably recite the words properly the first time, so they do not need to repeat any words."

"Suppose you try moving just a little bit from your regular place in shul and see if you can tolerate that?" I proposed.

"I've tried it already," Ari replied in a defeated tone of voice. "It takes me so much longer to get through the davening that it simply isn't worth it."

"Maybe you should consult a *posek* and see if you are actually required to repeat words in *Krias Shema*," I suggested as I began sharing some of Ari's frustration.

"Look, the halachah is clear," Ari asserted forcefully. "If you do not pronounce the words properly, you have not fulfilled the mitzvah. And the rule of thumb is *safeik d'Oraisa l'chumra*. (When in doubt about a Torah-based command, one must assume the mitzvah has not been fulfilled properly and must be repeated.)

In subsequent sessions, I used the same approach in looking for wiggle room regarding his getting away for a vacation and his need to find another job. With both of those issues I was as unsuccessful as I was in helping him with his obsessional thoughts about *Krias Shema*.

After a few more sessions, it became painfully clear to me that I was not helping Ari, nor would I be able to do so using the approach I was taking. And since I had nothing else to offer at the time, I declared defeat and told Ari what he knew already — that I was unable to help him with his obsessional thinking.

Ari was quite gracious about the whole affair and told me not to feel inadequate. He said that he had very low expectations before he came and he recognized how difficult his case was. We ended on friendly terms.

About a year later, Ari called with some critical follow-up information. He told me that eventually he consulted a psychiatrist who prescribed a new medication called Prozac. Ari reported that it literally changed his life by freeing him of his obsessional thinking. He was now able to daven anywhere he chose and was able to keep up with any minyan. He no longer repeated words in *Krias Shema.* And, yes, he and his family finally got to go away for a much-needed and well-deserved vacation.

What I later learned was that Prozac was not a new medication. It had been on the market for some time and had been used successfully to treat depression. In fact, it was 70 percent effective in curing the symptoms of moderate and severe depression. What was discovered in the late '70s, however, when I had been working with Ari, was that Prozac also helps people suffering from OCD; only with OCD cases, the drug is 90 percent effective!

While medication is an extremely powerful weapon in the battle against OCD, it is not the only one which has been developed. There are also CBT (cognitive behavioral therapy) approaches which I have learned can also be effective, as illustrated by the next case example.

CHAPTER 36

The Role of CBT
— Nechama

Nechama was a petite, put-together woman in her late 30s, who made it clear to me at our first meeting that she was not coming to see me willingly.

"My husband made me come," she volunteered before I even asked. "He said he cannot take it anymore. And he sort of gave me an ultimatum. He said either I come to you for help or else. And I didn't want to find out what he meant by 'or else.' So that's why I'm here."

Nechama then proceeded to give me a classic illustration of obsessional thinking. "I kind of get anxious when milk and meat are not separated properly," she began somewhat sheepishly, downplaying her obsessional thinking and the behavioral havoc it was causing at home.

"What do you mean?" I probed.

"Well, when my husband buys milk, I need him to bring it home double-wrapped," she explained. "Otherwise I never know if it may have touched something accidentally."

"Is that all?" I probed further.

"Well, once the milk is taken out of the refrigerator," Nechama explained, "I always insist that it be placed only in one spot on the counter. That way I can have better control over it."

"Keep going," I prompted.

"Well, I also have to be the only one removing a *fleishig* pot from the refrigerator and putting it on the stove," Nechama continued. "Someone else in the family might not be careful about letting it touch something on the way to the stove."

"Is it the same thing for returning a pot from the stove to the refrigerator?" I asked.

"Of course," Nechama replied. "I cannot trust anyone else at home to do it properly."

"And what do you mean by 'properly'?" I asked.

"Well, someone else at home might touch a counter or a table on the way back to the refrigerator," Nechama elaborated. "After all, not everyone at home is as careful about *milchig*s and *fleishig*s as I am."

"And suppose someone else at home does touch a countertop or table with the pot?" I asked. "What happens then?"

"Then I have to scrub the entire countertop or table," Nechama sighed. "And that takes me a long time until I'm sure that it's properly cleaned. So, as you can imagine, I'd much rather avoid having to do all of that cleaning."

"Do you think everyone takes such precautions in their homes?" I asked gently.

"No, I don't," Nechama said bluntly. "But I just feel I have to have these rules followed at home for me to feel secure about the kashrus of our kitchen. I realize it may be a bit too much at times for my family, and that's why my husband gave me that ultimatum. But I feel I have to do things this way. And please don't tell me to just to stop, because I know I can't."

"You could get considerable relief from these disturbing thoughts if you took medication," I softly suggested.

"Don't talk to me about medication," Nechama warned. "There is no way I would ever consider taking any drugs. I'm too concerned about negative side effects. If you are going to help me, it can only be with talking. I'm not taking any drugs."

In our next session, I pointed out to Nechama that she was only paying lip service to her acknowledgment that her obsessional thoughts were irrational. On the one hand, she admitted that her rules were terrorizing her family and were quite abnormal. On the other hand, however, she believed that they were legitimate measures, given the conditions in her home. In order to overcome her challenge, she needed to be more committed to the notion that her thoughts were inappropriate.

"You must learn to label these thoughts as irrational," I instructed her. "Practice saying to yourself, 'That's my OCD talking.' And then add, 'And I don't have to always listen to such a harsh, critical boss.'"

"Furthermore," I continued, "you may not be able to hold back from giving in to these thoughts and acting on them. But you must always label them correctly and remind yourself that you do have choices here."

Nechama was quite skeptical that such a simple prescription could help. Nevertheless, she did agree to try it at home.

When she returned the following week, Nechama reported only minimal improvement. "I still needed to impose my rules. Although I did let my husband put the milk in the refrigerator himself once this week."

I sharply criticized Nechama's use of the word "minimal." What she saw as minor change, I pointed out, was the first crack in the wall of her OCD. "You are turning the tide," I enthused. Then we reviewed in greater detail her compliance with my instructions. At the end of the session, Nechama appeared a drop more hopeful than when we started.

It took another few weeks for Nechama to make more significant progress. Eventually, however, she did succeed in relaxing some, but not all, of her rules at home. Her obsessive thoughts were not eliminated. But they were enough under control that her husband no longer insisted that she continue the therapy. While she could have made further progress if she had continued, I was gratified to see that her husband was sufficiently satisfied with our results that he "allowed" his wife to end the therapy.

CHAPTER 37

The "*Lechem HaPanim*" Technique

— Duvi

Duvi was a happy-go-lucky *yeshivah bachur* who came to see me when he was eighteen years old. He came willingly at the suggestion of his parents, whom I knew socially. He was a tall young man with an awkward gait and a warm, bright smile that could light up the room.

At our first meeting, Duvi was very uncomfortable about revealing the true purpose of his coming. He began by talking about his learning, which had not been going well recently. In the past, he was at the top of his *shiur* at a well-known and well-respected yeshivah in the New York metropolitan area. It was clear to me that Duvi enjoyed his learning and was quite distressed that it was not going as well as it had in the past.

Duvi elaborated on the *chavrusos* he had in the past and how much he was envied by other *bachurim* in his *shiur*.

I listened attentively, understanding how appropriate it is for a *bachur*'s life to revolve around his learning. I was also mindful, however, that Duvi's learning was not why he had come to see me.

"Tell me, Duvi," I cut in to his seamless, rambling monologue. "What do you suppose is making it so hard for you to concentrate on your learning lately?"

Duvi squirmed uncomfortably in his chair. We had finally arrived at the reason for his consulting me and he clearly was not happy about it. After some hemming and hawing, Duvi struggled to respond.

"I don't usually look at myself in the mirror," he began with a chuckle. In fact, Duvi said just about everything with a chuckle. And that was one of the most charming aspects of his friendly, smiley personality.

"I was at a *chasunah,* actually, of a cousin," Duvi continued. "Hey, I think you know that cousin because he davens in the same shul as your brother-in-law."

Duvi was clearly getting sidetracked and going off on a tangent because he was embarrassed to tell me what was bothering him. If he never got to the point, however, there was no way I would be able to help him. I decided, therefore, that it was time to get Duvi back on track.

"I asked you why your learning has not been going well lately and you responded that you don't usually look at yourself in the mirror," I said, trying to help Duvi pick up the thread of his original thought.

"Oh yes, of course," Duvi laughed, realizing how far off course he had gone. "Well, uh, you see, I was at this *chasunah* of a cousin. Like I said, I think you know him. And, anyway, I was walking down the hall to the chuppah and I passed a mirror on the wall. Uh, heh, like I said, I really don't usually look at myself in the mirror. But, uh, I caught a glimpse of myself as I passed and...well, I noticed that my nose is really too big for my face."

There, it was finally out. Duvi was obsessed with thoughts about the size of his nose.

"Have you thought about this at all since then?" I asked, pretending not to have grasped already what was preventing him from learning the way he used to in the past.

"That's really all I think about now," Duvi confessed, confirming my diagnosis.

"Tell me how this impacts your learning," I probed gently, realizing that this was sensitive territory we were entering.

"When I try to get into the learning with my *chavrusa,* I keep thinking that he is looking at my nose and thinking to himself how it is too big for my face. I try to distract myself from that thought, but the more I try not to think about it, the more I end up thinking about it," Duvi said with a huge smile and a nervous laugh.

"Have you told anyone about this?" I asked.

"Well, I don't want anyone to know," he said seriously. "After all, this isn't really a normal thing. People might think there is something wrong with me. It might even affect me later regarding *shidduchim.* I did tell my father, though. And he just told me not to think about it."

"Would you want to have plastic surgery to shorten your nose?" I asked, trying to get a better understanding of his feelings about this.

"Oh, no," Duvi replied emphatically. "I'm not interested in any surgery." And that last word was said loudly with a tone of finality, as he almost shuddered at the thought.

Returning to his father, Duvi shared, "I don't think my father really understands that this is not something I can just make go away. I wish I could. I know it doesn't make any sense. But I can't seem to get this out of my mind."

As the session was about to come to a close, I asked Duvi how he felt talking to me about this issue. He replied that he was definitely uncomfortable at first. But once we got into it, it was a bit of a relief to finally share this with someone. He wasn't sure I could really help him. But he was willing to return to try and work on this with me.

At our next session, I introduced Duvi to what I call the *lechem hapanim* technique. I began by asking Duvi if he would be willing to try a little experiment in my office. He agreed.

"I'm going to mention something to you," I said. "And I want you to try not to think about that thing for just ten seconds. Do you think you can do that?"

Duvi chuckled and nodded his head. "Sure," he said confidently.

"Now, you can think of anything else," I instructed. "You can even think about your nose. The only thing you can't think about is the thing that I'm going to tell you. Are you ready?"

Duvi was now quite eager to play this little game with me. He smiled broadly and nodded his head affirmatively.

"Okay," I said. "What I want you not to think about is a pink elephant. And the ten seconds start now!"

I kept a close watch on the clock and indicated when the ten seconds were over. "Okay. Stop now," I said.

Duvi had been squinting his eyes during this time. He now opened them with a puzzled look on his face.

"So tell me, Duvi," I inquired. "Were you able to do that? Were you able to not think about a pink elephant for the entire ten seconds?"

"Uh, no, not really," Duvi replied with a defeated tone in his voice.

"Don't be disappointed in yourself, Duvi," I consoled. "The truth is, almost no one can do it. In fact, trying not to think of something usually makes it more likely that you will think of whatever you are trying to avoid."

Duvi was listening attentively and nodding in agreement as I spoke. Since I had his full attention, I continued.

"All you have been trying to do about your intrusive thoughts concerning the size of your nose is not to think about it. And you have been unsuccessful because no one can rid himself of unwanted thoughts by trying not to think about them.

"What you need to do is to try to *replace* one thought with another. This is what I call the "*lechem hapanim*" technique.

"You know what the Torah says about the *lechem hapanim*?" I asked.

Duvi shrugged his shoulders. He did not understand where I was going with this.

"Regarding the *lechem hapanim,* the Torah says (*Shemos* 25:30), 'lifanai tamid,' doesn't it?" I asked rhetorically. "That means the *lechem hapanim* had to be on the Shulchan constantly. But how, asks the Gemara in *Menachos* 96b, is that possible if the bread has to be removed every week on Shabbos, when it is given to the *kohanim* to eat? The answer is that the *kohanim* would bring a rack with twelve loaves on it over to the Shulchan. And then they would slide the new bread onto the shelves, pushing out the old at the same time. That way the old bread was removed and replaced with the new bread without there being even one second that the Shulchan stood without bread."

"So, uh, what does that have to do with me?" Duvi asked cautiously.

"My point is," I responded, "that you will have more success in controlling your thoughts about your nose if you attempt to replace those thoughts with something else."

"Like what?" Duvi wanted to know.

"Like something pleasurable," I explained. "Try to think a thought that gives you pleasure. It could be a pleasant scene, for example. Or it could be a situation that would make you happy. It could have happened in the past. Or it could be something that never happened, but would make you feel very good if it did."

Duvi took a moment to digest what I had said. He closed his eyes to help him concentrate. When he opened them, I knew he had come up with something. "It would be a pleasant thought for me to finish the *mesechta* we are learning this *zeman*," he said with a broad smile.

"Yes, that is a pleasant thought," I confirmed. "But why not make it finishing *Shas*?"

Duvi blushed at the thought. "Yeah, that would be something special," he said longingly.

"So let's make the pleasurable thought finishing *Shas*," I advised. "But we need to put more meat on the bones."

"What do you mean?" Duvi asked.

"I mean you need to fill in more details. You need to paint this picture in color, not black and white," I explained. "For example, where will the *siyum* take place? Who will attend? What will be served? You get the idea."

Duvi gave a squelched giggle and responded, "I guess it would be at the yeshivah. And the whole *beis midrash* would attend. And I guess the yeshivah cook would cater it."

"And what about your parents?" I asked. "Wouldn't you want them there too?"

"Oh sure," he shot back. "My whole family should come. Why not?"

"Good," I said. "Now here's what you have to do. Whenever you catch yourself thinking about the size of your nose, you simply switch channels in your mind to the mental image of your *siyum haShas.* Just like switching the *lechem hapanim.*"

"How will that help me concentrate on my learning?" Duvi wanted to know.

"That's an excellent question, Duvi," I replied. "The idea here is for you to gain some control over your intrusive thoughts. If you can switch your thoughts, which is something we all can do, then you will be automatically thinking less about your nose. And when that happens, you will be able to learn like you did before all of this started."

Duvi was skeptical, but willing to give this approach a try. He needed considerable coaching in this technique until he was able to employ it successfully. Once he did, however, he began to observe improvement in his ability to concentrate on his learning.

At that point, we took a break for the summer, as Duvi's yeshivah was relocating to the Catskill Mountains for July and August. After the summer, we met again for a follow-up visit and I was pleasantly surprised to learn that Duvi was much less disturbed by the obsessive thoughts about the size of his nose and was able to concentrate more on his learning.

Up to this point, we have been discussing only obsessional thoughts. While these thoughts often lead to unusual actions to accommodate the real or imagined stressors, the main pathology is the presence of intrusive, irrational thoughts.

The *C* in OCD stands for compulsive behaviors. These are actions which clearly have no rational or purposeful function; they are only performed by the sufferer as an unexplainable compulsion. While the person who experiences obsessional thoughts can often hide it from others, one who engages in compulsive behaviors is easily spotted as being abnormal. This adds to the stress and shame of having this condition, making those who suffer from it even more eager to overcome it. The next case example, therefore, is about someone who suffered from an unusually severe case of compulsions.

CHAPTER 38

Prescribing the Symptom

— *Sendy*

Sendy's parents lived far away and out of town. For that reason, I did not meet with them before I saw their son, something I normally like to do. For an underage adolescent, I usually ask his parents for necessary background information and try to establish an initial bond of trust with them. In lieu of the face-to-face meeting, I only spoke with Sendy's mother over the phone.

Sendy's mother described him as "having social problems." She explained that he needed help making friends in yeshivah. And since he was attending a yeshivah in New York, she asked if I would be willing to help him. Her request was simple and straightforward.

Sounds like a case of social anxiety, I said to myself. *This should be easy.*

Little did I know what I was in for. Nevertheless, I accepted the case and agreed to work with him.

Sendy was a seventeen-year-old *yeshivah bachur* who wore the typical uniform of a white shirt and black suit. That was where his similarity to other *bachurim* ended.

Entering my office, he walked with a jerking gait and practically fell into the chair he chose. Right away I noticed that he was making all sorts of what I naively thought were involuntary movements and motions. In fact, Sendy appeared similar to someone suffering from a neurological disorder such as Parkinson's disease.

His head jerked to the side periodically. One shoulder jerked up occasionally. And he made repetitive, purposeless motions with his hands.

When I asked Sendy what I could help him with, he repeated what his mother had told me. "I really like learning in Yeshivas Masmidei Torah," Sendy began. "The rebbeim are great. The dorm is nice. And I even like the food. But I'm having a hard time making friends and I've been there already for almost a full *zeman*."

"What was it like for you in elementary school?" I asked, trying not to get distracted by all of Sendy's weird motions and movements.

"Oh, in elementary school, I had loads of friends," Sendy replied proudly. "I'm a pretty outgoing guy and just about everyone in my class was my friend."

"So what do you suppose is causing your difficulty this year?" I innocently asked.

"Well," Sendy hesitated, "you see these movements I make sometimes? People stare at me and think I'm strange. It's not that I can't control myself. I could if I had to. But I just feel I have to move this way."

"So let me get this straight," I said, trying to absorb what I was hearing. "You make these movements *deliberately*?"

"Yeah," Sendy reluctantly admitted. "I know it sounds strange. But, like I said, I just feel I have to do it. Or else...oh, I don't know."

"Have you ever tried *not* to make these movements?" I asked, already anticipating the answer.

"Yeah, I have," Sendy said. "But if I go too long without making some of these movements, I feel I'd better. Do you know what I mean?"

"I think I do," I said. "You mean that you feel as if something terrible will happen if you don't make these movements. Is that correct?"

"Exactly," Sendy replied with visible excitement at finally being understood.

"So let me see if I am hearing you correctly," I said as the session was drawing to a close. "You feel guys are avoiding you in yeshivah because you are making all of these strange movements and motions. And you would like to stop doing all of this, but you feel you are practically forced to continue. So you'd like me to help you figure out a way to stop without feeling so anxious. Is that right?"

Sendy smiled broadly and shook his head to the affirmative. Then he replied, "You just said in a minute what I've been trying to say for almost an hour!"

Somewhere midway into our next session I broached the subject of medication. "You know, there are medications available today which I think could really make you feel much better. Would you be willing to try them?"

"Oh, no, no, no," Sendy responded emphatically. "I would never want to take pills for this. No way!"

"These medications are safe," I countered. "They are used by many people and have minimal side effects. Why wouldn't you be willing to give them a try?"

"If anyone found out that I was taking medication," Sendy explained, "they would think there's something wrong with me. And I certainly wouldn't want that. Then I would never be able to make any friends in the yeshivah."

So I offered what seemed to be the obvious counterargument. "Well, the way things are going now, Sendy, when guys see you making all of these motions, they probably are already thinking that something is wrong. But if you take medication, which no one has to know about, then you would be able to stop. And then you could resume a normal social life."

"Yes, they may *think* there's something wrong with me now. But they aren't sure. If I start taking pills, they would *know* there's something wrong with me and I would never be able to live that down. So, please, let's not talk about this anymore. It's making me too nervous."

Sendy did not appear to be a candidate for the CBT which worked so well with Nechama. And with medication taken off the table, I really felt at a loss as to how to help him. While I felt it was a long shot, I decided to try a technique called "prescribing the symptom."

This approach is categorized as a paradoxical intervention. It was first developed by pioneers in the family therapy movement of the '60s and '70s. In brief, a paradoxical intervention is an instruction a therapist gives which appears to be designed to accomplish the opposite of the therapeutic goal. When prescribing the symptom, the therapist directs people to perform the very behaviors they came to the therapist to eliminate. The rationale behind this strategy is that once any shift in the symptomatic behavior has been made, people are then empowered to make further changes.

Honestly, I was skeptical about how well this would work with Sendy. As I saw no other options, I decided to give it a try.

At our next session, I told Sendy that in order to help him with these unwanted movements and motions, we would need to first list and define them. He agreed.

With notepad in hand, I asked, "What is that you are doing now with your hand?"

"I'm snapping one finger against the other by shaking my wrist," he said. "See, like this."

Sendy then deliberately made that hand motion to demonstrate it for me.

"What do you call that one?"

"Uh, I don't know. I don't call it anything. I just have to do it."

"Okay. Well, let's call it a finger snap. Is that all right?"

"Sure. That's fine."

"Now, how often do you do finger snaps in, say, an hour?"

"I have no idea. I don't count them. I just do them."

"I understand. But we need to develop a baseline so we can monitor our progress. We can come back to this later. Now tell me, what is that you are doing with your head?"

"Well, I need to tilt my head this way and then kind of twist it to the side, like this."

Sendy then deliberately repeated the movement he described in order to demonstrate it for me.

"I suppose we could call that one a neck twist, couldn't we?"

"Okay. That's all right with me."

Altogether we identified about six different bizarre-looking movements Sendy made repeatedly and compulsively, although I cannot remember them all now. My first instruction to him was to try to count how often he makes these movements in a typical hour.

"But I don't make them the same number of times each hour," Sendy protested. "Each hour is different."

"Okay. So pick one hour each day and record the counts for those," I advised.

Sendy returned the following week with his lists. As he had warned me, there was a wide fluctuation in the frequency of these movements each day, and he was completely unable to identify the reason one day there were more and one day there were less. In lieu of a clear baseline, therefore, I suggested we simply calculate an average number from each of the days he had recorded. Once that was completed, I proceeded to prescribe the symptom.

"Now here's what I want you to do," I began. "I want you to pick one hour a day to try the following experiment. It can be any time during the day, although an hour during learning *seder* would be preferable. Tell me now which hour you would like."

"Well, I guess I would pick the first hour," Sendy replied. "That would be from 9:30–10:30."

"Good," I said. "Now we cannot work on all of these movements at once. As Chazal said, "*Tafasta merubah, lo tafasta*" (*Rosh Hashanah*

4b). So let's focus first on the finger snaps, since those are the most frequent. Okay?"

"Uh, sure," Sendy said, clearly confused about where I was headed with all of this.

"Every day, at the start of the hour you have chosen," I continued, "I want you to do all of finger snaps one after the other. Since we're not exactly sure how many you would do during any given hour, we'll use the average number we computed before."

"But it will look strange if I'm doing all of those finger snaps in the *beis midrash*," Sendy protested.

"Perhaps," I acknowledged. "But you are doing these finger snaps the same number of times every hour in the *beis midrash* anyway. Doing them a little more at one part of the hour shouldn't make that much of a difference."

"How is that supposed to help me?" Sendy wanted to know.

"Even though you'll be doing the same number of finger snaps as you would have done before," I explained, "by doing them all at the start of the hour, you will be controlling them instead of them controlling you."

Sendy was not convinced this would help, but he was willing to give it a try. We reviewed exactly what the exercise entailed and he left committed to implement the experiment.

The next week, Sendy reported on his homework. He was unsure as to whether he had completed the assignment properly. Nevertheless, it seemed to have helped, because he acknowledged, almost reluctantly, that during the rest of the targeted hour, he hardly snapped his fingers at all.

We used the same system to help Sendy gain control over his neck twists and all of the other strange motions and movements he felt compelled to do every day. While we did not succeed in eliminating his compulsive behaviors, their frequency was reduced by more than 50 percent from what they had been when we first met.

At that point, Sendy felt his compulsions were no longer interfering with his social life in yeshivah and he wanted to stop the therapy.

Considering the success we had achieved until now, I wondered whether or not I should attempt to convince Sendy to continue.

In order to help resolve my dilemma, I consulted a colleague, Dr. Rashi Shapiro. "To have reduced such major compulsions to less than 50 percent of where they were before you started, Meir, is quite an accomplishment," he said. "And to think you did all of this without the assistance of any medication is pretty remarkable. How much further do you really think you could get even if you did continue? I would let him end with you now so that he will not feel that his therapist is disappointed in him."

It was good advice and I accepted it. Sendy and I had one final session devoted to wrapping up and ending on a note of accomplishment and success.

Looking back now, many years later, I see how this case highlights the power and efficacy of prescribing the symptom when it comes to reducing compulsions even as bizarre and numerous as those from which Sendy suffered.

SECTION X

FAMILY CONFLICTS

CHAPTER 39

Facilitating Communication
— *Rivka and Yocheved*

In the animal kingdom, all members of the same species look alike. When observing the faces of two chickens, for example, it is difficult to tell them apart. Humans, of course, each have unique facial features that make it easy to distinguish one from another. The reason for this anomaly of creation is to remind us of the following fact of life. "[People's] attitudes are dissimilar, just as their faces are not similar to each other" (*Berachos* 58a). Elsewhere, Chazal put it this way, "Rabbi Meir used to say, 'In three ways each person is different from his friend: in voice, in appearance, and in attitude" (*Sanhedrin* 38a).

Whenever people hold differing opinions, there exists the potential for conflict. And this is nowhere more evident than in families, where members can see things very differently from each other.

Throughout my practice, I have witnessed families wrestle with a wide range of issues and concerns. In each case, I have seen that the best route out of the morass in which they find themselves is to help them improve their communication with each other. Poor communication is not always the cause of the problem; but, in most cases, it can be the solution.

I have outlined what I believe are the essential tools needed to achieve effective communication in my book, *Ten Minutes a Day to a Better Marriage: Getting Your Spouse to Understand You* (Artscroll/Mesorah Publications, 2003). For the benefit of those who have not yet purchased a copy, I will summarize the main points here.

Effective communication means communication where both sides feel heard and understood. And, for some families, this is a standard they cannot reach without outside help. In order to conduct effective communication, it is necessary for both sides to take turns being the speaker and the listener. And they must retain these roles for the *entire* time-limited session, whether in my office or at home, switching roles only after a minimum period of twenty-four hours.

The rules for speaker and listener are as follows: The speaker picks the topic, but must begin by expressing some positive feeling toward the listener. In addition, the speaker cannot raise his/her voice, use foul language, insult, or attack the listener. Finally, the speaker must clarify what (s)he wants from the listener and not simply complain or criticize.

If, after the session has ended, the speaker wants to continue or add something (s)he omitted or just remembered, (s)he must wait until it is his/her turn to be the speaker again, which is only after the listener has had his/her turn being the speaker.

The listener's job is more challenging. The listener must pay attention and demonstrate his/her understanding of what the speaker is saying by reflecting back everything the speaker says at regular intervals and by asking relevant, non-defensive questions. Reflecting back means repeating in his/her own words whatever the speaker said. And when reflecting, the listener may not simply summarize, but must include all of the details and/or examples used by the speaker. The listener is not required to agree with anything the speaker says, only to understand and reflect what (s)he hears. Finally, the listener may not challenge, disagree, debate, or even correct the speaker. The time for all of that is when the listener becomes the speaker at the next session, either at home or in my office.

We find a precedent for reflecting in Tanach. Shlomo *HaMelech* is approached by two women, each claiming to be the mother of a single baby. Then the *pasuk* relates, "And the king said, 'This one says, "The live baby is mine and yours is the dead one." And this one says, "No, yours is the dead one and my baby is the live one"'" (*Melachim I* 3:23). By repeating the claims of both women, therefore, Shlomo *HaMelech* was demonstrating his understanding of the conflict. (And according to the Malbim, he was also demonstrating his rationale for determining who was telling the truth and who was lying, which was later proven.)

When family members use these rules for effective communication, they are capable of resolving even long-standing conflicts, as illustrated by the case of Rivka and Yocheved.

Rivka was an anxious *almanah* in her mid-sixties, who lost her husband five years before we met. When she called to schedule the appointment, she explained that there was something she wanted to tell her thirty-something married daughter, Yocheved, who only agreed to listen if the two spoke in a therapist's office. My office was the agreed-upon venue for this communication session.

When I welcomed Rivka and Yocheved into my consultation room, it was apparent that the two had not been talking to one another in the waiting room. What I quickly learned was that the two had not spoken to each other in almost two years.

Rivka began by repeating what she had told me over the phone. Then turning to Yocheved, she said, "I've been waiting a long time to tell you this, and I have a lot to say—"

At that point, I interrupted Rivka and suggested that we set certain boundaries for this discussion. Rivka was frustrated and annoyed at my interference and wanted me to allow her to continue. Yocheved, however, very much appreciated my intervention.

I then presented the rules outlined above and suggested that they follow them to facilitate the discussion of what was clearly a very sensitive and controversial sticking point between them. Yocheved heartily agreed and Rivka begrudgingly acquiesced.

By mutual consensus, Rivka was the first one to be the speaker. She anxiously shuffled the note papers she had brought with her and began with a pressured tone of urgency in her voice.

"When your father, *a"h*, passed away, I was left all alone and felt helpless. I had relied on your father for everything while he was alive, and I didn't know how I would manage, both emotionally and financially. Then my sister, Aunt Helen, came over and reassured me that she and her husband would always be there for me for whatever I needed.

"I relied on them for many of my household expenses and most of my emotional support in the months that followed and I grew quite dependent on them, to say the least. Then one day, Aunt Helen announced to me that I was too dependent on them and that they could no longer continue offering me the same level of support.

"To say I was devastated and shocked would be putting it mildly—"

At this point, I cut in, turned to Rivka, and said, "I don't see what this has to do with Yocheved. Since we only have a limited amount of time, why not get to the reason you wanted to meet in my office."

"This is part of what I want to tell her," Rivka replied, clearly irritated by my comment. "I need to give some background information in order for what I have to say to make any sense."

I leaned back and let Rivka continue.

"So where was I?" Rivka asked herself. "Oh yes, Aunt Helen. Well, when Aunt Helen told me that, I felt as if I had been hit by a truck. I didn't know why she was doing that. I may have been very dependent on them during that time, and I can understand it may have been too much for them. But to cut me off like that left me feeling even more desperate and confused."

Throughout the session, Yocheved was doing a pretty good job of listening attentively and reflecting accurately whatever her mother was saying. At times, Rivka cut Yocheved off before she had even finished. When I called this to her attention, Rivka complained, "But there is so much more I want to say and we're running out of time."

"Yes," I said, "we are running out of time. But why continue speaking if Yocheved has not followed what you said so far? The reflecting can be annoying. But it is necessary. I see this is a complicated matter with a long history, and we are clearly not going to resolve this in one session. I am prepared to meet with you both to resolve this impasse, which I am sure has been quite painful for both of you."

Condensing what Rivka had to tell Yocheved over the next few sessions, this is how it sounded.

"After Aunt Helen pulled the rug out of from under me, I was quite desperate. And when I asked her for an explanation, she said she had spoken with your brother, who had supported their decision to act that way. So I think you can understand why I felt abandoned by him. Looking back now, I probably should have confronted him directly about this. But, as I said, I was feeling lost, helpless, and quite confused. And I didn't have your father to discuss all of this with.

"Hopefully, you can understand why I felt I needed to distance myself from your brother and his family, who I saw as not really caring and supportive of me. I know you both must have thought I was simply paranoid at that point. Perhaps if you understood what I was going through, then you would not have judged me so harshly."

Yocheved had a tough time holding back while she was the listener. Nevertheless, she succeeded in following the rules for being a good listener. The following session, when her turn came to be the speaker, she added a whole new layer to the conversation.

As Yocheved put it to her mother, "I can understand what you went through after Tatty was *niftar.* Or, maybe I can't understand. But I can *try* to understand. What I cannot understand, however, is why you felt the need to besmirch our whole family by discussing all of this dirty laundry with the *rav*. Once he got involved, we were all embarrassed by the way you had portrayed us. You made us out to be disrespectful children who were ignoring our responsibility of *kibbud av v'eim*. And now my husband feels he can no longer daven in the shul he's attended since we got married.

"Furthermore, if you felt I was mistreating you in any way, why couldn't you come and discuss that with me directly? Why did you feel you had to first go to the *rav*? You were making assumptions and then acting on them. I have always dealt with you and spoken to you with *derech eretz*. To have the *rav* think of me as disrespectful was very, very hurtful. I cannot speak for my brother, but I certainly never spoke against you to Aunt Helen. And I don't see why I should be blamed for the way she treated you."

When Rivka's turn came to speak again, she responded, "My purpose in coming here was not to rewrite history. I went to the *rav* because I was desperate. And you should never know what it feels like to be an *almanah* and have someone pull the rug out from under you.

"What I'm looking for now is just to have a normal relationship with my daughter and grandchildren. I haven't seen your children in over a year and I miss them terribly. We don't need to dredge up everything from the past all the time. Let's just try to move on from now. Can we at least just go out for coffee once in a while?"

To this Yocheved responded the following week, "I would also like to have a relationship with my mother. And I want my children to know their bubby. But whenever I tried to have a civil, pleasant relationship with you, you kept bringing up the whole story with Aunt Helen and then you started in criticizing me for what you imagined was my role in Aunt Helen cutting off her support. It got to the point where I just couldn't take it anymore. I would be happy to go for coffee once in a while, as long as I feel safe. And, by the way, that's why I insisted on meeting first in a therapist's office. Because that was the only way I could feel safe speaking with you."

After two months of this structured communication in my office,

Yocheved felt safe enough to meet her mother for coffee. And that neatly coincided with my summer vacation. I recommended that we meet again upon my return to assess how things were going.

When I returned, we had our final meeting. During my vacation, Rivka and her daughter met several times for coffee and once for lunch. They never completely resolved their conflicting views of what had transpired after Rivka's husband had passed away. They did, however, succeed in reestablishing their relationship. They were clearly on track to repair much of the damage caused by their poor communication during that stressful period in their lives five years earlier.

Rivka and Yocheved were both adults, and, as such, they were both confident and articulate in speaking with each other. However, when the child is younger, the challenge of bridging the communication gap is much greater, as illustrated by the next example.

CHAPTER 40

Facilitating Communication, Part II

— Izzy

Early in the dawn of my career, after I launched my private practice, I met with local rabbanim to inform them of my services. Most of those meetings ended with my being told that they would prefer to refer people to an older, more experienced therapist.

When I met with Rabbi Gold, the *menahel* of one of the largest *mosdos hachinuch* in Brooklyn, however, I felt more encouraged because he gruffly informed me, "I don't believe talk therapy really helps. Medication can help. But just talking doesn't help."

At least he doesn't have anyone else he prefers to refer to, I told myself. *If he ever does need to refer someone, maybe he'll consider me.*

A few months later, Rabbi Gold did call — to refer his nephew, who had a serious stuttering problem that was making him anxious and socially withdrawn. "I cannot cure his stuttering," I confessed to Rabbi

Gold, "but I can try to help him with his anxiety and social withdrawal."

After six sessions, the nephew saw no improvement and was unwilling to continue. Not only did I experience that as an utter failure, but I also felt I had burned a bridge with Rabbi Gold. *I guess he'll never refer anyone else to me again*, I thought.

A couple of months later, Rabbi Gold proved me wrong when he called again. This time, however, he was calling about his son Izzy. Izzy was fourteen and learned in Rabbi Gold's yeshivah. He had always been a top student, well-liked by classmates and rebbeim. Two days before, however, there had been an incident that completely baffled Rabbi Gold.

He had come home unexpectedly in the middle of the day and found Izzy playing hooky. When Rabbi Gold demanded an explanation, Izzy did not respond. Rabbi Gold was a forceful, no-nonsense administrator and was not used to getting stonewalled by anyone. Later that night, he again asked Izzy for the reason he was home when he should have been in yeshivah. And again, Izzy was mute.

The next day, Izzy stayed home and remained there until Rabbi Gold called me. Rabbi Gold was determined to get to the bottom of this out-of-character behavior. So he called and asked me to speak with Izzy. There was one condition, however. I would have to speak with Izzy at their home as Rabbi Gold was uncomfortable with the prospect of Izzy being seen coming to my office.

I consented to Rabbi Gold's condition and scheduled an appointment for a home visit. When I arrived at the Gold home, Izzy was in his bedroom and refused to come out. Rebbetzin Gold showed me to Izzy's room and left us alone.

Izzy was crouched beside his bed in the far corner of his room. I sat down on his bed and gently asked if he would be willing to talk with me. He shrugged his shoulders noncommittally. Then I asked if he could tell me what was bothering him. Again, he shrugged his shoulders.

This is going to be a very one-sided conversation, I thought. *I suppose I'll have to try to guess what is going on with him.* Did it have to do with him and his father? I asked.

Izzy looked up hopefully and nodded affirmatively.

"Am I correct in assuming that it's hard for you to talk to your father?" I wondered aloud.

Izzy looked up again, nodded, and then buried his face in his hands, sobbing audibly.

I waited until he stopped crying. "Would you be willing to meet me again in my office?" I asked. Again he nodded affirmatively.

"Would it be all right if your father comes too, so we can all discuss this together?" I asked.

"Yes, I'll go," were the first and only words he spoke to me the entire time I was there.

Rabbi Gold called me later that day. "So what did you find out?" he barked into the phone.

"I need to meet you both together to discuss this," I replied. "But the next time must be in my office. I already discussed this with Izzy and he said that he is willing to come."

"Just tell me when we should be there and I'll come too," Rabbi Gold shot back.

Two days later, I sat with Rabbi Gold and Izzy in my office. "Let's get right to it," Rabbi Gold began. "Tell me what's wrong with my son. I'm his father and I need to know what the problem is. I know you met with him earlier this week, so please tell me now. That's what we're here for."

I hesitated to tell Rabbi Gold what I was thinking. He was older and somewhat intimidating. He had a rough, almost dictatorial manner which made me feel I had better weigh my words. Nevertheless, I felt he needed to hear the truth in a direct, unadulterated fashion. So I took a deep breath and said, "Rabbi Gold, your son is afraid of you."

Rabbi Gold looked as if I had just punched him in the stomach. I braced myself for his reaction to my blunt words, while I regretted having taken that approach.

Rabbi Gold whipped around to face Izzy and demanded, "Is that true?!"

Izzy turned his face to the wall and looked as if he was trying to escape. I felt frozen in place as I watched this intense family drama unfold in front of me. Izzy eventually turned back to face his father and simply nodded. Then he burst into uncontrollable sobs.

Rabbi Gold reached over and grabbed Izzy in a bear hug as father and son wept unabashedly in each other's arms. Tears welled in my eyes as well as I witnessed this powerful reconciliation between them.

"You taught me something very important today," Rabbi Gold said to me in a much more toned down and humble manner. "I know what I have to do now...and I thank you for your help." With that, he got up and walked out of my office with his arm around Izzy.

I never spoke with Rabbi Gold or Izzy again. But over the years, I have passed them on the street several times. Rabbi Gold and his son either never noticed me or chose not to acknowledge that we knew each other. Because I always take my cues from my patients, I never tried to greet either one of them, assuming they would prefer me not to do so. However, whenever I have seen them together, their animated conversation has always suggested to me that the ice broken between them in my office has remained that way.

CHAPTER 41

Facilitating Communication, Part III

— Dina

A while back, we had some major repairs made to our home. During a lull in the work, I approached the contractor with a question that had been bothering me.

"Tell me, Tzion," I began, "I'm curious about something. Before we took you for this job, we shopped around and got estimates from other contractors, and your estimate was by far the lowest. How can you afford to do this work for so much less than the going rate?"

"I'll tell you the truth," Tzion replied, adjusting his baseball cap. "I always give low estimates in order to get the job. Then I make it up on the 'might-as-wells,' for which I charge the standard prices."

"What do you mean by 'might-as-wells'?" I asked.

"Whenever anyone does repairs or renovations," Tzion explained, "there are always jobs they add on which were not part of the original contract. They figure, 'If we're already doing this, we might as well do that too.' And it's on the 'might-as-wells' that I make up the difference. For example, you hired me to straighten out your floor and repair the ceiling in this room. But after we started, you figured you might as well replace all of the windows in it too and put spotlights in the living room at the same time."

Therapy often works the same way. Someone comes for help with one issue. Then, when that is taken care of, they continue or return for help with something else. Such was the case with the Hirsches.

Rebbetzin Hirsch met with me at her husband's urging. She had lost her older sister eight months earlier and simply could not move on from her grief. She was tearful all day, lethargic, and unable to complete her normal tasks as a housewife and mother to their five children. Recognizing that his wife's bereavement was abnormal, he recommended that she seek professional help.

During a round of individual therapy, I explored the roots of Rebbetzin Hirsch's complicated bereavement which we traced back to her conflicted relationship with her mother. The brief, but intense at times, treatment was successfully completed in a few months, after which she was able to return to her normal high-functioning state.

Shortly after the termination of my work with Rebbetzin Hirsch, she called about a family conflict which she said disturbed her more than the depression she had just overcome. Her fifteen-year-old daughter, Dina, was acting up; she and her husband wanted my guidance on how to deal with it.

I suggested that I first meet with Rebbetzin Hirsch and her husband without Dina. At that session, Rabbi Hirsch, a well-respected mesivta rebbi at a local yeshivah high school, first thanked me for helping his wife get back to herself following the *petirah* of his sister-in-law. Then he and his wife painted the sad, but not uncommon, picture of what was going on at home.

Dina had been a good, but average, student throughout elementary school. She posed no behavioral problems at home or in class, and the reports from teachers were more or less positive up to and including eighth grade. In ninth grade, Dina gravitated toward a "bad crowd," which the Hirsches believed had a negative influence on her.

More specifically, Dina had become somewhat disrespectful toward both of her parents. In school, she wore the required uniform. At home and on weekends, however, Dina was dressing in a manner which the Hirsches felt skirted the edges of what they considered acceptable for a Bais Yaakov girl. Finally, Dina's grades were slipping recently, which was viewed by both parents as a clear red flag.

The Hirsches were very concerned about where Dina was headed with all of this. They feared she might be headed for the ranks of "at-risk" youth which had garnered so much attention at that time in the community.

I recommended that we try some family therapy with the three of them. Both were skeptical. They had hoped I would meet with Dina alone and try to straighten her out. I explained that she would be less receptive to me, a total stranger, and whatever rebelliousness she demonstrated toward her parents would only be increased toward me. Finally, there were issues in their relationship with their daughter that needed to be addressed. What better way to accomplish that than to have all three of them in the room together?

Rabbi and Rebbetzin Hirsch were not convinced. Nevertheless, they consented based on the trust I had earned through my previous successful work with Rebbetzin Hirsch. Then we scheduled appointments that would not conflict with Rabbi Hirsch's teaching schedule and Dina's school hours.

When the four of us all sat down together, I proposed that we follow the same format that was described in chapter 1 of this section ("Facilitating Communication"). This time, however, since there were three family members present, I directed that at each session, one parent would be the designated observer, not actively participating. Each week, Dina would either be the speaker or the listener. And when Dina was the speaker, we would alternate between her speaking to one parent and then the other. I reviewed the rules and all three of the Hirsches agreed to give it a try.

I suggested that we start with Dina being the first speaker, and I also recommended that she choose which parent she wanted to assume the role of listener. Dina picked her mother. For the rest of the session, she spoke and Rebbetzin Hirsch reflected and asked relevant questions.

The gist of Dina's agenda was as follows: "I feel sometimes that you do not trust me. You also treat me like a little kid. I know I'm not an adult, but I'm more an adult than a child and I resent your being on top of me all the time. For example, whenever I say I want to go shopping, you always insist on coming along. All of my friends go shopping themselves or with other friends. But you never let do that and that is so embarrassing for me."

When it was her turn to be the speaker, Rebbetzin Hirsch first tried to defend herself, saying, "As your mother, I need to supervise your clothing purchases to make sure they stay within the bounds of proper *tzenius*."

When Dina became the speaker again, she proposed that she would be willing to return any purchase her mother deemed unacceptable. She wasn't making an issue of *what* she bought, but rather *how* she shopped. Rebbetzin Hirsch found that proposal acceptable.

When Rabbi Hirsch was the listener, Dina had this to say: "What really ticks me off is the way you never give me a straight answer whenever I ask permission for something. For instance, if I want to go to a friend's house to study, you always say, 'I'll have to ask Mommy.' Why can't you decide for yourself? Then I have to wait until you get around to asking Mommy. And then sometimes it's too late already for me to go."

Rabbi Hirsch, a soft-spoken, gentle man, was less defensive than his wife had been. And when it was his turn to speak, he told his daughter how proud he was of her in general, and how articulate she was in the family therapy sessions in particular. He added, however, that he consulted with his wife because he was a firm believer that parents must be unified in dealing with their children. He wanted to support his wife and he often deferred to her.

When Dina spoke again to her father, she pressed her point further. "Sometimes I get the feeling that you do not want to hurt me by saying no. And that's why you never give me a straight answer. But I ask you because I really want to know what *you* think. I'm not trying to rebel against you and I'm not trying to play you against Mommy. I just want to know what my father really thinks. I know it may surprise you, but I really want to know what my father thinks!"

Dina's voice quivered as she said that last sentence and then she could not continue. Rabbi Hirsch reached out for Dina's hand as she choked back tears. Rebbetzin Hirsch grabbed a tissue for herself and one for Dina; then she dabbed the corners of her eyes.

"I know it's out of turn," Rabbi Hirsch said after a brief silence, "but I must tell you, Dina, that I never knew you felt this way. And I will make a concerted effort to give you my opinion the next time you ask for it."

The following week, all three Hirsches reported that the previous session had been pivotal. Since the previous session, they had started conducting similar communication sessions at home. As a result, they felt ready to continue on their own. Rebbetzin Hirsch put it this way: "We all feel that the lines of communication are now open, thanks to you, Dr. Wikler. Isn't that right, Dina?"

Dina blushed slightly, smiled, and nodded her head.

I congratulated them on their progress and agreed that they were ready to end their meetings with me. I then suggested that they return in three months for a follow-up to ensure that the gains they had made remained permanent; all three heartily agreed.

After our final session three months later, I have maintained annual contact with the Hirsches, initiated by them. Every *erev Rosh Hashanah*, like clockwork, I receive a warm, gracious greeting on my answering machine from Rebbetzin Hirsch, wishing me a *kesivah v'chasimah tovah* and thanking me once more for my help. And when I return her call, she briefly fills me in on family milestones and simchahs.

CHAPTER 42

The Parents' Support Group

— *Aryeh*

I recall as a young man the first time I noticed a one dollar bill taped to the cash register of a retail store. *Why is that there?* I wondered. Is that a spare single the cashier will use to make change? If so, then why not just keep it in the register with all the rest of the cash?

When I finally built up the courage to ask, I was rewarded with the answer. That was the first dollar bill received in payment from a customer after the store first opened, the proprietor explained. It was customary to save such an item as a memento, taped either to the outside of the cash register or to the wall behind the counter.

In a similar vein, I vividly recall many of the details from my work with one of the first young families I met with after completing my graduate school training. Ezra and Rechy Rosen were in their mid-twenties. Ezra was a newly minted accountant and Rechy taught preschool.

The Rosens initially sought help in overcoming a minor marital hurdle. When that was resolved in relatively short order, they left feeling more committed to each other. They also left me feeling greatly encouraged and convinced that I had chosen the right career. Upon terminating *all* of my work with the Rosens, however, I also faced one of the first ethical challenges in my career.

The Rosens were both highly intelligent, articulate, and about my age. We shared a similar sense of humor in addition to many areas of interest. I had only recently moved into the neighborhood and had not yet built a large cadre of friends in the area. As a result, I was tempted to continue my contact with the Rosens on a strictly social basis.

Technically, that would not have violated the professional ethic of not maintaining dual relationships, since our professional relationship had ended. *But what if they'll need my professional help again in the future?* I wondered. Then my befriending them now would not be in their best interest as it would prevent me from being able to work with them again. For their sake, then, I made the difficult choice of resisting my urge to socialize with them.

Three years later, my choice was vindicated. They were noticing some behavioral issues with their six-year-old, Aryeh. I agreed to see him for an evaluation. My assessment was that he was a bit precocious and independent-minded. He was not outside of the normal range, and I did not recommend any further counseling or therapy. If their concerns remained, they should contact me again, I advised.

About ten years later, they did just that, calling me while in crisis. I was sorry to hear they were in distress. And I was curious to learn if their current issue was related to the marital work we had done years before.

When they arrived, they volunteered without my having to ask that their marriage was as solid as ever, and they thanked me again for the work we had done thirteen years earlier.

"What can I help you with today?" I asked.

"It has to do with our teenage son Aryeh," Ezra said, getting right to the point. "He must have been around six years old when we saw you last. Now he's sixteen and taller than me. You wouldn't recognize him. Starting around his bar mitzvah, he's been very disrespectful to both of us. He's irresponsible about his chores at home, and we don't even ask him to do very much. He's also not doing well academically in yeshivah; his rebbi this year complains that he often looks spaced-out."

"He's also very disruptive at home," Rechy added. "For example, he often teases and starts up with his younger siblings. The whole family is on edge because of him. We are at our wits' end as to what to do about this. Ezra suggested that we meet with you and I also thought it was a good idea."

"Tell me," I probed, "it sounds as if this has been going on for a while. Was there anything in particular that served as the *makkeh b'patish* and made you call this week?"

"The truth is that we had a major confrontation Friday night," Rechy revealed, looking at Ezra as if to ask permission to open that can of worms.

Ezra nodded his approval and Rechy continued. "You see, we daven in a shul where some of the men wear hats on Friday night and others wear only yarmulkes. Ezra, of course, always davens in a hat. And since his bar mitzvah, Aryeh also wears his hat to shul. Well, Ezra was ready to leave for shul and he was waiting at the door for Aryeh. When Aryeh came out, he wasn't wearing his hat. Ezra reminded him to get it. And then Aryeh said he wasn't going to wear it. He said not everyone in shul wears a hat and he didn't want to wear one either. Ezra very calmly and firmly said, 'But *we* do.' Aryeh refused.

"Then they both started shouting. One thing led to another, and before anyone realized what was happening, they started hitting each other. Aryeh ran out of the house and did not return until we were finished with the seudah. We're all so stressed out about this, I can't tell you."

"How horrible!" I said, shaking my head. "Ezra, would you like to add to what your wife just said?"

"I guess I kind of lost control," Ezra confessed. "But he really gets under my skin sometimes and then I just lose it."

My first choice was to try to see the three of them together for some family therapy. After commiserating with the Rosens, that is what I proposed. While Ezra and Rechy were open and even keen on the idea, Aryeh was totally unwilling. "I don't have any problems," he reportedly told his parents. "If you want to talk to him, you can go yourselves."

My second choice was to see the Rosens alone and work with them. In the weeks that followed, I tried to walk the tightrope of achieving the proper balance between being supportive and empathic while still nudging them away from the authoritarian parenting styles in which each had been raised.

"Don't I have a right to set the rules in my home?" Ezra asked almost pleadingly. "After all, if I ever said to my father, *a"h*, one-tenth of what Aryeh says to me, I would have had my head handed to me."

"Of course, as parents you have the right," I replied. "You also have the right to enter an intersection if your light is green. If, however, you see a tractor trailer barreling down the cross street and ignoring his red light as he approaches the same intersection, you would be *dead* right to proceed. Similarly, considering what is going on now in your home, it would be foolish and counterproductive for you to 'lay down the law' to Aryeh. You could end up pushing him even further away than he is now."

My approach with the Rosens was only partially successful. On the one hand, they felt encouraged each time they met with me. As Rechy put it, "We try not to go straight home after we leave your office. We want the good feeling to linger as long as possible because we know that whatever hope or encouragement we feel here will vanish as soon as we walk in the door at home."

On the other hand, Aryeh was continuing to deteriorate. The term "at-risk" had not yet been coined. If it had, he would have been the poster child. First, he stopped wearing tzitzis. Then his yarmulke came off after yeshivah. Eventually, he even stopped putting on tefillin and dropped out of yeshivah altogether, going to work in the local pizza shop instead.

I really felt sorry for the Rosens and empathized with the pain of their disappointment. As Chazal understood thousands of years ago, "A degenerate child in one's home is worse than the war of Gog and Magog" (*Berachos* 7b). I desperately wanted to help them.

During one session, I thought out loud. "I really think you both need more than I can offer. You need the guidance and support that you can only get from other parents going through the same crisis. As Chazal say, '*Tzaras rabbim chatzi nechamah*' (*Devarim Rabbah* 2:14). You need to join a support group for *frum* parents of acting-out teenagers."

The Rosens were agreeable, but did not know where to find such a group. I offered to look into the matter myself. I did considerable research until I discovered that no such support group existed anywhere in the community. So I made a commitment to the Rosens and myself that I would start such a group. I composed a short advertisement about it and placed it in a popular English periodical.[1]

In response to the ad, I received numerous calls. Clearly, I had identified an unmet need in the community. Most of the people who called met the requirements of being *frum*, with an at-risk teenager living at home. Few of the callers, however, felt they could "come out of the closet" to meet with other parents in a group setting.

Three other couples, however, were willing to give the Parents' Support Group a try. They joined the Rosens for the first meeting of what turned out to be an ongoing weekly support group that I led in my office for eighteen months. Not all couples stayed in the group for the entire year and a half. But as couples left, others joined to replace them.

---

1. For a more detailed description of the Parents' Support Group, see my article, "Parenting a Troubled Adolescent in a Torah Home," *The Jewish Observer* (November 1991: 20—25).

During the meetings, parents shared their frustrations, torment, and fears. They also shared their insights, strategies, and successes. Each set of parents had an adolescent child who was teetering on the edge of going off the *derech* or who had already gone off completely, *r"l*. At each session, parents took turns venting and complaining about the challenges they faced at home. They also supported each other, and offered concrete suggestions and advice.

As a result of their participation in the group, parents reported gradual and incremental progress. This child stopped smoking marijuana. That child resumed attendance at shul on Shabbos. And still another child announced his intention to pursue a GED (high school equivalency certificate).

I have not kept up with all of the parents since they participated in the Parents' Support Group over thirty years ago. I have had contact with the Rosens, however, although not as a result of socializing with them. Over the years, Ezra has referred friends, neighbors, and their children to me. When making the referral, Ezra sometimes takes the opportunity to fill me in on the latest developments in his family.

So what happened to Aryeh in the end? Well, he fully returned to Yiddishkeit a couple of years after the Parents' Support Group disbanded. He married a Bais Yaakov girl with a similar history and moved to Lakewood, where they are raising their six children. Aryeh is now a real estate developer and attends a *daf yomi shiur* every morning before *shacharis.*

Of course, there is no way to know for sure what brought that about. Aryeh and some of the other troubled youth might have found their way back to Yiddishkeit even if their parents had not joined the Parents' Support Group. I believe, however, that the group played a significant role in bringing about a similar happy ending for all of the parents who participated.

LIVING WITH DIFFICULT PEOPLE: PARENTS, SPOUSES, AND CHILDREN

CHAPTER 43

The Difficult People
— Narcissistic and Borderline Personality Disorders

Personality disorders are persistent conditions where the individual exhibits maladaptive ways of thinking and behaving that interfere with his normal functioning. People suffering from these conditions have difficulty establishing and maintaining healthy relationships with friends, coworkers, and relatives. They are not delusional, depressed, or overly anxious. In most cases, they can be helped with conventional psychotherapy.

The two personality disorders that pose the greatest challenge to therapists and family members alike are narcissistic and borderline personality disorders. And while these conditions constitute less than 5 percent of an average therapist's caseload, they will typically take up over 50 percent of that therapist's consultation sessions with his or her supervisor.

As with all personality disorders, in order to qualify for a diagnosis of narcissistic or borderline personality disorder, someone would need to display most or all of the symptoms of that disorder. In other words, someone could exhibit only a few narcissistic or borderline features in his personality and not technically qualify for the full-blown diagnosis. While the impairment for such people is clearly not as great, it nevertheless can pose serious challenges for their friends and family.

Finally, these two conditions represent clusters of symptoms with considerable overlapping. To facilitate the discussion of these disorders, however, they will be described separately.

As the term suggests, someone suffering from **narcissistic personality disorder** is very self-absorbed. He or she has a distorted view of his or her entitlement, expecting special favors and treatment as a matter of course. Such people often feel underappreciated and not treated with adequate respect. In order to feel that they are being treated fairly, they often expect an inordinate amount of attention, approval, and/or sympathy from others. When they do not receive it, they are resentful and complain (i.e., "You think *you're* tired?! What about *me*?!").

In many cases, narcissists are also preoccupied with their appearance and how they are viewed by others. While everyone wants to be liked and appreciated, these people make it a primary focus of their lives. Much of what they do and think is directed toward achieving this goal. And they often see themselves as appearing more attractive and being more talented than they actually are.

In addition, narcissists demonstrate a marked lack of empathy. In other words, they find it hard — and in some cases are completely unable — to understand the feelings of others, which is the necessary ingredient to achieve the *middah* of being *nosei b'ol im chaveiro*, being able to share someone else's burden (*Pirkei Avos* 6:6). As a result, they are often clueless as to how obnoxious their behavior is to those around them.

It is not clear why some people become narcissistic. In some cases, having been overindulged as children is a contributing factor. In other cases, however, emotional deprivation and an absence of healthy nurturing are predisposing influences.

Family and social relationships with narcissists are characterized as being markedly unbalanced. In other words, friends and relatives must give 90 percent of the time, while receiving only 10 percent of the time for the relationship to be maintained. As a result, these relationships are strained at best, while conflicted and tense in the worst cases.

Finally, narcissists are absolutely allergic to criticism. They are never wrong and they never make mistakes, at least from their point of view. As a result, they hardly ever see the need to apologize for anything and they rarely accept responsibility for any failed relationship.

To find excellent examples of narcissists, we need look no further than the political landscape, which is literally strewn with such people. Positive outcomes from therapy with such individuals are extremely hard to come by. Their friends and relatives are more likely to consult therapists than the narcissist himself or herself.

Borderline personality disorder is less common, but even more problematic than narcissistic personality disorder. While it occurs in only a small fraction of the population, it causes the therapist most of his work-related stress if he has such a patient.

Borderlines tend to have pervasively unstable and intense relationships. They are highly impulsive and unpredictable. They experience bouts of intense anxiety and depression, often triggered by the chaotic state of their relationships. At times they may idealize someone, demonstrating intense loyalty, admiration, and affection. And at other times, they may denigrate, disparage, and express intense hostility toward the same person.

The reason for this roller coaster behavior is because borderlines often feel threatened with abandonment by their friends and relatives (i.e., "You just don't care about me!"). This concern, of course, can also be a self-fulfilling prophecy, as borderlines make unrealistic demands on those around them, which often causes the very rejection they fear.

Borderlines are also characterized by their inappropriate and excessive anger. They often lose control of their tempers, and they will explode with little or no provocation. At times these episodes will take place in public, causing shame and embarrassment to their friends and relatives. This makes those who interact with a borderline feel as if they are constantly walking on eggshells and trying to avoid the hidden minefields in the relationship.

Borderlines can also be manipulative, as they attempt to control others and prevent the feared abandonment. This can even include, but is not limited to, making suicidal threats and/or gestures. In extreme cases, actual suicidal attempts are made.

Such people are also extremely sensitive to criticism and can perceive even innocuous statements as highly critical. They feel easily threatened and, in more extreme cases, can appear to suffer from paranoia.

There is no clear, known cause for borderline personality disorder. It does not seem to have a genetic origin. But early childhood trauma is definitely a major contributing factor in many, but not all, cases.

One of the most confounding features of this disorder is the fact that all of the symptoms described here can, at times, be kept hidden. That means that someone with this condition can temporarily conceal these symptoms, coming across as completely normal and healthy. As a result, acquaintances, neighbors, and some extended family members can be totally surprised to hear that close relatives, friends, and coworkers are having so much difficulty with this person. In addition, the borderline may get engaged and married before exhibiting the full range of his or her symptoms to the spouse.

Finally, therapists can often misdiagnose a borderline, assuming he is suffering from simple anxiety and/or depression. Only after getting better acquainted with this person will the true nature of his disorder become apparent.

Treatment for this condition is so challenging and stressful that many therapists attempt to avoid working with someone they suspect may be borderline. And even when such a person is accepted — wittingly or unwittingly — for treatment, the therapy usually ends in disappointment for both sides. Once again, it is the friends and relatives of borderlines who consult therapists much more often than the borderlines themselves, as will be illustrated in the chapters that follow.

CHAPTER 44

Feeding the Narcissism
— Hillel

An administrator of a major Jewish communal organization called one day and left me a message to return his call. I was flattered by the call, expecting to be invited to address one of the large public forums his organization often sponsored.

When I returned the administrator's call, I was surprised, but no less flattered to learn the purpose of the call. He wanted to refer his brother Hillel, a married father of four in his late thirties, to me for treatment. Apparently, Hillel had been fired from his most recent job as sales manager of a large office furniture distributor. Hillel had been insubordinate, stubborn, and arrogant, and was now unemployed for the past two months. Hillel's wife, Fraydie, was losing patience with him and making noises about divorce. The administrator was seeking my assistance in saving his brother's marriage.

"Sounds like things have been deteriorating rapidly," I observed. "Have your brother give me a call and I'll see what I can do. I'm not hopeful, based on what you've told me. But I will certainly give it my best shot."

The next day, Hillel called, with considerable reluctance in his voice. "My brother said you wanted to meet with me," Hillel said.

I chose not to correct Hillel and simply scheduled an appointment to see him. When he arrived, he appeared beaten and defeated. "What can I help you with?" I asked.

With a disgusted look on his face as if to say "you should know without my having to tell you," Hillel replied, "I'm depressed."

"That's terrible," I said. "How long have you been feeling that way?"

"Ever since I lost my job," Hillel said with a shrug of his shoulders. "I suppose I shouldn't say I 'lost my job,' I should say I was fired. And for no good reason, I might add."

"Why do you think you were fired?" I asked.

"Because my boss is too insecure," Hillel shot back. "He thinks he's so smart that he knows everything. And I guess he just couldn't stomach it if anyone else shared a different point of view. I had some very good ideas that could have helped him take his business to the next level. The ideas I had would have benefited him, not me. But he was so uptight about running things his way that he just didn't like it if I made any suggestions about how to do things differently at the office. So I guess you could say we had a personality clash. Only we would not have had to clash at all if he hadn't been so insecure and threatened by my great ideas."

Putting together what I had heard from his brother with what I was hearing from Hillel, it became clear to me that I was sitting with a classic narcissist. Hillel displayed all of the symptoms of inflated self-image and an exaggerated sense of entitlement. He would, therefore, have poor insight potential and would not respond well to any corrective criticism, however much I sugarcoated it. My only option, therefore, was to do what some call "feeding the narcissism." In other words, I would offer unconditional acceptance and approval. The theory behind this approach is that sometimes, if the narcissist feels adequately "fed," he can step up to the plate and accept more appropriate levels of responsibility. It was the only arrow in my quiver.

"It sounds as if your boss simply did not appreciate what you had to offer," I said.

Hillel sat up straight. He clearly was not expecting to hear that from me. "Hey, you seem to get it," he said with a faint smile tickling his lips.

"How long have you been out of work?" I asked.

"I'd say it's about two months already," Hillel replied, shaking his head.

"I'm sure this has been difficult for you," I soothed. "I'm just wondering, have you done anything to try to find another job?"

"Yes, it has been difficult," Hillel confirmed. "In fact, it is even difficult for me to get out of bed in the morning. As I mentioned, I've been feeling very depressed about all of this. So I usually don't get out of bed until shortly before *chatzos*, just to be able to daven *shacharis*. To be honest, I don't always even make that. Then I have to daven two *minchah*s."

"Wow," I said. "You really are depressed! I see you are going through an even tougher time than I originally thought."

"You know," Hillel said, pointing his finger at me. "I think you really do get it. Not everyone understands me like you do."

"How about your wife?" I asked. "How's she dealing with your being out of work?"

"Are you kidding?" Hillel replied, raising his voice. "She's the real reason I'm feeling so depressed. Let me try to explain this to you. As I mentioned already, it's difficult for me to get out of bed every day. If I do manage to get up before *chatzos* and daven *shacharis,* I'm so exhausted that I feel like going back to bed after breakfast. But then I push myself and go through the want ads in the paper. And that's about all I have energy for these days.

"Then my wife comes home from work and I ask her when she thinks she'll be ready to serve dinner. So she practically jumps down my throat! 'Why don't you pick yourself up and get another job already,' she almost shouts at me, as if I'm a lazy good-for-nothing."

"Sounds like you don't get much respect at home," I observed.

"Hey, you really *do* get it," Hillel said, this time with an unabashedly broad smile.

"I guess your wife doesn't appreciate how hard it is for you just to get out of bed each day," I said.

"That's right," Hillel agreed. "My kids don't get it either. They come home from school and want me to help them with homework and stuff. But I just cannot deal with any of that now. Even my brother gets on my case. And he's beginning to sound just like my wife."

"Sounds like no one really understands what you are going through," I said, shaking my head.

"That's right again," Hillel confirmed. "But I get the feeling that you understand what I'm going through. Maybe I should bring my wife here so you can kind of straighten her out. Can we arrange that, Doc?"

"Uh, no," I said. "I'm sorry but that's not something I do. You see I work with people to help them deal with their friends and family. I don't speak for them. I can help you deal with your wife, if you like. But speaking to her for you is not something I would ever do."

"I understand," Hillel said. "No need to apologize. It makes sense. I have to learn how to deal with her myself."

Over the next few weeks, I assumed the same posture with Hillel, accepting and supporting his feelings, whatever they were. At one point, Hillel's brother even called out of concern.

"My brother tells me you are encouraging him not to look for work now. Is that true? I sent him to you so that you could get him off his backside and start contributing to the family finances again."

"I'm sorry, but I don't have your brother's permission to speak with you," I said respectfully. "All I can say is that I am trying my best to help him. I cannot confirm or deny anything he tells you about our sessions."

After a few more weeks, Hillel came in and told me he was getting bored sitting around the house all day. He was thinking about his old job and decided that he would do better working independently.

He was always a pretty good keyboard player, so he decided to try working as a one-man band.

Hillel contacted a friend who was a photographer and asked if he could recommend him for simchahs, which he did. Then one job led to another, and before long, he was fully employed playing for bar mitzvahs, *sheva berachos*, and even some *chasunah*s.

Hillel's arrogance remained intact after his brief round of therapy. He did manage, however, to pull himself together and get back to work after the temporary setback of his unemployment.

Once he was out of the house for part of the day and contributing to the family finances, Fraydie found it more bearable to stay married. And while I never received the follow-up thank-you call from Hillel's brother to which I felt entitled, I nevertheless judged him favorably. I attributed his not calling to his misunderstanding the confidentiality protocol in therapy. I took satisfaction in the fact that Hillel's marriage had been saved and he was gainfully employed at what appeared to be a stable occupation.

Once Hillel started working, he stopped meeting with me. I did not hear from him or anyone from his family after Hillel terminated his therapy. I only learned of the ongoing nature of his new line of work by seeing him play at some simchahs where I happened to be a guest. At each occasion, Hillel chose not to acknowledge me, and I took the cue from him and pretended not to know him.

CHAPTER 45

Studying
Kibbud Av v'Eim

— *Reena*

In most cases, when a child has a borderline parent, the child understands that something is terribly wrong at home, but is unaware of the parent's diagnosis. At other times, especially when the child grows up, the child realizes that his or her parent's erratic, irrational, and inappropriate behavior is due to the parent suffering from borderline personality disorder. Reena was a perfect example of the latter category.

Reena was in her late twenties, a petite, put-together, married mother of three. As her father-in-law was a prominent *chassidishe rebbe*, she was reluctant to consult a therapist. She felt that too many people were aware of her *yichus*, and she was concerned that she might be identified upon entering or exiting my office. Nevertheless, due to the dilemma in which she found herself, she felt she had no alternative other than seeking professional guidance.

"I just don't know what to do anymore," Reena sighed at the initial consultation. "I know my mother is a borderline. And I want to fulfill my obligation of *kibbud av v'eim.* But I'm afraid it is going to destroy me in the process."

"How do you know your mother is a borderline?" I asked. "Has she been diagnosed by a mental health professional?"

"No, she won't go to a therapist," Reena replied. "I certainly wish she would. It would probably make my life a lot easier. But she would never go."

"Then how do you know what her diagnosis is?" I persisted.

"To tell you the truth, I googled her symptoms," Reena said. "I always knew she was different from other mothers. She seemed overly attached to me when I was growing up. She wanted to know all the details about what was going on between me and my friends. And she never shopped alone; she always took me with her. She didn't treat any of my brothers or sisters like that. In fact, she kind of ignored them, which they hated. Don't get me wrong — I liked the attention. But it always felt excessive.

"Then, when I got older, I learned about BPD and looked it up online," Reena continued. "My mother has all of the classic symptoms. She loses her temper and screams for the slightest little thing. She never apologizes. She is always criticizing and putting others down, especially my father. And she's not ashamed to do it in public, which is really embarrassing. Frankly, I can't understand why my father puts up with it. But that's really none of my business."

"From your description," I said, "she does sound like a borderline. And, apparently, she's been one for quite some time. So what prompted you to call me now? Exactly what were you hoping to accomplish?"

"After I got married," Reena said after taking a deep breath, "an awful lot changed. My mother started treating me like her enemy. As much as she was attached to me while I was single, she has become openly hostile to me since I moved into my own home. Now I can do nothing right. She even criticizes my clothing. She is always visiting my nieces and nephews, bringing them gifts and nosh. But she never visits my kids. In fact, my baby was born five months ago and she has not even come over to see him.

"You want to know why I called now. The answer is that we have a simchah coming up in the family. My uncle, my father's youngest brother, is getting married, and I will be coming with my husband and children. My mother already told me that she will totally ignore me there unless I apologize to her for not giving her a better birthday present last month. I got her a sweater that I thought she could wear. But she felt it wasn't a personal enough present for her special birthday. She just turned fifty.

"I cannot tell you how many times I've apologized to my mother for things that I did which really weren't bad or wrong. But at this point, I'm so fed up that I just can't take it anymore. What I'd really like to say I know I can't, because it would be disrespectful. But to apologize for buying my mother a sweater for her birthday?! Give me a break!"

"What does your father say about all of this?" I asked. "Do you speak about your mother with him?"

"Are you kidding?" Reena asked rhetorically. "I talk to my father about this all the time. He agrees that my mother is being unreasonable. But he just wants there to be shalom, so he always asks me to be *mochel* and to be *mevater*. He keeps promising me that if I just go along with what my mother wants 'this one time,' I'll see that things will get better. But that never happens.

"At this point, I really think that my father is part of the problem," Reena continued, getting all riled up. "If he would stand up to her, maybe she would cut out all of this craziness."

"You can't really reason with someone who is being unreasonable," I pointed out. "And, anyway, as you said yourself, your parents' relationship with each other is really not something you can change."

"I'm not trying to change their relationship," Reena protested. "I just wish my father would admit how sick my mother really is.

Perhaps I could bring him here and you could convince him. You seem to understand what we're all going through."

"If your father wanted to consult a therapist," I said, "he could have done that long ago. Yes, he may be in denial. But for now, the denial may be working for him. So let's get back to you. Tell me what questions you have."

"Okay," Reena said, pulling her thoughts together. "What really confuses me is what my responsibilities are regarding the mitzvah of *kibbud av v'eim.* I mean, if not for that, I wouldn't feel forced to give in to my mother's crazy demands all the time. In fact, I might not even attend that simchah altogether. The last time we were at a simchah, my mother refused to even greet me. And that was when I came over to her. It was so embarrassing for me and my husband. People asked me what was going on and I had to make up a story. This is all so stressful, not only for me, but also for my husband.

"My father is always saying he understands how I feel," Reena continued, "but then, at the end, he always tells me, 'She's your mother and you have to respect her.' So I'm really torn about this. Do I really have to do everything my mother wants even if drives me crazy?"

"I'm not going to *pasken* that *shailah* for you," I said. "But this much I can tell you: Like all other mitzvos, the mitzvah of *kibbud av v'eim* does have limits. It's not exactly a blank check. And children are not their parents' possessions. There's an excellent article on this subject written by a colleague of mine.[1] I have a copy here I'd like to share with you. Once you've had a chance to read it, let's meet again so we can discuss this further."

Reena read the article and scheduled another appointment. When she came in, she appeared much less stressed-out than the first time we met.

---

1. Benzion Sorotzkin, "Honoring Parents Who Are Abusive," in *Chinuch: Beyond the Surface* (CreateSpace Independent Publishing Platform, 2015), 173–191. Previously published in *Nefesh News* (January 2004): 17–20.

"I read the article you gave me," Reena said, "but I still have some questions. For example, if I do attend the simchah and my mother starts attacking me in public, how should I handle that? I mean, I know I can't answer back and say what I want to say. So how can I protect myself and still not disrespect my mother?"

"The best thing you can do is simply walk away," I advised. "I'm not talking about sticking around for a while and then leaving. I'm talking about walking away as soon as your mother becomes abusive. Even if your mother doesn't get the hint, you will suffer less. And as the article clearly demonstrates, children are absolutely not required to allow parents to abuse them."

I met with Reena for a few more sessions, during which we discussed self-protective strategies she could use in other scenarios where her mother attempted or succeeded in insulting, attacking, or embarrassing her. When we eventually ended and had our final session, she indicated that what she found most helpful was the article I had given her to read. It had empowered her by convincing her that children are not required by Torah law to allow parents to abuse them even if the parents are not fully in control of their behavior.

CHAPTER 46

Healthy Disengagement and Asking Questions

— Gavriel

As stressful as it is to have a borderline parent, at the end of the day, children can and should achieve independence from parents. When someone is married to a borderline, however, that is not an option. As a result, having a borderline spouse is especially problematic, as the case of Gavriel illustrates.

Gavriel was a neatly dressed married father of four and in his mid-forties when he first consulted with me. He had a boyish face and an innocent, compliant personality to match which made him appear much younger than his chronological age. He also had a somewhat passive nature, which is quite common among people who choose to remain married to borderline spouses. He was successfully employed as an accounts manager for a high-end specialty chocolate company. He got straight to the point at the start of the session.

"I know my wife is a difficult person," he began. "She's been that way ever since I married her eighteen years ago. I know she cannot change and I do not expect that of her. When I married her, it was for life. So please don't advise me to get divorced. I'm a devoted husband and father, and I would never break up our family by leaving my wife. But I'm finding it very difficult to cope with all of the stress and tension at home. I recently confided to my *rav* about what is going on at home and he recommended that I meet with you. I believe he already spoke to you about me. Is that correct?"

"Yes," I confirmed. "I did speak briefly with him. But perhaps you can fill in the details for me. In what way is your wife difficult?"

"Okay, let me give you some examples," Gavriel offered. "Well, for one thing, my wife is a screamer. She has a very short fuse and yells a lot at everyone, especially my oldest daughter. My wife is always finding fault with her and then they quickly become embroiled in these incredible shouting matches. The other children cower in their rooms and I also find it very painful to watch. If I attempt to defend my daughter, my wife turns on me with even greater ferocity. And the same thing happens if I just try to calm her down."

"Have you ever tried to get help in the past?" I asked.

"Oh, sure, many times," Gavriel replied. "We've been to three different marriage counselors over the course of our marriage. Each time the story is the same. My wife picks the therapist. She spends the whole session bashing me, which is all right if it helps her to vent. But then, if the therapist suggests that I get a chance to speak, she becomes indignant and accuses the therapist of siding with me. If the therapist backs down, we continue. If not, my wife refuses to continue the counseling.

"If I suggest we see someone now," Gavriel continued, "my wife will say she is no longer willing. She says, 'If you want to go, then go yourself. You have plenty to work on that needs changing.' So, actually, that's part of the reason I'm here today. Perhaps you can suggest things I can and should be doing to improve the situation at home."

"If this has been going on for so long," I asked, "then why are you reaching out now for help? What happened that made it more unbearable?"

"That's a good question," Gavriel said reflectively. "I suppose it's a combination of things. First of all, the shouting matches between my wife and daughter have definitely escalated recently. Furthermore, I feel all of this is taking a toll on me. And, finally, it has begun to affect me at work. I do cold-calling at work, trying to open new accounts. I don't know if you've ever tried cold-calling companies. You need a thick skin to do that kind of work. And, if I do say so myself, I'm pretty good at it. But lately, I'm finding it harder and harder to make these calls. And I know it has to do with the stress I'm experiencing at home."

"Give me some other examples of how your wife is difficult," I suggest.

"Well, let me see," Gavriel said, scratching his temple. "Whenever we go out to a simchah, she suspects me of looking at other women. And she's always checking my cell phone to see who I've been speaking to. She also finds housekeeping a bit of a challenge, and our house is terribly cluttered with all of her stuff — newspapers, magazines, and papers — that sort of thing. She also is almost always complaining about something. And no matter what I do to try to please her, it never seems to be enough, or at the right time, or in the right way. For example, if I tell her about something that happened or that I heard, she will often pressure me to get to the point. But then at other times, if I am brief and leave out details, she complains that I'm not forthcoming and I'm forcing her to interrogate me."

At this point in the session, I reached for my copy of the DSM, the *Diagnostic and Statistical Manual of Mental Disorders* published by the American Psychiatric Association. Turning to the section on borderline personality disorder, I read the list of symptoms out loud. "I would never diagnose someone I haven't seen," I said. "But you tell me. Do you believe your wife fits this description?"

Gavriel didn't hesitate. "She sure does," he stated emphatically.

"Then she may be a borderline," I observed.

"So what does that mean for me?" Gavriel wanted to know.

"It means that you are correct in what you said earlier — that you can't change her," I explained. "It also means that there is nothing you did or can do to reduce her outbursts. So, at least you don't have to blame yourself for them."

"Okay, that's comforting," Gavriel said almost to himself. "But is that it?"

"No, not at all," I said. "It also means that her condition is something you are going to have to learn to cope with so that it doesn't interfere with your work. And you are going to have to learn how you can minimize the impact of all of this on your children."

"That's exactly what I came for," Gavriel stated emphatically. "I see our time is up for today. So can we discuss how I do that next time?"

"Absolutely," I confirmed. And then we scheduled an appointment for the following week, the same day and time.

At our next session, Gavriel began by telling me that during the previous week he found another answer to my question as to why he found his wife's behavior more difficult to deal with now.

"My son's rebbi called two days ago," Gavriel reported. "He said he was concerned because my son seemed spaced-out in class and was not fully participating with his classmates during recess. Then he asked if there was anything going on at home lately that could be causing him to be so withdrawn. I told him I'd look into it, because I don't want to wash my dirty linen in public. But apparently my wife's screaming has been affecting my son more than I realized, which really raises this to a whole new level."

"Sounds like your son could use some help of his own," I said. "Do you think your wife would agree to let him see a therapist?"

"I'm not sure," Gavriel said, shaking his head. "She might feel threatened by that. But my son's yeshivah has a guidance counselor. I think I'll suggest to the *menahel* that my son see him. That way my wife will not have to be involved."

"The guidance counselor might want to communicate with you and your wife," I pointed out. "Perhaps it would not be such a good idea to do this behind your wife's back. Maybe you could tell her that you spoke with your son's rebbi, which is true. And then, based on that, you followed up with the *menahel*, who arranged for the guidance counselor to get involved."

"I like that," Gavriel said with a shy smile. "I think that sounds much better. Getting back to me, what advice do you have for me to help me cope better?"

"I've been thinking about your predicament," I told Gavriel. "And I have two suggestions for you. The first is that you really need a better support system. I mean you are on the front lines of a major conflagration every day. Just to keep your sanity, you need to be meeting with people who can be empathic, encouraging, and supportive on a regular basis. I would like to recommend, therefore, that you enter a therapy group where you can meet and work with others in a safe atmosphere under the guidance of a properly trained group therapist."

Most people are initially resistant whenever I recommend group therapy. Gavriel was different. He liked the idea right away. And his gentle, outgoing nature made him a perfect candidate. I gave him all of the details and instructed him to contact the group leader to arrange for a consultation so that he could learn more about the group, as well as meet and get a feel for the group leader.

"The second suggestion I have for you," I continued, "is to work on making a healthy disengagement from your wife. What I mean by that is that you are too invested in what your wife thinks of you. You said yourself that whatever you do to please her is never enough. And the more you attempt to achieve that unrealistic goal, the more stress you will be adding to your life. What you need to do is invest in activities and interests outside of your home and try to care less about what your wife thinks of you. That way you will be able to distance yourself from her verbal abuse while at the same time being emotionally available to your children.

"I have been thinking of attending more *shiurim* at my shul," Gavriel mused. "Is that what you had in mind?"

"I didn't have anything specific in mind," I shared. "But that sounds like a great plan. By investing more time and energy in your Torah learning, you will feel less vulnerable to your wife's mood swings."

Gavriel very conscientiously followed through on both of my suggestions. In a very short time, he not only began attending more *shiurim* at his shul, but he also got himself elected as an officer. Also, the group I referred him to accepted him, and he threw himself into that as well, finding it to be a valuable resource and safe haven.

At another session, Gavriel described another recent escalation of his wife's harassment. "She has done this in the past," he said, consulting notes he made for himself on his smartphone. "But she is definitely doing it more lately. And that is that she's kind of making rumblings about divorce."

"What do you mean by 'rumblings?'" I asked.

"She's making vague references without actually coming out and threatening me," Gavriel explained. "For example, she says things like, 'I'm done,' 'It's over,' or, 'I guess we're finished now.' I know she doesn't mean it and would never initiate a divorce. But it is very unpleasant to hear things like that. And I know it upsets the kids when she speaks that way in front of them."

"Tell me how you respond when she does that," I said.

"I don't really have a good response," Gavriel said, shrugging his shoulders. "Sometimes I try to defend myself. Sometimes I try to cajole her. But most of the time I just try to ignore it by changing the subject or talking to one of the kids about something else. I know I'm not handling these incidents properly. How would you suggest I react?"

"I call this kind of behavior 'sniping,'" I said, presenting one of my favorite metaphors. "A sniper is one who hides behind a rock or a tree and shoots at his target. The victim is at a terrible disadvantage because he cannot see the sniper and therefore cannot properly defend himself. In a similar fashion, therefore, some people use sarcasm or innuendo to express their hostility. It's very disarming."

"Yeah, that's exactly how it makes me feel — helpless," Gavriel said, nodding his head. "So what can I do at such times?"

"You have to respond by asking questions," I replied. "What that means is that you need to draw the sniper out more into the open in order to effectively deal with him. And the way you do that is not by commenting, but by questioning. In other words, you ask things like, 'What did you mean by that?' 'So, what are you proposing?' Or, 'Just what are you trying to tell me?' In that way, you double bind the other person, who has only two choices. Either she can withdraw her comment by saying something like, 'Oh, I didn't mean anything.' Or, she is forced to be more explicit. Either response benefits you. If she backs off, that is clearly to your advantage. And if she becomes more direct, then it will be easier for you to deal with the direct attack."

"Well, suppose I do what you say and she wants a divorce?" Gavriel asked.

"Then you can continue to ask questions," I advised. "For example, 'When do you want to do this?' 'How did you expect me to react to this?' and 'How were you planning to deal with child custody, division of property, and family finances?' Needless to say, these questions should be posed to her without raising your voice or displaying any other signs of anger. Even if your wife does not back off and she increases her attacks, it is still better for your wellbeing and your children's stress levels that you not continue to assume such a passive stance in the face of any verbal abuse."

"And suppose she erupts and unleashes a tirade against me?" Gavriel asked. "How should I react to *that*?"

"You can say, 'Let's discuss this later' or 'I cannot speak with you when you talk that way to me.' Then, if she continues unabated, you simply pick yourself up and walk out of the room. And if she follows you, you leave the house. No one should have to tolerate verbal abuse.

"I once asked the late Kosonier Rebbe, Rav Meshulam Rottenberg, *ztz"l*, why in the Rosh Chodesh *bentshi*ng we ask for '*chaim shel osher* *vechavod.*' I thought we were supposed to flee from honor.

"He then explained to me that there are two types of *kavod*: 1) being in the limelight, like receiving an award at a dinner, and 2) the more basic *kavod habrios*, not being insulted or embarrassed.

"It is the latter form of honor that we daven for in the Rosh Chodesh *bentsh*ing. In English, we call that self-respect, and that's what you need to more actively protect."

After a few more sessions, Gavriel ended his individual therapy with me. He reported that his son was making progress with the yeshivah guidance counselor. His daughter also entered therapy with a private adolescent therapist, with his wife's approval. And, according to the therapist running the group Gavriel joined, he was already becoming a star member, making valuable contributions each week, while growing personally as well. He was learning to be more assertive and less passive in his responses to his wife.

CHAPTER 47

Supportive Housing
— *Nachum*

From the case histories presented thus far, one could get the mistaken impression that diagnosing borderline personality disorder is a simple, straightforward affair, requiring little training, education, or expertise. Unfortunately, that is definitely not so. Many times even seasoned mental health professionals can be misled by the borderline's ability to temporarily conceal and control his symptoms, as was the case with Nachum.

Having a borderline parent or spouse presents serious challenges, as was illustrated by the previous examples. Having a child with BPD, however, can be an even greater ordeal for parents and siblings.

Nachum was a short, stocky teenager who was quite unathletic. He was more cerebral and had a passion for chess, his favorite pastime. After a few months at an out-of-town yeshivah, Nachum was sent home. His parents, Alex and Blima, never really got the story straight as to why he had been sent home. Something happened which neither

Nachum nor his rebbeim were willing to discuss in detail. After whatever happened, Nachum became withdrawn, depressed, and unable to concentrate. As a result, the yeshivah felt he would be better off at home.

Nachum's parents arranged for him to meet with a well-known, veteran *frum* therapist, and Nachum began seeing this therapist on a weekly basis. Nachum's symptoms of depression and the sudden onset of these symptoms suggested that Nachum had suffered some recent trauma. As much as the therapist probed this possibility, Nachum steadfastly denied that any trauma had occurred. *Perhaps after he feels safe and secure with the therapy*, his therapist reasoned, *Nachum will trust me enough to reveal what really happened that prompted his being sent home.*

After a couple of months of weekly sessions, the therapist had learned a lot about Nachum's dissatisfactions with his parents and siblings, but nothing more about the yeshivah episode. At the same time, Nachum started complaining that he was really suffering from multiple personality disorder, a rare condition in which a person switches back and forth between two or more totally distinct personalities, similar to Dr. Jekyll and Mr. Hyde. Nachum had researched this diagnosis online and was convinced that it applied to him. His therapist, however, saw this preoccupation as a form of resistance to treatment and a distraction from the therapeutic work which needed to be done.

At this point, Nachum's parents were becoming impatient with the lack of progress he was making in therapy. They also wanted guidance as to how they should be treating him at home. He was sleeping late, not enrolling in any local yeshivah, and spending most of his time playing chess online. Nachum's therapist felt that working with Alex and Blima at the same time he was seeing Nachum could interfere with Nachum's treatment. Therefore, he referred them to me.

Their son was seventeen when I first met with Alex and Blima. They were confused, anxious, and overwhelmed by Nachum's condition, and they had a slew of questions for me. How could I help them if Nachum was working with another therapist? they wanted to know.

"I'm getting a full description of Nachum's behavior from you," I said. "In addition, I've also worked with many other adolescents and their families. And, finally, I will be in touch with his therapist to fill in any missing pieces."

Once they were reassured, Alex and Blima painted the picture of what Nachum was like at home. "He taunts his older sister and two younger brothers," Blima said with desperation in her voice. "And he is provocative with us, as well. He doesn't go to shul anymore and he often comes to the Shabbos table without his yarmulke. He is angry at both of us, accusing us of not caring for him and favoring his siblings. He has lost touch with his friends, and he doesn't seem to want to do anything other than play chess.

"And now he's on this kick that he has multiple personality disorder," Alex added. "We've spoken with his therapist, who doesn't agree. And from what we've read, he doesn't really have any of the symptoms. But what do we know? Either way, we need advice about what to do with him at home. Our other three children are embarrassed to have their friends come to the house."

I encouraged Alex and Blima to avoid advising or criticizing Nachum and to let his individual therapy take its course. In the weeks that followed, however, things continued to deteriorate. I was not meeting Alex and Blima on a regular basis. "When you have questions, call me," I had instructed them.

Two months later, they called for another appointment. When they came in, they informed me that Nachum had stolen money from his older sister. "Our other children don't feel safe at home anymore," Blima said, almost in tears.

Then they informed me that Nachum's therapist recommended medication. He had referred Nachum to a psychiatrist, who had prescribed an antidepressant. "I guess we'll need to give the medication a chance to kick in," I advised.

Three months later, there was still no improvement. I met again with Alex and Blima. At this point they looked worn down by Nachum's erratic, unpredictable behavior. He had gotten a part-time job at a local pizza shop. Unfortunately, that lasted little more than a week. He was now back at home, playing chess and starting up with his siblings, especially his younger brothers.

"One thing we haven't tried yet," I pointed out, "is family therapy. How would you feel about meeting here with Nachum? Do you think he would agree to come?"

Alex and Blima were uncertain as to whether he would agree to see another *frum* therapist, although they very much liked the idea. We scheduled an appointment, and to everyone's surprise, Nachum agreed to participate.

After a couple of weekly family sessions, Nachum asked if he could see me for individual therapy instead of his current therapist. He felt he could relate better to me. I told him I would have to speak to his therapist about that first, which I did. His therapist encouraged me to work with Nachum. He felt he was making little headway. "Perhaps he just needs another approach," Nachum's therapist said.

When Nachum came without his parents, he was resistant, sarcastic, and doing a good job of demonstrating how difficult he could be. He called after the session to apologize for his offensive behavior and to schedule another appointment, which he missed without canceling. Then he called to reschedule and skipped that appointment as well. *So much for needing another approach*, I thought after the second missed appointment.

Alex and Blima called for another appointment a few weeks later. This time they informed me that Nachum had made an unsuccessful suicide attempt by overdosing on the medication the psychiatrist had prescribed, and he had been hospitalized briefly. Upon discharge, he requested to see another psychiatrist.

He had also enrolled in and dropped out of a local junior college. And he had stolen money again, this time from his father's wallet.

"Our children are asking us to get Nachum to move out," Blima said, clearly ambivalent about it herself. "On the one hand, I certainly understand where they are coming from. Everyone is so on edge whenever he's home. But on the other hand, I can't just kick him out of the house. He's still our son. We just don't know what to do."

"I think what you need for Nachum now is supportive housing," I suggested.

"What's that?" Alex wanted to know. "No one ever mentioned that."

"It's a subsidized, supervised residence for young people like Nachum who temporarily cannot live at home," I explained. "He can come home for Shabbos whenever he wants and whenever you feel he is ready. It will help him gain some much-needed independence. And it will give you and your children a breather. There's a *frum* social service agency in Brooklyn that runs such a program. Here's their number. Call them and see if Nachum would be eligible."

It took quite some time to complete all of the paperwork and fulfill all of the requirements. Nevertheless, a few months later, Nachum moved into one of the supportive housing units run by the agency I recommended. As part of the intake procedure, Nachum had to be evaluated by the agency's psychiatrist, who felt Nachum was not suffering from depression or multiple personality disorder, but from BPD.

The next time Alex and Blima met with me, they shared the new diagnosis suggested by Nachum's new psychiatrist. Like Yosef HaTzaddik's brothers when they heard the words, *"Ani Yosef"* (*Bereishis* 45:3), I was dumbstruck. And then all of the pieces of the puzzle called Nachum fit together. His shifting from idealizing to denigrating one therapist after another, his provocative behavior, his suicide threats and attempt, and his inappropriate hostility toward his family all pointed so clearly to the diagnosis of BPD. How could I and other experienced mental health professionals have missed what was now so obvious? The answer was that borderlines can often control and conceal their symptoms enough to mislead even the most qualified therapists.

Nachum is still a borderline. Currently, however, he is more north of the border, so to speak. He still occasionally talks of suicide and he is still living in supportive housing, which is giving his parents and siblings a bit of a respite. He also still tests and taunts his parents from time to time, although not as often as in the past. But he is also now attending college and has a part-time job as a deliveryman for a local drug store. He has been weaned off all medications by his current psychiatrist and is not missing them. And, most importantly, Alex and Blima are learning how to minimize the chaos in their lives caused by having a child with BPD.

Alex and Blima still meet with me from time to time. They come in to share their triumphs and their challenges. I try to guide and support them as needed. Nachum's future is uncertain. But each time Alex and Blima come in, the three of us acknowledge what a game changer it was when Nachum's diagnosis was finally nailed by his second psychiatrist, and how helpful it has been that Nachum is still living in supportive housing.

ADULT SURVIVORS OF CHILDHOOD ABUSE

Letter Writing
— *Bracha*

Approximately one-third of the adults who were abused as children — physically, verbally, or both — have no lasting emotional or psychological wounds. The rest, however, may suffer from a wide range of symptoms, including depression, social withdrawal, low self-esteem, passivity and dependence, indecision and fear of failure, excessive need for reassurance, and excessive anxiety. Someone who experienced many of these was Bracha.

Bracha first came to see me the year after she returned from seminary in Eretz Yisrael. "I don't feel ready to start *shidduchim*," she explained. "I know that's what I'm supposed to be doing now, but I just don't feel ready."

"And what do you feel is holding you back?" I asked.

"I'm just too anxious," Bracha said. "I worry a lot about everything. And the thought of having to make such an important decision kind of overwhelms me."

"But you don't have to decide about marriage on the first date," I countered.

"I know that," Bracha said, waving her hand dismissively. "But six or eight dates can go pretty quickly. And if I don't feel I can make that decision now, I don't even want to get started."

"So what prompted you to want to meet with me now?" I asked.

"Well, for one thing," Bracha replied, "I just got back from seminary and all of my friends are heavy into *shidduchim.* And the other reason is that I was told to get help by Rav Elyashiv."

"You met with Rav Elyashiv while you were in Eretz Yisrael?" I asked in wonderment.

"Not really," Bracha said. "My cousin, who is learning in Brisk, went for me. Actually, he told me he was going to Rav Elyashiv with an important medical *shailah* regarding his mother, my aunt. When I heard that, I asked if he would speak to him about me too."

"What did your cousin say about you?" I asked.

"He told Rav Elyashiv that his cousin just finished seminary," Bracha said, "and that she has *mit di nervin* and isn't sure if she should start *shidduchim.* What should she do? And he answered, 'Tell her to speak with a *psycholog.'*

"Then, when I came home, I asked my mother to find someone for me to talk to and she came up with your name. So that's why I'm here."

Bracha's anxiety was more of the free-floating variety. She worried what people thought of her. She worried how events in the future would work out. And she even worried, at times, that she was worrying so much, she would lose her mind.

It took quite a while just to catalogue all of Bracha's anxieties. And during this time, she repeatedly looked to me for reassurance that she was *not* going crazy. Although I was never able to prove it to her, my conviction that she was not having a breakdown was comforting to her. Unfortunately, it did not translate into her being able to fully calm herself down.

"I was so anxious this week," is how Bracha began almost every session we had. As the session got under way and we dug into the specifics of her worries, however, we were able to address them and, at least temporarily, reduce her elevated level of anxiety.

One day a few months later, Bracha introduced a new worry to her already long list. She sometimes experienced a mental image that was very disturbing to her. And the more she fought this mental picture, the more it took hold of her.

My first thought was that this was a mental obsession that could be treated with standard CBT (cognitive behavioral therapy) techniques. "Tell me what the mental image is," I instructed, getting ready to shift into CBT.

Bracha blushed and looked as if I had asked a question that was too personal. "I can't tell you," she whispered, looking down at the floor.

This doesn't look like garden-variety OCD, I thought. The shame and embarrassment Bracha was experiencing suggested that her visual image related to some earlier childhood trauma. While she was clearly uncomfortable sharing the content of that mental picture with me, I understood that in order for us to be able to address it, she would have to.

As Reb Elimelech of Lizhensk wrote in his *Tzetel Katan* (par. 13), "[One should] tell every time to the one who is guiding him on the ways of Hashem and even to a trusted friend all the thoughts and wicked ruminations that are contrary to the Holy Torah which the *yetzer hara* brings up in his mind and heart.... And he should not hold back anything due to embarrassment. And it will come about through telling these things that it will succeed in breaking the power of the *yetzer hara* so that it will not overpower him the next time. [And this recommendation is also beneficial because of] the good advice that he can receive from his friend, which is the way of Hashem and a wonderful remedy."

Nevertheless, it was critical for me not to push Bracha too hard to reveal what she was unready to share. I certainly did not want her to be traumatized all over again by my efforts to help her. So I gently asked her, "Why would you not want to share this with me?"

"I'm too embarrassed," Bracha answered, confirming my suspicions.

"I understand that it would make you uncomfortable to tell me," I validated, "but in order for me to help you with this, I really need to know what it is."

"I really want to tell you," Bracha said, her eyes pleading with me, "but I just can't."

How can I make this easier for Bracha? I wondered. *She needs to feel safe. But she also needs to share this with me.* I struggled with this dilemma for a few moments and then came up with a plan I had never used before.

"Suppose we don't talk about this anymore," I suggested, and I saw Bracha relax slightly. "Instead, let's write to each other. How would that make you feel? Are you willing to try that?"

Bracha smiled. She was clearly intrigued by the idea. "Okay," she said, looking hopeful.

I took out two pads of paper, giving her one and keeping the other for myself. On mine, I wrote, "How do you feel about this idea of communicating by writing instead of speaking?" Then I showed her what I had written.

Bracha quickly took a pen and wrote on her pad, "This is much better."

Then I wrote, "Can you describe the thoughts that you have which cause you so much discomfort?"

Bracha chewed on the back of her pen. She looked at me, at the pad on her lap, and then back to me. Taking a deep breath, she wrote the following words, "a part of person's body."

I needed no more evidence. Bracha had been abused as a child. She was clearly struggling with the aftermath of that trauma and she needed help to heal.

I leaned back in my chair and asked her directly, "Who abused you?"

"I don't know if you would call it abuse," Bracha replied with great hesitation.

Once the ice was broken, however, it did not take long for her to tell me all of the details of how her older brother had abused her when she was nine years old. As is typical of adults who were abused as children, Bracha downplayed the seriousness of what she was telling me and defended her brother at the same time. She had very warm, positive feelings toward this brother, with whom she was in close contact. She admired and looked up to him for being a well-respected *talmid chacham*, loving father to his children, devoted husband, respectful son, and pillar of his community. She consulted him frequently for advice and *shailos*, and did not want to jeopardize that relationship in any way.

As more details of the abuse emerged in our work, it became increasingly difficult for Bracha to deny the truth of her having been abused by her brother. Eventually she accepted the reality of her having been traumatized by the incident and its aftermath.

One detail of her parents' handling of the situation was critical for understanding the complicated dynamics of Bracha's family. Immediately after the episode with her brother, Bracha ran to her mother to report what had happened. Without being explicit, she indicated that something terribly wrong had transpired between them. Her mother listened without displaying any visible reaction. Desperate to feel protected, Bracha pressed her mother for reassurance.

"All right," Bracha's mother barked in an angry tone of voice. "I'll speak to him."

Perhaps Bracha's mother was not angry at all. Perhaps she was frightened and overwhelmed. Perhaps she was confused and anxious. And perhaps she felt helpless to deal with an issue of such magnitude. Nevertheless, the impression Bracha received from her mother's cold, rejecting manner was that she was in some way responsible for what had happened. And while most victims of child abuse tend to blame themselves for what happened, this guaranteed that Bracha would be left with free-floating, excessive guilt feelings that fueled her heightened anxiety from that day forward.

In order for Bracha to heal the psychological wounds of her having been abused, it was necessary for her uncover, face, and finally deal with her ambivalent feelings toward her brother, whom she dearly loved. And for her, confronting her brother was simply out of the question. He would undoubtedly deny that it had ever happened. The rest of the family would rally around him, and she would risk being ostracized permanently.

Looking for a way to thread that needle, I recalled the letter writing we had done in the early phase of our work. I then proposed a variation of that approach.

"How would you feel," I asked one day during the second year of my work with Bracha, "if I asked you to write a letter to your brother?"

"Oh, I could *never* do that," Bracha objected. "Then there would be a written record of what happened, and it would only be used against me. I would be too frightened of the consequences."

"I'm not talking about actually sending it to him," I clarified. "What I'm talking about is writing a letter expressing your feelings toward your brother, but not sending it to him."

"Then what's the point?" Bracha wanted to know. "Just to get it off my chest?"

"Yes," I replied. "But that's not the only reason I'm recommending it. You can also bring it with you next week, if you feel comfortable doing so, and we can discuss it."

Bracha immediately agreed to write the letter. And she even seemed eager to do it.

The following week, she came in with a four-page, handwritten letter. "Do you want to see it?" she asked as the session began.

"I'd prefer you to read it to me," I suggested.

For the next few weeks, we went over Bracha's letter to her brother line by line. After reading each sentence, she would stop and elaborate on what she really meant and wished she could say. By the time we had completed going over her letter, she had clarified, validated, and accepted the full range of her ambivalent feelings toward her brother.

Somewhere in the middle of this phase of my work with Bracha, her mother called me.

"I'm not calling to ask you anything about Bracha," her mother began. "I know you cannot share anything with me, and I respect her privacy. But I must say, by the way, that I am seeing a tremendous improvement in her since she began therapy with you. She is much less anxious and much more confident than she has ever been. My husband and I are grateful to you for what you've done for her."

"Then what is the purpose of your call?" I asked.

"I'm calling about myself," Bracha's mother said. "I see you know what you are doing and I would like to meet with you myself, if I may."

"Does Bracha know you're calling me?" I asked. "And may I tell her that I spoke with you?"

"Oh, absolutely!" Bracha's mother exclaimed. "I would never do anything behind her back. By all means, feel free to tell her."

"Let me discuss this with Bracha," I suggested, "and I'll get back to you."

At my next session with Bracha, I told her about my conversation with her mother. Then I asked, "How would you feel if I saw your mother?"

"I suppose I'd have mixed feelings," Bracha answered with some hesitation. "On the one hand, I'd feel good that my mother was seeing a competent therapist. On the other hand, I guess I'd feel uncomfortable, wondering what she might be telling you about me or what you'd be telling her. But I wouldn't want to interfere with your *parnassah* and getting another patient."

"Don't worry," I said. "You don't have to decide for me. I just wanted to hear your feelings about this. I plan to tell your mother that I won't see her, but I'd be happy to refer her to a colleague."

Bracha was both pleased and surprised. "Why won't you see her?" she asked.

"You're entitled to have your own therapist, without having to share," I explained. "Besides, I see your mother's request as a lack of respect for your boundaries. From some of the things you've told me already, I see that personal privacy is not always respected in your family, and I want to prevent, not participate, in that."

Somewhere toward the end of the second year of our work, Bracha announced that she felt ready to start *shidduchim*. Shortly after that, she became engaged to the first *bachur* she dated.

Bracha chose not to disclose to her *chasan* the work she had done with me. "He doesn't have to know about my brother," she said. "After all, they're friends from yeshivah, and I don't want to disrupt that in any way."

In order to have a clear conscience going to the chuppah, Bracha decided she wanted to end her therapy before her wedding date. Although she still suffered from some anxiety and indecision, she was very proud that she had been able to decide to get engaged without undue vacillation.

When reviewing the work we had done, Bracha cited my decision not to see her mother as having made her feel safe and protected. She also pointed to the letter writing as having been very liberating and helpful, enabling her to talk about what she really wanted and needed to discuss.

CHAPTER 49

Confronting the Abuser
— Leah

Perhaps because Leah was one of thirteen children, she had a gentle, easygoing, and passive personality. While this enabled her to be well-liked, it also made her vulnerable to the manipulation of peer pressure. And this was at least partially responsible for an episode that took place during her last month at seminary in Eretz Yisrael.

Some of Leah's roommates decided to pull an all-nighter in studying for a major exam. As the only girl in the room who wanted to get some sleep, she was outvoted. The next night, these same girls decided to party in the room until the wee hours of the morning. During the following night, an air raid siren woke everyone, after which Leah had a hard time falling back to sleep. With three nights of almost no sleep, Leah began behaving in a hyperactive manner and speaking incoherently, which alarmed her roommates.

The dorm counselor was called. Leah was not acting herself. And without knowing about the three consecutive nights of sleep deprivation, the dorm counselor suspected Leah was having a breakdown of some kind. To be on the safe side, the dorm counselor called Hatzolah. Their ambulance took Leah to a psychiatric hospital where she was diagnosed with bipolar disorder and placed on medication.

Three days later, under intense pressure from Leah's parents, the hospital discharged her and she returned home to New York without completing the year. With a three-day psychiatric hospitalization and a diagnosis of bipolar disorder added to Leah's *shidduch* resume, her marital prospects looked bleak. As a result, three years later, she and her parents agreed to a *shidduch* proposal from a *bachur* who had issues, but who came from a good family.

Fortunately, or unfortunately, depending on how you look at it — the engagement did not last. Two days after the *vort,* the young man got cold feet and broke it off.

Now Leah had a broken engagement added to her *shidduch* resume, which hit her very hard. She found it difficult to cope with the shame and disappointment. It was hard for her to keep working as a babysitter at the local community center. At this point, her parents suggested she speak with a therapist.

Leah was in her early twenties when I first met with her, and she did not fit the profile of someone with bipolar disorder. In fact, when asked for her treatment goals during the initial consultation, Leah said she wanted to get off the medication she was taking.

"I'm not sure you really have bipolar disorder," I observed. "Have you ever had any other manic or depressive episodes besides that one in seminary?" I asked.

"No, I haven't," Leah confirmed. "And I'd rather not be on medication if I don't need it."

"I agree with you," I said. "The episode you had could have been triggered by the sleep deprivation and not bipolar disorder. But if you are bipolar and do need medication, going off it could risk another hospitalization."

"I'm willing to take that risk," Leah responded confidently.

"Then you'll have to discuss it with your psychiatrist," I cautioned, "to make sure you wean off it gradually, in a safe manner. And we'll have to meet regularly so I can monitor how you're doing, because I may notice an episode coming on before you do."

Leah did both. She met with me weekly while following her psychiatrist's instructions. Two months later she was completely off her medication.

During the initial consultation, Leah had also expressed an interest in learning how to get over the broken engagement so she could move on with her life. In addition to monitoring her medication reduction, therefore, we also focused on what prompted her to become engaged to someone who had so many red flags in the first place. Certainly her diminished *shidduchim* prospects played a major role. But her passive personality was also a factor. When the young man expressed an interest in getting engaged, Leah felt she could not disappoint him even though her gut told her it was a mistake.

It was during our exploration of the origins of Leah's passivity that I first learned she had been abused by an older male cousin. This illustrated once again that the perpetrators of child abuse are most often someone the victim knows well, as opposed to a total stranger.

The abuse had taken place in Leah's home on three separate occasions. After the third episode, she informed her parents, who responded appropriately by insuring that Leah was never alone with that cousin again. Leah was nine or ten years old when this happened. And although she felt protected by her parents afterwards, they never thought that she might need professional help to deal with the emotional aftermath of those episodes.

After we reviewed these incidents and discussed her feelings during and after each one, we focused on the impact they had on her. Clearly these experiences contributed to her passivity and the suppression of her feelings. And while these traits were vital as survival strategies in her childhood, they were not serving her well in adulthood. Her engagement, for example, was a good illustration of how much she was hurt as a result of her overly passive and conciliatory nature.

Just when I thought we had completely uncovered the roots of Leah's passivity, she opened a whole new window into her past. "Could experiences with peers also affect someone's development?" she asked.

"Of course," I replied. "But it depends on many factors. Tell me what you have in mind."

"Well, starting in second grade," Leah began, "I was the target of bullying by some of the tougher girls in my class."

"How long did this go on and what was the nature of the bullying?" I asked.

"It lasted at least one, maybe two years," Leah said. "I don't recall exactly. But it involved teasing, making fun, and name calling. I just remember that I hated going to school. But I never told my parents about it. I'm not sure why I didn't. And I don't recall how it finally stopped."

"That certainly set the table for the abuse that came later," I said, validating the mistreatment to which Leah was subjected in elementary school. This led us into a few more sessions of examining the ramifications of her victimization at such a young age.

At one point after the therapy had progressed, Leah asked me quite directly, "So how can I learn to be less passive? I don't want to go through the rest of my life handicapped by these experiences of abuse."

"Basically," I said, "there are two ways to accomplish that goal. The first is to recognize how you came to be so passive. You may have been born with a somewhat passive nature, which contributed to your being targeted in the first place. After each episode of abuse, however, that passivity was reinforced, as you needed to suppress your feelings about it in order to cope. That's important to bear in mind so that you don't blame yourself for the consequences of others' misbehavior. Based on what we've done so far, I'd say you've already accomplished that. And the second way is to focus on the here and now by pushing yourself to be more assertive wherever possible."

"How do I go about that?" Leah asked.

"I want you to make a note of situations this week," I instructed, "that fall into the following three categories: situations where you wanted to assert yourself, but couldn't; situations where you tried to assert yourself, but failed; and situations where you asserted yourself and succeeded in getting whatever it was that you needed."

For the next few weeks, Leah and I reviewed her various episodes of success and failure. Regarding the former, we examined what had helped or enabled her to speak up or stick up for herself. And regarding the latter, we examined what held her back or interfered. Then we discussed how she could handle a similar case differently next time.

After working on being more assertive for a while, Leah asked me one day, "Do you think it would be a good idea for me to confront my cousin about the abuse?"

I praised Leah for having the strength and courage to even raise that issue with me. Then I walked her through a full consideration of the advantages and disadvantages of doing that. On the one hand, I pointed out, she could gain considerable self-confidence, as well as closure. And it could empower her, helping her to heal from the victimization.

Moshe *Rabbeinu* promised *klal Yisrael* just prior to *Kri'as Yam Suf,* "As you see Mitzrayim today, you will never again see them" (*Shemos* 14:13). Similarly, by confronting her cousin, Leah could hope to never feel intimidated by seeing him ever again. On the other hand, however, it could also trigger a setback.

"Why would it trigger a setback?" Leah wanted to know.

"Well," I said, "suppose he denies the whole thing and says it never happened? And suppose he claims you fabricated the story just to besmirch him? That could traumatize you all over again, opening up the old wounds from the abuse."

Leah sat in silent reflection. She clearly wanted to do whatever she could to advance her healing. She did not, however, want to jeopardize any of the gains she had made in therapy.

"How would you feel if we worked on preparing you for that confrontation?" I suggested.

Leah liked the idea and threw herself into the next phase of our work with the same enthusiasm she had displayed throughout. For the next few weeks, therefore, we considered all the possible defenses with which her cousin might respond to her accusations. We also reviewed how she could counter each one.

"How do I know when I am ready?" Leah wanted to know.

"When you feel confident enough," I replied, "that even if he denies the whole thing, you will not feel diminished in any way. Then you're ready."

"Where should I do this?" Leah asked at another session.

"Wherever you feel most comfortable," I advised. "Remember, this is about your taking care of your needs, not anyone else's."

"Could I do it here in your office?" Leah asked.

"Sure," I consented. "But he would have to agree. And from what you've told me about your cousin, I don't know if he would go along with that arrangement."

The following week, I was happily proven wrong. Leah informed me that she had called her cousin, requesting a meeting in my office. He had asked what it was about and she told him that there was something she wanted to say to him that she could only say in her therapist's office. He then asked if he could bring his rebbe, and Leah said she would get back to him because she wanted to discuss it with me first.

"He probably suspects what this is about," I speculated. "If I'll be there to support you, it's only fair that he should have someone to support him. But I'll make sure that doesn't obfuscate the proceedings."

Over the next few days, we coordinated all four schedules and set a date for the meeting. I had one more individual session with Leah before the joint session so that we could run through one final rehearsal. After that she told me, "I think I'm as ready now as I'll ever be."

While I had worked with many adults who were abused as children, this was the first time a confrontation between a perpetrator and his or her victim had ever been arranged in my office. *If I'm feeling tense*, I thought, *I can't even imagine how the others are feeling.*

When we all sat down, I opened the meeting by thanking Leah's cousin and his rebbe for cooperating with Leah's request for the meeting. Then I said, "I think Leah has something she would like to say to her cousin, so why don't we get straight to that now."

Leah turned to her cousin, looked him in the eye, and accused him of having abused her. Both Leah and I were relieved to hear that he did not deny what happened. Then he surprised both of us by volunteering an apology, tepid as it was. Finally, he made a vague reference to hoping Leah would not use his apology as a confession, indicating that he was frightened she might bring criminal charges against him.

Leah assured her cousin that she had no wish to see him serve time in jail. She did, however, want him to take full responsibility for the psychological damage he had inflicted on her. When asked what specifically she wanted to see from him, she replied that she was having a hard time paying for her therapy and she wanted him to foot the bill, if not for the past sessions, then at least going forward.

At this point in the meeting, the cousin's rebbe spoke for the first and only time. He reaffirmed the cousin's willingness to accept responsibility for his past actions. Leah's need for therapy, however, may not have been caused solely by her cousin. In addition, because her cousin was currently unemployed, it was not realistic to expect him to pay the entire fee each week. Therefore, the rebbe proposed that the cousin assume responsibility for only a portion of the fee.

Leah accepted the rebbe's proposal and then a dollar amount was successfully negotiated. Before the meeting concluded, Leah also insisted that her cousin take responsibility by absenting himself from any extended family gathering which Leah could be expected to attend. He accepted this unconditionally. I then thanked everyone for attending and adjourned the meeting.

When we reviewed the meeting at our next session, I praised Leah for the courage and confidence she displayed in confronting her cousin. How was she able to do that? I asked.

"The rehearsals really helped," Leah said with a smile.

"And how did you feel about the meeting overall?" I asked.

"I was pleased with the way I handled myself," Leah began. "But I was disappointed with my cousin's apology. He sounded so insincere. He was clearly scared, and it felt good to see that. But I think I would have preferred that he show more remorse. Nevertheless, on the whole, I think it went well. And his contribution will certainly help me pay your fee each week."

Buoyed by the success in confronting her cousin, a few weeks later Leah told me she was considering doing something similar with the former classmate who had been the ringleader of the bullying in elementary school.

First, we walked through what she wanted to say to this woman. Leah was not as clear about this as she was regarding her cousin. After some back and forth with me, Leah decided that she simply wanted this woman to know how much the bullying had affected her at the time.

The next issue we discussed was the venue for the meeting. Leah did not want to hold it in my office for two reasons. Firstly, she could not envision this woman agreeing to meet in my office. And secondly, requesting that could project an image of weakness on Leah's part. Nevertheless, Leah wanted a neutral, safe venue.

"How about meeting in a pizza shop?" I suggested.

Leah liked that idea. Then we discussed how she would set up the meeting with this woman over the phone.

"Why not simply tell her there's something you want to discuss with her that you would prefer to talk about in person?" I proposed. "That way, she won't follow up by asking what you want to discuss."

Leah liked that wording. Then we brainstormed all of the possible responses her former classmate might have, as well as how Leah could deal with each one. When we finished, she was eager to arrange this as soon as possible.

The following week I was surprised to learn that Leah had already met with her former classmate in the pizza shop. "Tell me how it went," I urged.

"It went better than I expected," Leah announced proudly. She went on to describe how apologetic her former classmate had been and how satisfying it was to hear it. The former classmate asked for Leah's *mechilah* and Leah unconditionally granted it.

Leah spent another few months finishing the work of building her self-confidence and improving her self-esteem. Then a *shidduch* came up that sounded very appropriate. I figuratively held her hand through the dating until she got engaged. Leah is now happily married and busy raising her two (so far) children.

CHAPTER 50

Overcoming Denial

— Tzippy

As strange as it sounds, adults who were abused as children by their parents are even more likely than others to deny or downplay the mistreatment they received. The reason for this is twofold. Firstly, it is vitally important for children to be able to see their parents as good, loving, and protective. To see them in any other light threatens the foundation of their sense of security.

The second reason is that acknowledging that their parents had been abusive would automatically evoke feelings of resentment. And these negative feelings could potentially threaten the positive, loving feelings the children desperately cling to in order to support their fractured egos.

If the children believe that their parents were not abusive, then the mistreatment they received from them must be explained in another way. Sometimes the children blame themselves, thinking they were inadequate or not good enough. At other times, they make excuses and find justifications to exonerate their parents. While this enables the children to maintain their positive image of their parents, it also keeps them stuck in their old patterns of thinking and behavior that are, at times, self-destructive. The goal in such cases, therefore, is to help the children relinquish their denial and accept the reality of their sad history, thereby allowing the process of healing to begin.

A perfect example of this process is Tzippy, a single *baalas teshuvah* in her mid-twenties, who came to me on the recommendation of her *rav*, with whom I was privileged to enjoy a close relationship for many years. When I first met Tzippy, she was unemployed, living in an inadequate basement apartment, and struggling with feelings of depression. At the time, she claimed she was looking for work.

Tzippy had an MBA in accounting and had passed all four parts of her CPA exams. Due to her depression, however, she did not feel she could handle a full-time accounting job, and all the prospective employers were not willing to hire a new worker on a part-time basis.

Tzippy's parents were not completely irreligious. As a result, she felt comfortable returning home for just about every Shabbos. In truth, however, her parents paid only lip service to accepting her newly *frum* lifestyle and there were many challenges to her Shabbos observance that she had to face whenever she went.

Tzippy's unemployment and her dreary weekday living conditions both contributed to her feelings of hopelessness. While she wanted to get married, she felt she could not even date in her current emotional state. She also felt stuck in more ways than one.

"If you can't have the best," I told Tzippy, "then you have to accept second best. What I mean by that is that if an accounting job is not what you can find right now, you have to consider something else. Not working is simply not an option for you."

With considerable support and encouragement from me, Tzippy took a job as a secretary/administrative assistant at a local Bais Yaakov high school. Once she was working, she was able to afford to move into an above-ground apartment. She was still depressed, but considerably less so than when we first met.

Early in our work, I also explored Tzippy's family dynamics. "Tell me about each of your parents," I suggested. "I need to learn about your family."

"I grew up in a typical traditional Jewish family," Tzippy said with a weak smile. And that sweeping generalization was already a red flag for me.

"Tell me more about your parents," I suggested. "Let's start with your father."

"Oh, my dad is a loving father and husband," Tzippy said. "He's retired now, but he used to be an ophthalmologist. What more would you like to know?"

"How does he get along with your mother?" I asked. "If he's at home now and not working, that could put a strain on their relationship."

"Well, actually, it's better now than it used to be," Tzippy said. "When I was younger, they used to argue sometimes. But over the last couple of years things have gotten much better between them."

"And what kinds of things did they used to argue about?" I asked.

"Well, my father used to have a bit of a drinking problem," Tzippy reluctantly revealed.

"How old were you when he had this drinking problem?"

"Oh, I'd say from when I was about six years old until a couple of years ago," Tzippy said matter-of-factly.

"What made him stop?"

Tzippy took a deep breath and said, "Actually, he had a major heart attack from all of the drinking. And that's really why he had to retire and give up his practice."

"And what was it like for you when your father had too much to drink?" I asked.

"Um, well, he used to yell a lot," Tzippy said as if she were making a confession.

"And who did he yell at?" I asked. "Was it only your mom? Or did he yell at you too?"

At that point, Tzippy put all her cards on the table. She described in great detail how her father would verbally abuse her. And, as if that were not enough, whenever her older brother would ridicule or taunt her, her father would support her brother and blame her for the conflict. This further compounded the emotional abuse.

"Sounds like your father was an alcoholic," I observed. "And you were certainly abused by him when you were growing up."

Instead of feeling validated and supported, Tzippy took great umbrage at my use of the word "abuse." She stiffened in her chair, denied having been abused, and tried to walk back the portrayal of her father that she had given me. I then tried, unsuccessfully, to convince her that the term was appropriate by citing the examples she had shared with me. When we ended the session, however, she told me she was not ready to schedule another appointment. She would call me during the week to schedule it.

After not hearing from Tzippy, I called her the following week. She was still not ready to schedule the next appointment. At that point, I expected never to see her again and began castigating myself. *I guess I blew it*, I thought. *I should not have been so blunt in characterizing her father as having been abusive. She was apparently not at all ready to hear that.*

About three weeks later, Tzippy called and requested another appointment. When she came in for that session, she filled me in on what had transpired during the break in her therapy.

"After our last session," Tzippy began, "I made up my mind not to continue seeing you. I was very turned off by your telling me I had been abused. I don't see myself that way. And I am not comfortable with someone applying that term to me."

"So what changed your mind?" I asked.

"Well, I spoke about it with my *rav* — I discuss everything with him," Tzippy explained, "and he told me not to let that interfere with our work. He said that he sees you've already helped me, and I should trust you and continue the therapy. I still don't see myself as having been abused. But since I trust my *rav* on everything else, I guess I should trust him about you as well."

I reset the "cruise control" for a much slower speed, and I proceeded more gently and with greater caution. Over the next few weeks, we spoke more about Tzippy's family history. Gradually, she came to acknowledge the fact that she had, in fact, been emotionally and verbally abused by her alcoholic father.

Once Tzippy's wall of denial finally came down, she was easily able to see the connection between her traumatic history and her current difficulties. This then enabled her to engage in and complete the work of healing the emotional wounds of her childhood abuse.

Around that time, she landed an entry-level, full-time position at a prestigious accounting firm in Manhattan. Her extended work hours, coupled with the gains she had made, prompted her to terminate her therapy.

Two years later, Tzippy asked to see me again. Her father and brother continued to harass her at times. She was, however, now better equipped to protect and defend herself. But that was not the reason she had called.

A *shidduch* had been proposed between Tzippy and a *yeshivah bachur* from a similar background. They had seen each other a few times already and Tzippy was seriously considering getting engaged. The young man was extremely sensitive, caring, and gentle, apparently the diametric opposite of her father and brother. The commitment inherent in becoming engaged, however, terrified her, causing her to be gripped with indecision. In desperation, she reached out to me.

When we met, Tzippy outlined both sides of her dilemma. Had she discussed this with her *rav*? I wanted to know. And had he met the *bachur* himself?

Tzippy told me that her *rav* had met the young man in question. Unfortunately, however, that complicated the matter for her because her *rav* wholeheartedly approved of the *shidduch* and was pushing her to get engaged even though she did not feel ready.

I tried to be supportive without giving advice, which is what Tzippy seemed to need and want. I did, however, try to help her clarify her own feelings, fears, and frustrations. It took her a few weeks longer than someone without a history of abuse for her to make up her mind. And throughout her period of indecision, the *bachur* was mercifully patient, demonstrating how unlike her father he really was. When she finally decided to accept the *bachur*'s proposal, she was feeling more confident and self-assured. The week before her *chasunah,* she terminated with me for the second time.

A few years later, I ran into Tzippy, her husband, and their three children. She was still working at the same firm, but had cut back her hours to part-time, and her husband was still learning in kollel.

SECTION XIII

SUBSTANCE ABUSE AND BEHAVIORAL ADDICTIONS

The Process of Addiction

How do people become addicted? Why do some people develop addictions and others do not? And what are the risk factors that make someone susceptible to becoming an addict? These are the questions which will be addressed in this chapter.

All addictions can be grouped into two categories: substance abuse and behavioral addictions. Substance abuse includes all situations in which someone has developed a physical addiction to something that is inhaled, smoked, injected, or swallowed. Familiar substances to which people develop addictions are alcohol, cannabis or marijuana, prescription pain killers, opium, heroin, tobacco, tranquilizers, and cocaine. Typical behavioral addictions include gambling, texting, social media, and viewing inappropriate images on the Internet.

Regardless of what the person is addicted to, there are some features that are common to all addictions. Firstly, the substance or behavior to which someone has become addicted consumes an inordinate amount of the person's time, attention, and financial resources. At best, time and money are squandered. At worst, people's careers, family relationships, and even their very lives are totally destroyed by the addiction. The craving is literally uncontrollable as the addict spirals downward until he or she hits rock bottom, which is often too late to salvage their jobs, family ties, and even lives.

In addition, the addict usually finds it necessary to spin a web of deceit in order to maintain the addiction. He is not only dishonest with others, but he is also dishonest with himself. He deceives others so that they will not try to pull him away from his addiction. His own thinking turns into a form of massive denial — that he doesn't have a problem, that he isn't hurting others, and that he isn't hurting himself.

In dealing with those who try to help, the addict is not only deceptive, but often manipulative as well. For example, suppose the addict is living away from home and is currently unemployed and penniless. He may complain that he has no money even to buy food. Well-intentioned relatives then feel sorry for him and agree to sponsor a meal or two. In desperation to avoid the painful symptoms of withdrawal, however, the addict will use the money to feed his addiction and not himself.

The denial exercised by the addict can take many forms. "I'm not really addicted," he may assert. "I can stop anytime." Another version of denial is, "It doesn't control me. I only smoke/drink/gamble, etc., when I want to." Just like a chain-smoker denies his addiction by saying, "I'm not addicted; I quit every Shabbos," so too another kind of addict will claim that he can stop whenever he chooses.

Another form of denial is when the addict tries to downplay the seriousness of his addiction and the damage it is causing to himself and others. Chazal, of course, understood this form of denial very well. As they put it, "[When] a person commits an *aveirah* and repeats it, then it appears to him as if it is now a permissible act" (*Yoma* 86b).

Moreover, if and when the addict attempts to quit, the withdrawal symptoms are so intense that his good intentions are thwarted. The longer he resists the temptation to return to his addiction, the more severely he feels the withdrawal symptoms until it becomes an insurmountable challenge to quit completely.

Finally, the high which the addict receives from his addiction tends to diminish over time. In order to get the same high as before, the addict then needs to increase the amount and/or the frequency of his addictive behavior. As a result, addictions tend to get worse and not better if they are left untreated.

How do people become hooked in the first place? A common misconception is that people become addicted to substances or behaviors because they've been influenced by a "bad crowd." In other words, it is thought that because a person associated with bad friends or acquaintances, this person, who otherwise would not have developed an addiction, did. This way of thinking is another form of denial.

With the exception of prescription pain killers initially taken following surgery, most addictions are caused by emotional traumas or deficits in one's childhood. More specifically, there is a profile for the addictive personality, a person who is more likely to develop an addiction later in life.

The addictive person is someone who suffered from some form of physical or emotional abuse as a child and was not helped to overcome the sequelae in adolescence or adulthood. The emotional pain and suffering from the childhood abuse or neglect becomes so intense that the person seeks some way to deaden the unwanted feelings. The addiction then becomes an attempt to dull or eliminate the intolerable pain. What makes addictions so difficult to overcome is that they are temporarily successful in calming or tranquilizing the agony. At least for a few moments or hours, then, the addict experiences some relief. And before the person realizes what has happened, he becomes physically habituated to the substance or behavior.

A good illustration of this process is the common addiction to smoking cigarettes.[1] There are few adults today who can honestly say they never took a puff when they were younger and a friend offered them a try. In the vast majority of cases, the first-timer coughed violently, threw away the unfinished cigarette, and silently swore never to try it again.

In a minority of cases, however, the person trying the cigarette persevered and forced himself to finish the cigarette. Then he repeated this unpleasant process some other time until he got used to inhaling the smoke without coughing and gagging.

What is the difference between these two cases? Why do some try once and never go back? And why do some push past the discomfort and become addicted?

The answer is that smoking cigarettes offers the side "benefits" of looking cool, being accepted by a group of nonconformists, and engaging in an activity that looks and feels rebellious. Someone who feels dissatisfied with himself or his life would find those "benefits" appealing. And someone who is suffering from the aftereffects of abuse or neglect would find those "benefits" vitally necessary for survival.

In both cases, people were offered cigarettes by others. Those who were emotionally secure rejected smoking after the first puff. And those who were looking for something to deaden the emotional pain in their lives latched onto the quick fix of group acceptance and looking cool until they developed a physical addiction to the nicotine content in the cigarettes.

If parents are concerned that their children not become smokers — and they most certainly should be — then they would accomplish more by cultivating a warm, close relationship with their children rather than micromanaging their children's choice of friends.

Similarly, alcohol, drug, and behavioral addictions develop in the same way. Someone may experiment with these substances first

---

1. I would like to thank Dr. Benzion Sorotzkin for this illustrative example.

because of their availability. Open bars at *chasunahs*, for example, provide an easy, socially acceptable gateway to later alcoholism for those youth who are already at risk.

In the case examples that follow, the seed of addiction was planted by easy access. It took root and blossomed, however, as a result of landing in soil made fertile by child abuse or severe emotional deprivation. And it was watered by years of struggling alone with the pain of the childhood trauma without having access to any therapeutic relationship.

CHAPTER 52

"*Shailah* Therapy"
— *Label*

Sometime during the early phase of my career, I met with Label, a tall, distinguished mesivta rebbi in his early forties. Label was always neatly dressed in a black suit, white shirt, and stylish, but conservative, tie. He had a long, neatly trimmed beard, and his serious countenance made him appear as if he were posing for his profile to be added to Mount Rushmore.

When I first met Label, the expression on his face made it clear to me that he wanted to be anywhere but my office. With excruciating difficulty, he explained why he had come.

"I've been struggling with something for years," Label began, weighing each word. "I've been trying to stop for the longest time. And I finally felt forced to face the reality that I am fighting a losing battle. I simply cannot do this on my own. I've come to you to ask if you think you can help me."

I acknowledged how difficult this clearly was for him and then encouraged him to continue.

Label took a deep breath and bit the bullet. "I look at inappropriate images," he confessed. "This started even before I got married. I passed a newsstand in Manhattan one day as a teenager and bought a filthy magazine. I knew it was wrong, and I felt terribly guilty about it at the time. A few days later, I threw it away and promised myself I would never do that again. Unfortunately, I was not able to keep that promise and I have been breaking it ever since.

"I thought this would stop when I got married. In fact, I was hoping it would stop because it went against everything I believe in. Even though I'm married for sixteen years and have five children, *kein ayin hara,* it hasn't gotten any better. Maybe it's even gotten worse over the years."

This was all in the pre-Internet era, before such material was as easily accessible as it is today. And the thought of Label having to risk embarrassment by making these purchases drove home to me how much he was suffering from his addiction.

"Don't try to tell me how this is affecting my marriage," Label warned me. "I know it myself. My wife knows nothing about this and I could never share it with her. Besides losing all respect for me, she would not be able to cope with the shock. But keeping this from her all these years has created an emotional distance between us that we both feel. She has mentioned it at times. And when she does, I try to change the subject or blame it on other factors. But I know the truth. It's my habit that's causing the rift between us."

While I certainly could not guarantee the outcome, I agreed to work with Label to try and help him extricate himself from his terribly destructive habit. Over the next few weeks, Label opened up more and more about how much he was suffering from his addiction.

"You know I'm a mesivta rebbi," Label said to me one day. "Do you have any idea how hypocritical I feel every day sitting in front of my class? They are looking up to me as a role model. I am trying to teach them Torah. And a day doesn't go by that I don't think to myself, *If they only knew the truth about their rebbi.*

"And as if that weren't bad enough," Label continued, "lately I've achieved some recognition in the world of *chinuch*, and that has only compounded my sense of shame."

When I asked Label to elaborate, he filled me in on the recent successes he had achieved in his highly competitive field. He had been invited to speak, for example, at *chinuch* conferences and conventions. His addresses were well received and sparked further invitations. In a way, he was becoming a *mechanech*'s *mechanech*. All the acclaim he was receiving in person and in print only exacerbated his self-recriminations.

"In order to help you," I pointed out, "I really need to learn more about your early childhood."

Label was initially reluctant to go there. "I have an uncle who is a well-known therapist," he said. "I remember him privately telling us how he often worked with people he knew he could not help, just to fill his schedule. I also recall how he would chuckle when he said that. Before we go down that road you're suggesting, I want to be sure you are not doing the same thing with me. You know, it is not easy for me to pay your fee each week. I don't earn that much as a rebbi and I have a large family. But if this will help me, I'm prepared to make the sacrifice."

"I've already told you that I cannot guarantee the outcome of our work," I replied. "But I can assure you that if I ever determine that I cannot help you, I will not hesitate to let you know. I would consider it highly unethical for me to do otherwise."

Over the next few weeks, we delved into Label's early childhood history. What emerged was a painful account of distance and disappointment.

"My father is retired now," Label reported. "He worked very hard as a plumber, and he needed to put in extra hours just to make ends meet. He was not very assertive with his boss, who clearly took advantage of his more passive nature. As a result, he was hardly ever home when

I was growing up. But it wasn't so much his absence that affected me. It was the way he dealt with me when he was home that hurt me the most.

"He always seemed self-absorbed or disinterested in me. I'm not really sure which it was. We hardly ever spoke unless my mother insisted he reprimand me for some minor infraction. I do recall wanting to have a connection with him. After all, he was my father. I remember, for example, once asking him to learn with me on a Shabbos afternoon. I must have been about nine or ten years old at the time. Now I ask you, how many nine- or ten-year-olds ask their fathers to learn with them? I don't think there are too many. But I was so desperate for any contact with him that I approached him and made that request.

"He brushed me away with his hand and gave me no excuse. I suppose I would have understood if he had said he was tired and wanted to nap. But he gave me no reason. And he didn't even say, 'Maybe later.' He just said no and that was it.

"I think I tried other times as well. Each time it was the same. I guess I never wanted to accept that he didn't want to learn with me and I kept trying. But each time he refused, it hurt even more. And it was not because he didn't know how to learn. He did. But he just never felt any connection with me. And that hurt me deeply."

It was clear that Label felt emotionally starved. He felt rejected by his father, and he was clearly searching for a close connection with someone. This search led him to the wrong place, replacing in fantasy what he felt he could never achieve in reality. Then, after he married, harboring his secret fostered a distance which left him feeling even more unfulfilled.

When I shared this interpretation with Label, he wholeheartedly agreed with it. It seemed to really hit home, and he left that session deep in thought.

The following week, however, Label burst my bubble of satisfaction when he said, "I don't see how having a better understanding of why I fell into this hole is going to help me get out of it."

I agreed with him that insight alone would not enable him to achieve his goal of breaking free from his addiction. It could, however, point us in the right direction. I then suggested that we focus more on his unsatisfying marriage. If he succeeded in getting more fulfillment from his relationship with his wife, I proposed, he might not need to turn elsewhere.

Again, Label was skeptical, but willing. He did not, however, agree to invite his wife to join him for marital therapy. He was too fearful that by doing so, she might discover the reason he came to see me in the first place. And all of my reassurances of confidentiality did not convince him to reconsider.

We then focused on what Label could do to remove the barriers he put up which prevented him from achieving the closeness he so desperately craved. I encouraged him, for example, to compliment his wife more often and buy her small presents. While Label accepted that these small steps could bring couples closer together, he could not bring himself to make these gestures. And after a few more weeks, it became perfectly clear that this would not be a fruitful approach.

At that point, I regretfully shared with Label my assessment that conventional psychotherapy would not be effective in helping him overcome his addiction. And mindful as I was of what he had told me at the outset about his uncle, I did not want to delay informing him of my conclusion.

Label took a few moments to absorb the bad news. Then he generously responded, "I have no complaints against you. I know you tried your best. But this was what I was afraid of before we began. At the end of the day, I'm really back where I started. So, what would you recommend I do now? Is there no hope for me?"

"*Chas v'shalom,*" I said. "Where there's life, there's hope."

At that time, just as there was no Internet, there were no programs like what the excellent Guard Your Eyes website offers now that assist those similarly addicted to break free from their addiction. In addition, there were no Twelve-Step meetings under *frum* auspices, such as

Project Safe in Brooklyn. The only Twelve-Step programs for people such as Label were conducted in non-Jewish settings.

After conferring with colleagues, I learned that they also concurred that conventional psychotherapy was ineffective in curing addictions. The only hope for recovery was actively participating in a Twelve-Step program, modeled after the original Alcoholics Anonymous.

"I believe you need to join a Twelve-Step program," I told Label. "They have meetings in just about every neighborhood, so you should be able to find one conveniently located."

"I could never do that," Label shot back emphatically.

"Why not?" I asked.

"Because the meetings are all conducted in non-Jewish houses of worship," Label asserted indignantly. "How would it look for someone dressed like me to be seen going into such a place? It would be a terrible *chillul Hashem*."

"If you have a question about that," I suggested, "then why not ask a *shailah*?"

"I could never do that either," Label protested.

"Why not?" I asked.

"Because I would be too ashamed to ask any *posek*," Label responded almost pleadingly.

"You don't have to ask in person," I pointed out. "Many people ask *shailos* anonymously today. You can simply call any *rav* and ask your *shailah* over the phone."

"You don't seem to understand," Label said, clearly frustrated with me. "I present at *chinuch* conferences and conventions where all of the *gedolim* attend. Any *posek* whose opinion I trust would be able to recognize my voice. So I don't have the option of calling anonymously."

I felt checkmated and did not know what to try next. After a few tense moments, Label broke the silence. "The only way I could ask the *shailah* is...if you asked it for me," he said.

My practice has always been to encourage people to ask their own *shailos*. Nevertheless, all rules have exceptions, and this case seemed to be one for which I would make an exception. I asked Label who he would want me to ask on his behalf, and he named a *gadol* with whom he knew I had a personal relationship. I said I would contact that *posek* and get back to Label as soon as I had an answer. Then Label suggested we suspend our weekly meetings until after I received a *psak* for him.

The next day, I met with the *posek* and presented the *shailah*. Basically, what I asked was whether someone would be permitted to enter a non-Jewish house of worship in order to attend a Twelve-Step meeting to facilitate his recovery from an addiction like the one Label had. The *posek* asked a few basic questions and then told me to call back in three days.

Did the posek need three days to research the shailah? I wondered, but did not have the courage to ask. As instructed, I waited three days and then called him again.

The *posek* said, "It definitely is not a *chillul Hashem*. I could have told you that three days ago. The reason I needed three days is because I wanted to think about whether it might be a *kiddush Hashem*, and I believe now that it is a *kiddush Hashem* for goyim to see how much a Yid is bothered by something which to the larger society is normal, acceptable behavior. That is what you should tell your patient. And you may even say so in my name."

As soon as I got off the phone, I called Label and repeated to him what the *posek* had said. "Are you ready to schedule your next appointment?" I asked at the end of our conversation.

There was a long pause. "No, I'm still not ready to meet with you again," Label said softly. "I need time to think about all of this. I'll call you when I'm ready."

After three weeks of waiting, I was both curious and concerned about Label. I was hesitant to call him because I did not want him to think I was motivated by self-interest like his uncle. Finally I decided to call, but not to offer him an appointment.

"I just wanted to hear how you're doing," I said when he picked up the phone.

"Thank you for asking," Label said, assuaging my concerns. "Actually, I'm not doing well at all."

"What do you mean?" I asked.

"Well, I've been very depressed since I spoke with you three weeks ago," Label explained. "But I don't think it's anything you can help with. So that's why I didn't call you. As a matter of fact, I really don't see any reason for me to continue meeting with you at all."

"I certainly respect your decision," I replied. "But if you are planning to terminate with me now, perhaps we should have one final session to wrap things up. It is something I always recommend whenever I end with someone. If you are feeling very depressed now, it may be even more important for us to have that final session."

To my surprise, Label readily agreed to this. When he came in, he elaborated on what he had told me over the phone.

"When I said I wanted you to ask the *shailah* for me, I never suspected that you would agree. Then when you said you would, I was sure the *rav* would never consent to my entering a non-Jewish house of worship. But when you called and gave me his *psak,* I realized I could no longer avoid attending those Twelve-Step meetings. Then I had to either quit my habit once and for all or pursue the only path left for me to overcome my addiction.

"That's when I threw out everything I had and committed myself to never buying any more. Now, I know I've made similar promises to myself which I never kept. This time I know it's different because I know if I don't keep my promise this time, I will have no more excuses for not attending the meetings."

I shared Label's uncertainty and I told him so. At the same time, I certainly wanted to believe that he would keep his promise, and I wanted to do whatever I could to reinforce his commitment.

"How would you feel," I asked, "about calling me in three months just to let me know, either way, how you are doing?"

Label liked the idea and said he looked forward to speaking with me then. Three months later, almost to the day, Label called and happily reported that, so far, he had kept his promise. Then he thanked me again for helping him overcome his addiction by agreeing to ask his *shailah* for him.

When I got off the phone, I said to myself, *What I was unable to accomplish with conventional psychotherapy, I was able to achieve simply by asking a shailah.* And I promised myself not to attempt curing someone's hard-core addiction again with psychotherapy alone.

Twelve-Step Programs

— Eli

Eli suffered from a hard-core addiction to gambling. Although he never sought my help in overcoming that addiction, and I never learned of it until he had already conquered it, his case history illustrates so many dynamics of addiction that I felt it deserves inclusion here.

One of Eli's rebbeim referred him to me shortly after Eli married his first wife, Miriam. They were having marital difficulties and the *rav* hoped I could save the marriage.

"Have either one of them call me to schedule the appointment," I advised.

When I first met with Eli and Miriam, both in their early twenties, it became clear right away what the cause of the stress in their relationship was.

Miriam spoke first. "I really want to make this marriage work," she said with urgency in her voice. "I care very much for Eli and want to please him. But somehow, no matter what I do, it just doesn't seem to be enough."

"Do you speak about this together?" I asked. "Have you asked what Eli would want you to do differently?"

"Oh, all the time," Miriam exclaimed. "But that's exactly the problem. Whenever I ask Eli, he tells me he doesn't know. Or, sometimes, he just doesn't answer at all—" Miriam stopped abruptly to choke back her tears, as she reached for a tissue.

Turning to Eli, I asked, "Tell me how you see the marriage."

Eli smiled nervously. "Can I speak about this with you privately?" he asked. "I'm not comfortable speaking about this in front of Miriam."

"You really need to be open with each other in order to resolve your issues," I pointed out.

"I'm not trying to be stubborn about this," Eli said with an uncomfortable smile on his face. "But I think you'll understand why I feel this way once you hear what I have to say."

"I'm okay with that," Miriam interjected as she got up to leave. "That's fine with me."

Miriam walked into the waiting room and closed the door behind her. Once I was alone with Eli, he told me what he could not say in front of his wife.

"I just don't find her attractive," Eli confessed. "And I think you can understand why I felt I couldn't say that in front of her. It would hurt her too much. Believe me, I feel terrible about this, but I just don't feel I can stay married to Miriam if I feel this way."

"Does Miriam have any indication you feel this way?" I asked.

"Well, I've told her that I think I made a mistake," Eli said, "but I haven't explained about the other part."

"Do you think she won't be hurt if you end the marriage?" I asked, trying to conceal my dismay at what I was hearing.

"No, of course not," Eli acknowledged. "But I'm sure it would hurt her more if she knew *why* I felt it was a mistake for me to have married her."

"I hope you don't mind my asking," I said, "but why did you get engaged if you didn't find her attractive?"

"Well, it's a long story," Eli answered and sighed.

"I'm listening," I encouraged. "Please tell me."

"Well," Eli began, "we first met on a blind date. I wasn't really that interested in continuing, but the shadchan was very pushy and I didn't have any strong reasons to say no. So I agreed. And that story repeated itself for another four dates. At that point, I really felt I couldn't keep this going anymore and wanted to end it. But before I had a chance to tell the shadchan, she told me that Miriam was ready to get engaged and I shouldn't disappoint her.

"I didn't want to hurt her. But I was also scared to death about getting engaged. I reached out to my uncle for advice, and he assured me I would feel differently after we got married. He said it was normal to feel scared, and I should just ignore those feelings and go ahead with it, which I did. And that's why I'm here now."

"Do you want my help to get out of the marriage," I asked, "or to help you decide what you want to do?"

"I guess a little bit of both," Eli replied hesitantly.

"How would you feel working with me individually on this?" I asked.

"I think I would prefer it," Eli said with a wide grin.

The session was almost over and I suggested we call Miriam back into the office. Eli agreed.

"Eli shared some of his feelings with me," I said to Miriam. "And he is willing to meet with me individually to address these issues. How would you feel if I met with him alone, without you?"

"Whatever you think would help us best is fine with me."

"I don't know how long I will need to see Eli," I told Miriam. "But however long that will be, I will not be communicating with you at all. Therapy works better when there is complete confidentiality. Are you okay with that?"

"If you think it could help our marriage," Miriam said with her voice quivering, "then I'm all for it."

When I started working with Eli individually, I proposed we first explore why he was so out of touch with his feelings. He readily agreed. Then, in very short order, he spilled out the long history of his childhood abuse.

"My father abandoned my mother when I was about six years old," Eli reported with little emotion. "He just picked himself up and walked out. I really can't blame him. If I hadn't been so young and helpless, I would have done the same thing. My mother wasn't the easiest person to get along with.

"I guess my mom was pretty stressed out by having to care for my younger brothers and me by herself," Eli continued. "She wasn't working and had to rely on relatives and the government for support. But I shouldn't be making excuses for her. She used to beat me every day when I came home from yeshivah. She was a very sick woman and she still is. Only now I don't have to live with her and I can support myself.

"I wouldn't even say I'm angry with her for what she did to me. She didn't know any better. And I guess she couldn't control herself. Who I'm angry with are all those adults in my life who knew what she was doing to me and did nothing to stop her. Some of my teachers and rebbeim must have realized something was wrong at home by the way I came dressed and without a coat in the winter. And my aunts and uncles certainly knew what was going on because they witnessed it on occasion. But no one ever did anything to save or help me, and I cannot forgive them for that."

It took a couple of weeks for the full story to emerge. When he was finished, I pointed out to him how all of that contributed to his marital problems.

"You were trained from an early age to deny your feelings," I told Eli. "In order to survive the abuse, you had to shut them off. That was necessary to enable you to get through the day. But now, as an adult, it is interfering with your ability to make important decisions, such as whether or not to get engaged. In addition, as you were being victimized, you needed to assume a passive, nonconfrontational stance toward others. Now it is difficult for you to assert yourself when you need to, such as when the shadchan was pressuring you."

Over the next few weeks, Eli learned to get more in touch with his feelings and act more independently. He left a job, for example, where he was only earning minimum wage and found more lucrative employment. And he also came to terms with what he wanted to do about his marriage.

"I've decided to give my wife a *get*," Eli informed me at the start of one session. "It's not fair to her for me to keep up this charade. It will be better for both of us if I do this now, before we have any children. I know this will hurt her. And I feel terrible about that. But to delay the inevitable will only hurt her more. It was a terrible mistake for me to get engaged to her, and it will only compound that mistake if I stay married to her. I plan to inform her of my decision this week."

I walked Eli through all of the consequences of what he planned to do, and it was clear that he had given this considerable thought. His mind was made up, and for him to feel so confident about a decision was definitely progress.

Eli's *rav* facilitated the process of the *get*, which was mercifully quick, but not painless. I continued meeting with Eli until shortly after his divorce. At that point, he felt he no longer needed my help and we stopped meeting.

About seven years later, Eli called, requesting an appointment. When we met, he explained the reason for his call. "I took a break from *shidduchim* for a couple of years after my divorce and then I started again. This time I didn't let anyone push me into anything that wasn't right for me, and I've gotten a bit more discriminating. I know now what I like and what I don't like, and this time I think I've found the right person. But before I do anything stupid, I thought I should come in and discuss it with you."

Eli went on to describe the woman he was dating. As a corporate lawyer, she was certainly very intelligent and accomplished. Eli definitely found her attractive and enjoyed her company. Unfortunately, however, she was also manipulative, controlling, and seemed to be taking advantage of him.

I did not want to burst Eli's bubble. I gently and gradually tried to help Eli see what was obvious to me. But before I had the chance to get Eli to see the full picture about her, she abruptly ended their relationship. At that point, Eli acknowledged that he had made another serious mistake regarding *shidduchim* and he signed on for another round of therapy.

As Eli filled me in on what had transpired in his life since we last met, it was clear that while much had changed, much had also remained the same. On the positive side, he had gone into the real estate development field and seen incredible success. Together with a partner, he was not simply renovating single family homes. Rather, he was developing multifamily dwellings and shopping centers all across the country. In short, he had become enormously wealthy in a very short time.

On the other hand, however, Eli was also being exploited by members of his family. Falling prey to their sob stories, he was supporting many of his mother's and siblings' extravagances. And while he wanted to set limits to their spending, he felt unable to do so. As a result, he was paying their bloated credit card bills each month with resentment. Once again, therefore, he was assuming the role of victim and felt incapable of asserting himself with his domineering mother. Interestingly enough, though, in the corporate world, Eli was successful in cutting deals which were very much to his advantage.

It was during this second round of therapy that Eli shared with me the recent history of his compulsive gambling. When he first entered the real estate field, he had access to large sums of money that had been put under his control by third party investors. Using some of these funds to feed his gambling addiction, he quickly found himself over his head in debt. Realizing on his own that this behavior could easily derail his nascent real estate career, he found and entered the Twelve-Step program Gamblers Anonymous.

"Now I make sure never to let a week go by without attending at least one meeting," Eli reported proudly. "My work takes me around the country. And one of the great things about GA is that you can find multiple meetings in just about every city. I've come to terms with the fact that I'm an addict, and I will never really be cured of this disease. So I know I have to keep going to meetings to make sure I don't have a relapse. You can just imagine how in my line, I have access to enormous amounts of cash. If I were to act out — even once — that could totally destroy my career."

Eli also attended his regular meeting whenever he was at home. In this way, he developed and maintained regular contact with his program buddies, who were available for support if and when he ever felt tempted to act out. In addition, Eli had a sponsor who was available to him by phone. This safety net of meetings around the country and supportive relationships succeeded in keeping Eli out of the gambling casinos which had threatened to destroy all that he had worked so hard to build.

Eli's case history is illustrative of the kinds of traumatic early life experiences that can lead to someone developing a serious addiction. His case also demonstrates the therapeutic benefit of regular attendance at Twelve-Step meetings, which is the only proven strategy for extricating oneself from the grip of a substance abuse or behavioral addiction.

EPILOGUE

OPEN LETTERS TO NEW AND PROSPECTIVE THERAPISTS

CHAPTER 54

Is the Mental Health Field Right for You?

After reading all of these case histories, some of you may be considering entering the mental health field by becoming a clinical social worker, clinical psychologist, mental health counselor, marital and family therapist, or psychiatrist. Whether you are standing on the threshold of making a career choice or you have already made your decision and have become a therapist, there are some insights and observations I would like to share with you based on my forty-five-plus years of experience working in and with the *frum* community.

If you cannot devote yourself to full-time Torah study because you lack *zitzfleish* or you need *parnassah*, then working as a psychotherapist is the greatest occupation you can choose for many reasons. Firstly, it enables you to partner with the *Borei Refuos* in healing and helping His children to overcome their hurdles and be all they can be to serve Him and lead more satisfying, productive lives. The satisfaction of being able to impact the lives of other people so profoundly is indescribable.

Today, for example, (as I was writing this chapter,) someone called to share the good news that his married daughter just gave birth to her first child, a baby boy. The mother of the baby had been abused as a child by a relative. As a result, after completing seminary, she informed her parents that she was not interested in getting married. Her distraught parents consulted with me, terrified at the prospect that their daughter might never marry.

After months of working with this young woman and her parents, she healed from her childhood trauma, which enabled her to enter *shidduchim* and eventually marry. The call from her father was the maraschino cherry on top of the ice cream sundae of satisfaction I enjoyed from working with this woman and her parents.

In addition, working in the mental health field is never dull or boring. Not only is every person unique, but also, every session with the same person is different from all others. As a result, each day is full of surprises and challenges for which you can never be fully prepared. Then you will be called upon to innovate, think out of the box, and use your talents and skills to their ultimate limits. This is work that requires you to be totally present, focused, and real throughout the day. You will need to use all of your emotions, social skills, intelligence, education, training, and experience in each session. And you will learn and grow from each therapeutic encounter, becoming more effective and helpful from one session to the next as your career blossoms and branches off in unanticipated directions.

Last but certainly not least, the mental health field affords an opportunity to perform the mitzvah of doing *chesed* each and every day. This in turn means that you are also fulfilling the mitzvah of *v'halachta bedrachav* (*Devarim* 28:9), imitating and following in the ways of Hashem. As Chazal have taught, "Just as He is merciful and compassionate, so too you should be merciful and compassionate" (*Shabbos* 133b). And there can be no greater act of mercy and compassion than helping someone to overcome the hurdles in his or her life.

To present a balanced picture of the mental health field, however, I really should include some of its drawbacks and disadvantages. Firstly, it is not a very lucrative profession. Starting salaries for therapists are embarrassingly low compared with the enormous cost of the graduate school education needed to enter the field today. Private practice, of course, can supplement your income. In the current competitive market, however, few therapists can hope to build a private practice up to the point where it can be their sole source of income.

Furthermore, as a therapist, you will be subjected to various digs and negative stereotyping by friends and family. "All therapists are a bit crazy themselves," "Therapists don't really care about people; they're only in it for the money," and "Therapists are always using their skills to manipulate others" are typical generalizations with which you will have to deal if you enter this profession.

In addition to the negative stereotypes, you will have to contend with glaring misconceptions about therapy and therapists. For example, "Therapists can read people's minds and they try to do it at all times." As a result, some people may feel exposed, vulnerable, and intimidated in your presence.

Others may suspect therapists of trying to psychoanalyze everyone they meet, and they may attribute nefarious motives to therapists for doing so. In other words, some see therapists as always attempting to manipulate others. Needless to say, this makes these people uncomfortable in your presence.

Moreover, some believe that therapists can figure out and fix all problems in no more than a single forty-five minute session, and if a therapist recommends any additional sessions, it is for mercenary motives only.

Finally, at the other end of the spectrum of misconceptions, there are those who believe that therapy solely consists of common sense repackaged in psychobabble. As a result, they are convinced that therapists possess no greater skills or insights than anyone else, and they give no greater weight to a therapist's opinion than their own on matters of mental health or family life.

The sense of frustration this latter misconception can evoke is illustrated by the following joke.

Two strangers are seated next to each on an airplane. One says to the other, "What line of work are you in?"

His seatmate replies, "I'm a rabbi."

"Oh," the first man says. "That's a simple occupation."

"How so?" asks the rabbi.

"Your whole job can be summed up in one sentence: 'Do unto others what you would have them do unto you.'"

"And what line of work are you in?" asks the rabbi.

"Oh, I'm an astrophysicist," his seatmate answers proudly.

"That's a simple occupation," the rabbi comments. "Your whole job can be summed up in the one phrase: 'Twinkle, twinkle, little star.'"

CHAPTER 55

Are You Right for the Mental Health Field?

Now some of you may be convinced that the mental health field is right for you. However, you need to consider the reverse question, "Am I right for the mental health field?"

In order to help you answer this question for yourself, I am presenting the following short checklist of questions addressing what I consider to be the traits necessary to be successful.

ARE YOU A PEOPLE PERSON?

Do you enjoy interacting with and meeting new people? Or are you intimidated in social settings? In order to succeed as a therapist, you need to feel comfortable with a wide variety of people, many of whom are not like you in any way.

Are you able to keep what people say confidential? No one will want to share intimate, personal information if he has the slightest concern that the information will be disclosed without his permission. What keeping things confidential means is, for example, that if your best friend's ex-spouse comes to you for a consultation, you will not breathe a word about it to your friend even though you are dying to do so.

ARE YOU AN EMPATHIC PERSON?

Can you understand how other people feel? Can you convey that understanding back to them in a meaningful way? Can you put yourself in someone else's situation and identify with their pain and struggle? That is what being *nosei b'ol im chaveiro* (*Pirkei Avos* 6:6) is all about. If you lack empathy, do not despair. Studies have demonstrated that empathy can be taught. Without it, however, you will have a difficult time connecting with people on an emotional level.

ARE YOU AN INDEPENDENT LEARNER?

Can you explore and research topics on your own? Or do you need to have someone else show you how to do everything before you can do it yourself? Since people are as unique as snowflakes, therapists need to be able to take what they learn in one case and then adapt it for application to another.

ARE YOU COMFORTABLE SETTING LIMITS FOR OTHERS?

Those who have unlimited compassion, caring, and concern will not survive in the mental health field. Just as parents need to set limits for their children, therapists need to set limits, at times, in order to be fully effective. In addition, they need to be able to maintain a proper balance between emotional closeness and distance. Too much of the former can lead to burnout. And too much of the latter will turn people away from you.

ARE YOU IN TOUCH WITH YOUR OWN FEELINGS?

The therapist's own feelings are a critical guiding light which can help him navigate the sometimes murky waters of the therapeutic process. If a therapist is not constantly in touch with his own feelings before, during, and after therapy sessions, he will miss valuable clues in recognizing when the treatment is going seriously off course.

ARE YOU ABLE TO TOLERATE A HIGH LEVEL OF UNCERTAINTY?

In accounting, two plus two is always four. In the mental health field, that degree of certainty is often unattainable. A therapist must be able to move forward with no clear road map or game plan other than instinct guided by experience. As with all other professions, the training received in any mental health graduate school only prepares one for the real learning which takes place on the job.

ARE YOU ABLE TO ADMIT ERRORS AND ACCEPT CRITICISM?

Those who are terrified of making mistakes should choose another career. It is not possible to learn how to ride a bike without falling. And it is not possible to become a successful therapist without making many mistakes along the way. Someone who is defensive when criticized by supervisors or colleagues will not learn what he needs to know. And someone who cannot apologize to clients or patients when necessary will not get very far as a therapist.

ARE YOU FLEXIBLE?

All rules have exceptions. And knowing when and how to break even your own rules is a vital skill for anyone entering the mental health field. If you are too rigid and cannot think out of the box, you will not be as helpful as you could be.

ARE YOU AN ARTICULATE COMMUNICATOR?

"Whatever" and "You know what I mean?" are common expressions that work in social settings. But unless you can be clear, concise, and say exactly what you mean, you will constantly struggle to make progress as a therapist.

CAN YOU ACKNOWLEDGE YOUR OWN LIMITATIONS IN SKILL AND EXPERTISE? AND CAN YOU CONSULT OTHERS WHEN NECESSARY?

Chazal said something which should give pause to anyone entering any health-related field. "The best doctors [are destined to go] to Gehinnom" (*Mishnayos Kiddushin* 4:14). The *Tiferes Yisrael* points out that this condemnation only applies to the "best" doctors. The reason for this is because doctors with a high standing and reputation often feel embarrassed to acknowledge any uncertainty. As a result, by not consulting with others, these top doctors can come to administer incorrect treatments that lead to the death of their patients, *r"l*.

CAN YOU TRUST YOUR OWN JUDGMENT EVEN UNDER PRESSURE?

This is not a contradiction to what was said above. A therapist needs to know what he does not know, but also have the confidence to assert what he does know.

Many years ago, for example, I was working with Yitti, a single woman in her early twenties, suffering from a classic case of anorexia. We had a solid therapeutic relationship and she was being monitored at the same time by an internist who specialized in eating disorders. Her weight was stabilized. But after eight or nine months of therapy, she still was not gaining any weight. Her parents became impatient and insisted she be hospitalized. I did not support that approach and neither did the internist. Instead, I recommended that the parents allow more time for the therapy to work.

At that point, the parents went "over my head," by approaching a prominent *rav* and appealing to him to force me on board with their plan. I was summoned by the *rav* without any explanation as to why he wanted to meet with me. When I arrived, he said, "I understand you are working with a woman who has anorexia neurosa?"

I chose not to correct his mistaken name for the disorder. Instead, I replied, "I'm really not at liberty to discuss whether or not I am working with someone without their permission."

"Okay," the *rav* said sternly. "You don't have to disclose anything about this case to me. But the parents came to meet with me about this. They told me that they want their daughter to be hospitalized and you are not cooperating with them. This is a serious condition, as I understand it. And I don't think a social worker should be making decisions about how to treat it. Therefore, I insist you do what the parents want. They say that the girl will only go into the hospital if you tell her to do so. Therefore, you must tell her to go into the hospital."

At the time, I did not feel that I could stand up to that *rav* and I buckled under his pressure. Following his directive, I advised Yitti to enter the hospital when I met with her next.

Yitti followed my advice and allowed herself to be admitted to the hospital chosen by her parents — one that had an inpatient unit for eating disorders — and she remained there for a full month. When she was discharged, she had barely gained two pounds, and her parents, who did not have any health insurance at the time, were forced into personal bankruptcy because of the astronomical hospital bill.

When Yitti came home, her parents forbade her to meet with me, and I never saw her again, although we did speak once on the phone after her discharge. I do not know what ever happened to her after that. I sincerely hope she received the help she needed. And I regret to this day that I did not have more confidence in my clinical judgment when I met with that *rav*.

ARE YOU INCORRUPTIBLE AND HONEST?

At times, the decisions you make as a therapist can have significant ramifications for all the people involved. As a result, some may attempt to influence you to alter your decisions in a way that will benefit them. In order to properly serve the best interests of your patients, however, it will be necessary for you to resist those attempts.

I recall, for example, one particular case in which I was asked by a matrimonial lawyer to conduct a psychosocial assessment of his client's suitability as a parent, which would be submitted as evidence for upcoming child custody litigation. His client's ex-wife was taking him to court to try to prevent him from having visitation rights with their son.

"I want you to be completely honest in your assessment," the lawyer requested. "If you feel the father is an unfit parent, I want you to say so. But if you deem him to be an adequate parent, then I want you to state that. I'll have my client call you to set up the appointments."

I met with the father, both alone as well as with his son. I also reached out to the mother to meet with her as well. Unfortunately, she refused to meet with me.

During the time I was preparing my child custody evaluation, two separate attempts were made to influence my assessment in favor of the mother. The first time was when the mother's father approached one of my close colleagues and asked him to speak to me about this case. My colleague told the father off and then added, "I see you don't know Dr. Wikler very well. Not even I could get him to write anything other than what he believes." When he got off the phone, he shared the conversation with me.

The second time was when a *rav* I knew asked to meet with me. When I came into his office, the *rav* said, "You are conducting a child custody evaluation for a divorced couple. I've known the father of the ex-wife for many years. He found out that I know you, so he asked me to put in a good word for him. Now, I am not familiar with the details of this case, but I wanted to accommodate him so that's why I asked to meet with you."

I was so infuriated by these two incidents that I complained about them to one of my *chavrusos*. "I can't believe that they would try to influence me *twice* by contacting people I know," I vented.

"It wasn't twice," my *chavrusa* said matter-of-factly. "It was *three* times."

"What are you talking about?" I asked, not grasping what he was hinting.

"The ex-wife's father called me too," he said. "First, I read him the riot act. Then I told him I wouldn't even tell you he had called, because I didn't want him to succeed in intimidating you through me in any way. But once you told me about the two other times, I figured you might as well know about the third."

Based on my interviews, I determined that the ex-husband was an above average parent. I stated as much in my report, which included all of the evidence on which I based my conclusions. Then I submitted the report to the lawyer.

A few weeks later, the lawyer called to say that the other side withdrew their complaint and the case never came to trial. He could not be certain, but he suspected that my report contributed greatly to the other side's decision to drop the litigation.

CAN YOU PUT THE NEEDS OF OTHERS BEFORE YOUR OWN?

At times, as a therapist, it may be necessary for you to make choices that will benefit the people with whom you are working, but which could put you at risk in some way. At such times, professional ethics dictate that you put the needs of others before your own.

I recall, for example, one case in which parents consulted me following the discovery that their ten-year-old son, Itzik, had been abused by one of his rebbeim. Initially, I provided support and guidance to the parents. Eventually, I also treated Itzik.

During the course of my work with this family, as more and more details of the abuse emerged, the parents wanted their son tested for an STD. They hesitated, however, knowing that seeking such a test would automatically trigger a police investigation, and they questioned whether they would be halachically permitted to do so, as the rebbi might be arrested.

I told the parents that I could not *pasken* their *shailah*. I did, however, recommend a well-known and respected *posek* for them to consult. The *rav* told them that parents have a right to seek medical attention for their child regardless of the consequences for the suspected perpetrator.

After receiving this *psak*, Itzik's parents had him tested. *Baruch Hashem,* the results were negative. Nevertheless, as Itzik was a minor, he was required to be interviewed by a forensic investigator, after which the rebbi was arrested. Three days later, he was released on bail and the entire episode triggered a minor earthquake in the *frum* community.

The *posek* was subjected to extreme harassment by some of the rebbi's supporters. Eventually, a panel of *dayanim* was assembled, which included one of the *gedolei hador* at the time, and a *din Torah* was conducted between the *posek* and leaders of the large, influential community to which the rebbi belonged.

As part of the *din Torah* proceedings, I was asked to testify. Doing so put me at risk with the entire community to which the rebbi belonged. Nevertheless, as it was both therapeutic and supportive for Itzik and his family, I unflinchingly agreed to testify. I was not asserting the rebbi's guilt, as I was not a witness to the abuse. Rather, as a mental health professional, I was testifying to my belief that Itzik had, indeed, been abused.

The *beis din* ruled that since there were no witnesses and Itzik's testimony was invalid as he was a *katan*, there was insufficient evidence to implicate the rebbi. They also determined that the parents could not press charges against the rebbi and the *posek* had to issue an apology. As a result of both, the local district attorney never brought the case to trial.

Not long after that, a leader of the rebbi's community informed me that had it not been for his direct and forceful intervention, I would have been targeted for the same harassment that had been directed at the *posek* a few months earlier.

I continued working with Itzik and his parents until they moved away, in part to escape the pressure and stress to which they were subjected as a result of this high profile episode. This family has kept in touch with me and recently invited me to Itzik's *chasunah* out of town, where he is now living and learning in kollel.

If you have answered all or most of these questions affirmatively, then you have what it takes to be a successful therapist. And we need you now more than ever to make this calling your career choice.

CHAPTER 56

Recipe for Success

If you have decided that the mental health field is right for you and you are right for the mental health field, there are three things I believe you need in order to be truly successful. And while there are certainly no guarantees in life, if you can put together all three of these ingredients, you stand the greatest chance of realizing your highest aspirations for your career as a therapist.

1. ROLE MODELS

Before your GPS can guide you to your journey's end, you must first enter the zip code or address of your destination. Similarly, in order to succeed in any career, it is extremely helpful if you have at least one good role model who is successful in that field. It is not necessary for you to have a personal relationship with that person, although that would certainly be preferred. Even if you only read about that person or observe him/her from afar, having a clear picture of what success in that field looks like will aid you in your climb up the ladder.

For me, and I am sure for many other therapists, that role model has always been Rabbi Dr. Abraham Twerski, MD. I still vividly recall the very first time I met him in 1975.

The occasion was a public forum sponsored by a large secular Jewish social service agency, in conjunction with their centennial celebration. In order to reach out to the *frum* community, the event was held in Boro Park, Brooklyn. Dr. Twerski was the guest speaker. And he was joined on the program by one of the agency's non-*frum* administrators.

I had heard of Dr. Twerski, as his reputation had preceded him. Seeing him in person, however, far exceeded all of my expectations. Dressed in his chassidish garb, with his long, flowing black beard, and knowing about his medical degree and psychiatric training, he personified for me the ultimate blend of Torah *hashkafah* and the highest level of professionalism in the mental health field. And that was all before he even uttered a single word!

When Dr. Twerski rose to speak first, I was totally mesmerized by his soft-spoken, out-of-town hominess and down-to-earth anecdotes during his note-less presentation. While I was a transfixed member of the audience, the agency administrator, who was the next speaker, was apparently intimidated by Dr. Twerski's grand-slam home run of a speech. When he spoke next, he stammered, stumbled, and seemed to feel upstaged by the *frum* psychiatrist from Pittsburgh, which only added to the charisma of the man I eventually learned to call Shea.

At the conclusion of the formal program, Dr. Twerski stayed to take questions from the long line of people waiting to greet him. When my turn came, I summoned all of my courage and asked, "Dr. Twerski, what in the world are you doing in Pittsburgh? We need you in New York!"

"I'm an out-of-town boy," he replied with his trademark humility. "I grew up in Milwaukee, Wisconsin. I could never live in New York. If I did, I would need at least six more just like me in order to survive. You see, I would get referrals from every *rosh yeshivah* and *chassidische rebbe.* And I would not be able to turn any of them down. It would be too much for me."

At that moment, coming face-to-face with such an outstanding role model, I felt energized like never before to devote myself to the field I had only entered three years earlier. And I could identify with Elisha HaNavi, whose life was totally transformed by his brief encounter with Eliyahu HaNavi (*Melachim I* 19:19–21).

Over the years, I have had the privilege of hearing Dr. Twerski speak on many more occasions, and even had the thrill of a lifetime to share the podium with him at the first national conference of *frum* therapists held in New York City in 1988.[1] In addition, I have gotten to know him personally, and I have visited with him more than once in his current home in Yerushalayim.

2. GOOD RABBINIC ADVISORS AND CLINICAL SUPERVISORS

Every occupation presents potential conflicts with halachah. I have a relative, for example, who is a businessman. He is literally on the phone at least once a day with his *rav* and *posek*, asking *shailos* pertaining to his business. And when it comes to professions needing rabbinic advisors, mental health is no exception.

As a therapist, you should never *pasken shailos* for others. If asked, you should refer patients to their own *rav* or *posek*. You need your own rabbinic advisors to help you resolve the *shailos* that have to do with your clinical work. In matters of halachah, it is always preferable to consult the same *posek* whenever possible, so that you both get to know each other and cultivate an ongoing relationship that will greatly enhance the process of your asking *shailos*.

It is not always feasible, however, to consult with only one *posek* consistently. Emergencies arise, for example, when your regular *posek* may be unavailable. Or one *posek* may have a better grasp of

---

1. See Steven Erlanger, "Orthodox Jewish Psychotherapists Face Conflicts," *New York Times*, April 25, 1988.

a particular matter than another *posek*. As a result, you will need to have access to more than one *posek* in order to insure you are taking the halachically approved approach in each case.

The nature of the potential conflicts between psychotherapy and halachah has been discussed elsewhere.[2] Suffice it to say here that during the course of my career, I have asked hundreds of *shailos* related to my practice.

Over the years, I have been privileged to meet and/or speak over the phone with many outstanding *poskim*. For example, I have consulted one or more times with: Rav Chaim Pinchas Scheinberg, *ztz"l*, *rosh yeshivah* of Yeshivas Torah Ore; Rav Yisroel Zev Gustman, *ztz"l*, *rosh yeshivah* of Yeshivas Netzach Yisrael; the Bostoner Rebbe, Rav Levi Yitzchak Horowitz, *ztz"l*; Rav Shlomo Brevda, *ztz"l*; Rav Chaim Kanievsky, *shlita*; Rav Shmuel Kaminetsky, *shlita*, *rosh yeshivah* of the Talmudical Yeshivah of Philadelphia; the Novominsker Rebbe, Rav Yaakov Perlow, *shlita*; Rav Dovid Cohen, *shlita*, *morah d'asra* of Congregation Gevul Yavetz; and Rav Yaakov Horowitz, *shlita*, *rosh yeshivah* of Yeshivas Beis Meir.

While you need rabbinic advisors to *pasken* the *shailos* that can and do arise in your clinical work, that is only one way in which cultivating relationships with *rabbanim* can benefit you. As Chazal have taught, "*Gedolah shimusha shel Torah yoser mei'limudah* — One gains even more from spending time with *talmidei chachamim* than from learning with them" (*Berachos* 7b).

After one halachic consultation I was privileged to have with Rav Chaim Pinchas Scheinberg, for example, I turned to leave and the *rosh yeshivah* called me back.

"Tell me," he said, "when you say '*Refa'einu*' in *Shemoneh Esrei*, do you daven for your patients?"

---

2. See my article, "Halachah and Psychotherapy," *The Jewish Observer* (May 1982): 8–11.

"Uh, no I don't," I replied, somewhat embarrassed by that unanticipated question.

"Well," he continued, "you really should, just as any doctor should be *daven*ing for his patients to have a *refuah sheleimah*."

That brief conversation took place over forty years ago. I am pleased to say that I have followed the *rosh yeshivah*'s advice ever since then, and I believe it has contributed in no small measure to the successes I have seen in my practice.

In addition to good rabbinic advisors, you will also need skilled, experienced clinical supervisors. In fact, the most important criteria in selecting your first job should be the quality of the supervision provided at that agency or clinic. And if you are working in a setting at which there is inadequate supervision, it is worthwhile to purchase your own. Good supervision is expensive. Even if you have to pay a large portion of what you earn in order to buy supervision, however, consider it the best investment you can make in your career, which will pay back dividends for the rest of your professional life.

3. PEER SUPPORT

One final ingredient must be added in order to maximize your chances of succeeding in the mental health field. That is, insuring that you have ample opportunities for peer support. Clinical practice can be stressful at times. You cannot rely solely on friends or family, who may never fully understand what it is really like down in the trenches of your caseload, and weekly supervision can never provide the same level of support that peers can offer.

If you work in an agency or clinic, peer support can be as easily accessible as your colleague in the next office or right down the hall. In private practice, however, it is not as readily available. Partly for that reason, I was hesitant to enter full-time private practice in 1984. I had heard and read that one can feel isolated and unconnected to collegial support in private practice. In order to avoid that pitfall, therefore, I formed a peer supervision group which began later that year and has been ongoing ever since.[3]

For the first year or two, the group had a fluid membership. After that, however, the membership has been remarkably stable, consisting of the same six members: Dr. Larry Bryskin, Dr. Rashi Shapiro, Dr. Benzion Sorotzkin, Dr. Gail Bessler, Dr. Elin Weinstein, and me.

We meet for an hour and a quarter once a week, where we take turns presenting one case to the group for clinical supervision. Each meeting begins with a few minutes of Torah study originally instituted to memorialize one of the founding members, Mrs. Yitti Leibel, *a"h*. It is followed by a brief follow-up on the previous week's case by the previous week's presenter. Then we get into the case for the present week, which takes up the bulk of each session.

Over the years, we have all found the group to be a rich learning experience. It never ceases to amaze me how much we can still learn from each other after all these years. We each have different training, areas of specialty, and skill sets. Nevertheless, we each have much to contribute to the case discussions each week.

In addition to sharpening our skills and helping us to keep focused in our clinical work, the meetings provide a handy networking opportunity to share news, information, and to socialize. Furthermore, we have shared each other's simchahs and have supported each other during times of personal challenge as well.

Last, but certainly not least, the group has proven to be an excellent source of referrals. As we are so familiar with each other's work, it is natural for us to refer more clients to each other than to those in the field with whom we are less familiar. As a result, these intragroup

---

3. For a fuller description of the history, format, and process of this group, see my article, "Sustaining Ourselves: An Interdisciplinary Peer Group for Orthodox Jewish Therapists Treating Orthodox Jewish Patients," *Journal of Psychotherapy in Independent Practice* 2, no.1 (2001): 79–86.

referrals have also provided us with the priceless opportunity to share cases with each other, meaning that two or more of us may be working with different members of the same family at the same time or with the same person using different modalities, thereby enhancing the services we provide.

If you have just entered the mental health field or if you are a veteran, experienced therapist, I would strongly recommend that you join a peer supervision group for all of the reasons mentioned above and more. And if none are available where you live, consider starting your own. If you do, I believe you will find it to be one of the best career decisions you have made since deciding to enter the noble, challenging, and highly rewarding mental health profession in the first place.

About the Author

D r. Meir Wikler is a psychotherapist and family counselor in full-time private practice, with offices in Lakewood, New Jersey and Brooklyn, New York.

In addition to having published over eighty articles in lay and professional journals, Dr. Wikler is the author of:

- *The First Seven Days: A Practical Guide to the Traditional Observance of Shiva for Mourners, Their Families and Friends* (United Hebrew Community, 1987)

- *Bayis Ne'eman b'Yisrael: Practical Steps to Success in Marriage* (Feldheim Publishers, 1988)

- *AiSHeL: Stories of Contemporary Jewish Hospitality* (Feldheim Publishers, 1994)

- *Einei HaShem: Contemporary Stories of Divine Providence in Eretz Yisrael* (Feldheim Publishers, 1997)

- *Partners with Hashem: Effective Guidelines for Successful Parenting* (ArtScroll/Mesorah Publications, 2000)

- *Zorei'a Tzedakos: Contemporary Stories of Divine Providence* (Feldheim Publishers, 2003)

- *Ten Minutes a Day to a Better Marriage: Getting Your Spouse to Understand You* (ArtScroll/Mesorah Publications, 2003)

- *Partners with Hashem II: More Effective Guidelines for Successful Parenting* (ArtScroll/Mesorah Publications, 2006)

- *Partners in Parenting: The Questions Parents Ask. The Answers They Need.* (ArtScroll/Mesorah Publications, 2011)

- *The Parenting Partnership: Parenting Questions on Tots through Teens and Beyond, Answered with Wit and Wisdom* (Hamodia Treasures/Israel Book Shop, 2013)

- *180 Rechov Yaffo: Bridge to a Bygone Era, 50 Stories of Emunah and Bitachon* (Menucha Publishers, 2014)

- *Wikler Classics: The Best of Dr. Meir Wikler's Heartwarming & Inspirational True Stories* (Feldheim Publishers, 2016)

Dr. Wikler has lectured throughout the United States and overseas to both lay and professional audiences on various aspects of mental health and family life in the *frum* Jewish community. His clinical work has been featured in several newspapers, including the *New York Times*, *Mishpacha*, *Hamodia*, and the *Jerusalem Post*. His lectures and *shiurim* are also featured on www.TorahAnytime.com.